Animals in Irish Society

Animals in Irish Society

Interspecies Oppression and Vegan Liberation in Britain's First Colony

COREY LEE WRENN

Cover art: Corey Lee Wrenn

Published by State University of New York Press, Albany

© 2021 State University of New York

All rights reserved

Printed in the United States of America

No part of this book may be used or reproduced in any manner whatsoever without written permission. No part of this book may be stored in a retrieval system or transmitted in any form or by any means including electronic, electrostatic, magnetic tape, mechanical, photocopying, recording, or otherwise without the prior permission in writing of the publisher.

For information, contact State University of New York Press, Albany, NY
www.sunypress.edu

Library of Congress Cataloging-in-Publication Data

Name: Wrenn, Corey Lee, author.
Title: Animals in Irish society: Interspecies oppression and vegan liberation in Britain's first colony / Corey Lee Wrenn.
Description: Albany : State University of New York Press [2021] | Includes bibliographical references and index.
Identifiers: ISBN 9781438484358 (hardcover : alk. paper) | ISBN 9781438484341 (pbk. : alk. paper) | ISBN 9781438484365 (ebook)
Further information is available at the Library of Congress.
Library of Congress Control Number: 2021938473

10 9 8 7 6 5 4 3 2 1

For Keeley
October 23, 2004–May 28, 2020

Contents

List of Illustrations — ix

Preface — xi

Acknowledgments — xv

Timeline of Anti-speciesism Efforts in Ireland — xvii

Introduction — 1

Chapter 1 Celticism, Christianity, and Animism in Gaelic Ireland — 19

Chapter 2 Human and Nonhuman Relationships under British Colonization — 45

Chapter 3 Activism for Other Animals in Ireland, Nineteenth and Early Twentieth Centuries — 79

Chapter 4 Modern Activism for Other Animals in Ireland — 109

Chapter 5 Nonhuman Animal Welfare and Irish Food Sovereignty — 141

Conclusion Human-Nonhuman Relationships in the Global Era — 181

Notes — 205

Works Cited — 209

Index — 239

Illustrations

Map of Ireland   xvi

1.1 Page from the Book of Kells. Source: Wikimedia Commons, scanned from B. Meehan, *The Book of Kells: An Illustrated Introduction to the Manuscript in Trinity College Dublin* (London: Thames and Hudson, 1994).   35

1.2 Children of Lir statue, Garden of Remembrance, Dublin. Source: Wikimedia Commons.   36

2.1 Wild and beastly depiction of Irish rebels by Thomas Nast. Source: *Harper's Weekly*, March 18, 1867.   61

2.2 Simian depiction of Irish rebels by Ó. John Tenniel. Source: *Punch*, December 14, 1861.   63

3.1 *The Trial of Bill Burns, under Martin's Act*, by P. Matthew. Source: Wikimedia Commons.   81

3.2 James Haughton. Source: Wikimedia Commons.   87

3.3 Frances Power Cobbe. Source: Wikimedia Commons.   95

3.4 Charlotte Despard. Source: A. Gardiner, *Pillars of Society* (New York: Dodd, Mead, 1914).   97

3.5 Kit Burns and his dog "fighting" ring. Source: J. McCabe, *Secrets of the Great City* (Philadelphia: Library Company, 1868).   101

3.6 Swill milk production as depicted by Frank Leslie. Source: *Illustrated Newspaper*, May 15, 1858.   105

4.1 Travellers in 1960s Ireland. This image is reproduced courtesy
 of the National Library of Ireland (TIL850). 123
4.2 Bobby Sands mural, Sinn Féin office, Belfast. Source:
 Gráinne McCormick. 126
4.3 Hunger strike memorial, Milltown Cemetery, Belfast. Source:
 author's collection. 129
4.4 Go Vegan World anti-dairy campaign poster. Source:
 Go Vegan World. 131
5.1 Aldi Love Ireland store flyer. Source: Aldi. 166
5.2 The College Vegetarian Restaurant advertisement. Source:
 Irish Times, September 11, 1900. 171
5.3. Jennie Wyse Power. Source: Wikimedia Commons. 172

Preface

In the summer of 2015, I began researching Irish countercuisine for a vegan encyclopedia project that would eventually publish with the *Routledge Handbook of Vegan Studies* (Wright 2021). I was living in Ireland at the time and was inspired to learn more about its cultural food history. To my surprise, I found that literature on the topics of veganism, vegetarianism, anti-speciesism, and animality in the Irish context was nearly nonexistent. This necessitated some creative thinking and deep research to solicit information on the experience of Nonhuman Animals and their relationship to Irish foodways and activism. As I finished the manuscript, I found that a single article was too limiting, as what I had begun to uncover warranted a deeper analysis. I was also designing a course on social movements in Ireland at the time, a project that necessitated over a year of preparatory research. What I found, or rather, what I did *not* find, further motivated the writing of this book. There is a robust body of social movement research underway in Ireland, and, yet, the Nonhuman Animal rights movement and veganism are virtually ignored. This is particularly interesting to me, given that the political structure of the American Nonhuman Animal rights movement is my main area of research. In this work, I have explored Britain's history as well, as it had such an influence over the formation of American anti-speciesist mobilization. Somewhere in between America and the United Kingdom, however, I had come to realize that Ireland had been lost to the discourse.

As the Nonhuman Animal rights movement has earned some degree of legitimacy in academic circles, there is finally an interest in exploring anti-speciesism beyond the reach of America and Britain. As many scholars have rightly indicated, colonialism has much to do with the fact that anti-speciesism has been remembered and researched as a uniquely American and British phenomenon. With power comes the privilege of dictating the historical record and cultural memory. As this book will chronicle, colonialism is also highly relevant to the shaping of speciesism and protest.

This book was also inspired by personal circumstance. I often receive comments from Americans and Irish alike who presume it is impossible to be vegan in Ireland, or that Ireland is somehow stunted in its treatment of other animals in comparison to other Western countries. Nothing could be further from the truth. Ireland has a vegan community that rivals many American and British areas. Every Saturday, a radical grassroots vegan education group sets up shop outside of Trinity College or in Temple Bar in Dublin, lining the pavement with eye-catching protest posters. Irish circuses no longer exploit Nonhuman Animals as entertainment, and foreign circuses visiting Ireland that do are subject to an uproar from unhappy citizens. I can even enjoy a vegan meal on Aer Lingus flights, while Dublin's airport, as of this writing, offers a fully vegan restaurant owned by "The Happy Pear." Also to my delight, the cultural commandant of Ireland, Guinness, changed its recipe to accommodate vegans (*sláinte* to Cavanaghs Bar in Cork, where I enjoyed my first pint). As I conclude revisions on this manuscript in 2020, Dublin had just been declared the most vegan-friendly city in the world according to TripAdvisor reviews (McCarthy 2019), and even Ireland's conservative food board had identified veganism as an increasingly normal and mainstream dietary lifestyle (Bord Bia 2018). Ireland, in other words, is a country defying stereotypes.

As an American, I am aware that the potential for me to misconstrue Irish culture or overlook important histories is high. I am also aware that, as a postcolonial state, Ireland has been unfairly subjected to a variety of unfavorable and inaccurate analyses by outsiders. I have attempted to circumvent this problem by sharing the manuscript widely with Irish activists, scholars, and friends. My status as an outsider, however, is certainly poised to threaten the credibility of the theses presented herein. It is hoped that my analysis is sufficiently objective as well as sympathetic, as the need for a vegan theory of Ireland is paramount. As this book was being prepared, Ireland was gearing up for its Food Wise 2025 plan to increase its animal-based agricultural output while its greenhouse emissions continued to exceed EU limits and mark it as a European leader in its contribution to climate change. The consequences are no abstractions; Irish weather has been rocked by increasingly extreme changes, including a major hurricane in 2017. Ireland's oceans and waterways have also been devastated, with aquatic life nosediving to unrecoverable levels. Meanwhile, over 100 million sheeps, pigs, cows, chickens, turkeys, gooses, dogs, cats, and other animals used for food, fashion, and scientific experiments are killed in Ireland *each year* (O'Donovan n.d.). Ireland's erasure from social movement research and its marginalization from activist consciousness is not simply unfair but potentially disastrous for the humans and other animals, both present and future, whose well-being depends on effective protest and policy-making.

Acknowledgments

I have many friends in Ireland to thank for this project, which began in 2015. Em Ryan, for instance, cat-sat for me on one of my trips to Ireland only to move there herself and become a dear friend. I must also thank tour guide Brian Matthews for sharing his wisdom in Irish history and culture during a two-week cross-country trip with my students in 2017, as well as Paul Murray (who graciously proofed the entire manuscript and salvaged my rudimentary Irish translations), Piers Beirne, Sandra Higgins, Hunter Liguore, Boria Sax, Francis Stewart, and Roger Yates for providing useful feedback and resources. I am indebted to Matthew Cole and David Nibert, who have been significant and generous mentors to me throughout my career. Both have offered invaluable feedback on my writing. My friends and colleagues Phil Carney, Aph Ko, Jon Pawson, Brian Snead, and Nic Vaz have, likewise, been an important source of support and feedback. My clever student, Gráinne McCormick, must be credited for graciously providing her image of the Bobby Sands memorial in Belfast.

As always, I must acknowledge my feline friends, Keeley and Trudy, who have kept me company and motivated. In May 2020, as this book was going through final revisions, Trudy was diagnosed with terminal breast cancer and Keeley (who was nearly 16) died after a long and profoundly heartbreaking battle with digestive difficulties. It is to them this work is dedicated. My mother, too, must be credited. As my best friend and most important mentor, she makes all things possible. I was finally able to take her to Ireland in 2019, and hopefully this book will make sense to her as a result! As for myself, I have fallen in love with Ireland and my time there has greatly enriched my life; it is my earnest hope that this book will help to reintegrate Ireland's contributions into anti-speciesist advancements and discourse.

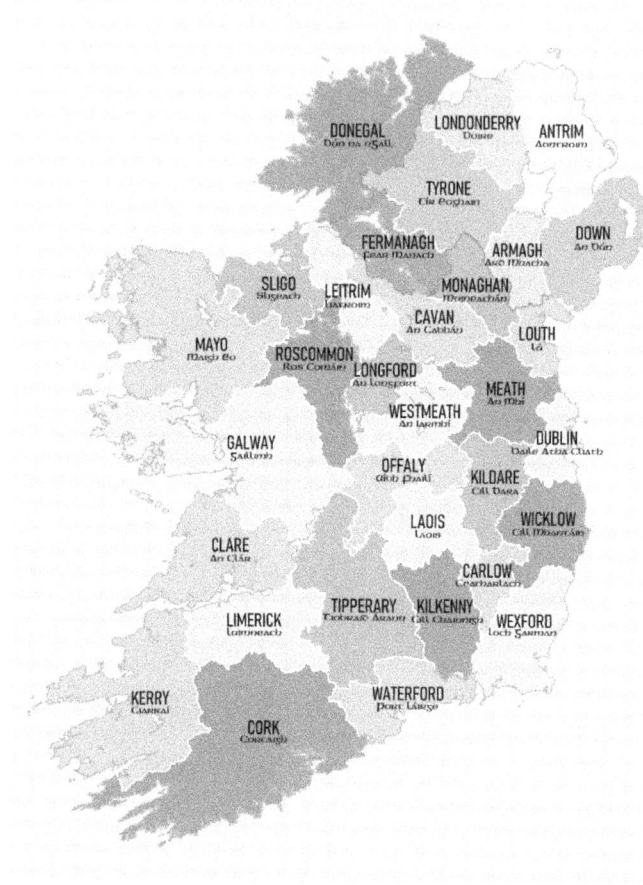

Map of Ireland.

Timeline of Anti-speciesism Efforts in Ireland

400s BC
Celts arrive with animist culture.

1100s
Normans arrive, implementing many agricultural changes.

1500s
Industrialized exploitation of "food" animals begins under British colonization.

1600s
Edmund O'Meara contests vivisection.

Britain passes law against tail-plowing and plucking sheeps.

Britain introduces "racing" and several blood "sports."

1700s
Popularity of blood "sports" denounced.

Irish silk weaving industry thrives.

1800s
Irish animalized by British and Americans.

British introduce "breeding" requirements and "shows" for dogs.

1822
Richard Martin passes Cruel Treatment of Cattle Act.

1824
Society for the Prevention of Cruelty to Animals formed with outreach to Ireland.

1831
Dublin "Zoo" opens.

1838
William H. Drummond publishes *The Rights of Animals, and Man's Obligation to Treat Them with Humanity*.

1870s
Belfast Vegetarian and Food Reform Society and Belfast Vegetarian Association form.

1874
Two Irish physicians disrupt vivisection exposition at the congress of the British Medical Association.

1876
Britain's Cruelty to Animals Act safeguards the institution of vivisection with licensure and regulation.

1880
George Bernard Shaw becomes a vegetarian and an advocate for other animals.

1890s
Irish Vegetarian Union in Belfast, Lisburn Vegetarian Society, Londonderry Vegetarian Society, and Dublin Vegetarian Society form.

1890
Irish Vegetarian Union joins Vegetarian Federal Union.

1891
Sunshine Vegetarian Dining Rooms and the College Vegetarian Restaurant open in Dublin.

1896
Representatives from Ireland speak at the International Vegetarian Congress at the Chicago World's Fair.

Timeline of Anti-speciesism Efforts in Ireland | xix

1900s
Modernization of food system dramatically increases "meat" consumption.

1909
Short-lived vegetarian community formed in Brown's Soapworks Irish Village in Donaghmore, County Tyrone.

1910s
Irish Vegetarian Union / Irish Vegetarian Society forms in Dublin.

Brown Dog Affair.

1916
Irish push for independence disrupts "meat" supplies.

1931
Bird Protection Act passed.

1932
Ulster Vegetarian Society forms.

1944
The Vegan Society launches in Britain, with outreach to Ireland.

1946
Dublin Vegetarian Society resumes operations following wartime abeyance.

1949
Irish Press dubs Moira Henry "The Only Vegan in Ireland."

Irish Society for the Prevention of Cruelty to Animals forms.

1960s
Jack McClelland, vegan athlete, completes several long-distance, record-breaking swims in Irish waters and launches chain of vegan-catering health food stores.

Industrialized food production establishes and extinguishes plant-based eating among poor.

1966
Irish Council against Blood Sports forms.

1972
Good Karma vegetarian restaurant opens briefly in Dublin.

1973
Jack McClelland and Brian Gunn-King appear on *Gordon Burns Hour* on Ulster Television.

Ireland joins the European Union, entrenching agriculture with subsidies and introducing new regulations.

1975
Margaret and Brian Gunn-King open International Vegetarian Union headquarters in Ballymena.

1976
Wildlife Act passed.

1978
Vegetarian Society of Ireland forms.

1979
Irish Wildlife Society forms.

1984
Warzone Collective opens in Belfast, serving vegan food.

1986
Cornucopia vegetarian restaurant opens in Dublin.

1989
Alliance for Animal Rights (AFAR) forms.

1991
Sanctuary status achieved for whales and dolphins in Irish waters.

1994
Animal Rights Action Network (ARAN) forms.

Rural Environmental Protection Scheme launched to encourage sustainable farming practices.

"Beef" Tribunal held, investigating irregularities in Irish "beef" industry.

1996
Control of Horses Act passed, targeting Traveller community.

"Mad" Cow Disease reaches crisis level, disrupting consumer trust and leading to mass slaughter.

2001
Celebrated Nonhuman Animal rights leader Tom Regan appears on the *Late, Late Show*.

Foot-and-mouth outbreak disrupts Irish economy and consumer trust.

"Culling" of badgers is officially sanctioned.

2004
Animal Liberation Front begins raids in Ireland.

2005
National Animal Rights Association (formerly Irish branch of the Coalition to Abolish the Fur Trade) forms.

2009
Vegan Society of Ireland forms.

Lisbon Treaty recognizes Nonhuman Animal sentience and improves welfare standards.

2010s
Cities across Ireland ban the use of Nonhuman Animals in circuses.

Vegan Information Project forms in Dublin.

"Love Ireland" campaigns launch in major grocery chains.

2013
Horse "meat" scandal disrupts consumer trust.

2015
Irish based Go Vegan World campaign launches.

ARAN folds.

2016
Irish Nutrition and Dietetic Institute acknowledges potential healthfulness of vegan diet.

Britain votes to exit the European Union, disrupting Irish animal agriculture.

2019
Dublin named world's most vegan-friendly city according to TripAdvisor.

Introduction

This is an alternate story of Ireland, one that centers its largest demographic—Nonhuman Animals—and their contribution to the country's development. This is not just a telling of nonhuman experiences, but, critically, how those experiences have also shaped that of humans, and how *ideas* about other animals influence Irish culture. This dynamic is a complicated and often conflicting one. Representations of Nonhuman Animals are copious and cherished in the story of Ireland, but their presence is also treated as marginal and overlooked by academics and policy-makers alike. The politics of postcolonialism compound this mixed acknowledgment of other animals, since Ireland, a marginal space itself, often goes ignored in general. Beloved though it may be in the modern global imagination, the adulation of Ireland as a "land of a thousand welcomes" is often patronizing. As Britain's oldest colony, Ireland is generally regarded in the postcolonial landscape as warm and friendly, quaint and simple, sometimes backward, and ultimately a peripheral player on the world stage. In other words, Ireland can easily be dismissed as inconsequential to political discourses and the humans and other animals inhabiting it remain understudied and underappreciated. This book aims to challenge this dual marginalization of Ireland's inhabitants. In a country so shaped by colonial foodways, what happens to Nonhuman Animals matters. The historical entanglement of human and nonhuman experiences with colonial oppression is a key factor in Ireland's social and political trajectory, while more than two centuries of Irish Nonhuman Animal rights activism and development in alternative foodways illustrate how the casualties of colonialism might successfully undermine longstanding systems of oppression.

I find the relative invisibility of Nonhuman Animals to be problematic, given their considerable importance to determining the human condition.

For that matter, Nonhuman Animals, as sentient persons who are vulnerable to human supremacy and colonial violence, could be greatly served by scholarly attention. Other sociologists agree. The sociological subfield of *animals and society*, which developed at the end of the twentieth century (Peggs 2012), examines the material role that Nonhuman Animals play in the historical progress (or regress) of human societies (York and Mancus 2013), the symbolic role that Nonhuman Animals play in the delineation of what it means to be human (Hobson-West 2007), and the possibility for Nonhuman Animal rights or liberation (Taylor and Sutton 2018). Sociology primarily seeks to qualify and quantify the influence of institutions, systems, and relationships on the making and maintenance of human society. Despite the countless ways in which Nonhuman Animals factor into these processes, the sociological discipline has largely overlooked the relationships between humans and other animals (Arluke 2002), thus opening the door to a great frontier of potential inquiry.

According to the critical *Marxist perspective* on social progress, both history and knowledge emerge as social constructions that serve to remember or manufacture reality in support of the prevailing economic system. Since the exploitation of Nonhuman Animals has undergirded most modern human societies, it is useful to critically analyze the making of meaning and memory for a more robust understanding of social relations. Historical records and experiences that do not contribute to this economic project are easily forgotten or erased. What is more, if they are deemed a threat, they are subject to vilification or trivialization. Nonhuman Animals have experienced all of these mechanisms of ideological control under a human supremacist system that sociologists refer to as *speciesism* (Nibert 2003). Telling the story of Nonhuman Animals in relation to human society is thus a political act of resistance, given its potential to unveil hidden systems of inequality.

The magnitude of nonhuman involvement in human society, from the injustice of colonialization to the consequences of climate change, is thus a story worth telling. Not all sociologists subscribe to a conflict-oriented Marxist perspective on society, but for those who do, systems of power and oppression are seen to constitute a creative dynamism that can propel a society toward more equitable social arrangements. Marx famously envisioned a society in which each inhabitant would be free to live up to their species potential. Indeed, it has been argued that Marx also recognized Nonhuman Animals as victims of economic oppression and that the degradation of humanity's most vulnerable was closely aligned with that of other animals (Foster and Clark 2018). Although Marx's plan for a more equitable future based on communal ownership over the means of production has for the most part failed to take root (contemporary scholars have rightly argued that Marx could not have predicted the complexity and magnitude of late stage capitalism) (Craib 1997), he did recognize that a reconfiguring of the false consciousness harbored by those laboring in the system would be a critical initial step in the dismantling of an oppressive social system.

In the twentieth century, political theorist and sociologist Antonio Gramsci expanded on Marx's observations from an Italian prison where he had been incarcerated for his socialist organizing. Gramsci, given his personal circumstances, was all too aware that entire cultures could be swayed by the dominant classes to suit their interests. Unlike Marx, however, he put a greater emphasis on the strength of *hegemony* (the domination of a particular power structure and its associated ideologies for the purposes of manipulating societal values and mores and, subsequently, the manufacture of a populace's consent to be ruled) in normalizing oppression (Adamson 2014). States, he recognized, could dictate and thus politicize culture for the purposes of preserving their power. This manufactured consent was far more potent than violent oppression, which could easily be recognized as coercive and unjust. It would not be enough to simply awaken oppressed persons to these hidden societal mechanisms, as Marx prescribed, or even for those persons to rise in revolt; they would need to create a *counter*-hegemony to facilitate change by normalizing alternative values and earning the consent of the people. Otherwise, social change was unlikely to be lasting, if it could be achieved at all.

Marx and Gramsci applied much of this political thought to the condition of the human populace, but the horrific conditions facing billions of Nonhuman Animals across the globe demonstrate just how insidious exploitative economic modes of production can be. Sociologists David Nibert (2013) and Bob Torres (2007) observe that other animals are doubly burdened by the complicity of the humans who exploit them for economic means and the cognitive and corporal manipulation of domestication that undermines their ability to protest their treatment. This is not to say that some Nonhuman Animals do not recognize and resist their oppression, as many of them do. Instead, I argue that it behooves scholars and activists alike to critically reexamine narratives of humans and other animals that normalize, rationalize, or otherwise apologize for inherently unequal and oppressive circumstances.

Although this effort is already well underway in the West and increasingly in the developing world, particularly with the rise of species-inclusive postcolonial studies (J. M. Davis 2016; Deckha 2013; Nibert 2013), many regions that are pivotal to the global economic exploitation of other animals remain seriously understudied, if not outright ignored. This book presents Ireland as an overlooked but critical site for the manifestation of global capitalist oppression. As Britain's first colony in the modern world system, many of the toxic anthropocentric patterns of power and brutality that reverberate across human-nonhuman relations today can be traced to this island. I argue that a serious examination of speciesism in colonial and postcolonial Ireland will illuminate the intersectional nature of oppression as a historical and contemporary phenomenon in human society. In doing so, I attempt to raise colonized humans and other animals from the margins of existing discourse and spotlight their sufferings, struggles, and contributions.

The Case for Irish Animal Studies

The importance of Nonhuman Animals to the Irish way of life is unmistakable. Outnumbering human inhabitants considerably, Irish cows sprawl across the countryside as they have since Neolithic times. Thousands of visitors board boats and brave the cold Atlantic waters hoping to spot whales off the coast of Cork or meet Fungi the free-living dolphin in Dingle's harbor. Motorists on the backroads of rural counties must navigate herds of free-roaming sheeps, and Aran "wool" sweaters have come to symbolize rural Irish life. Wolfhounds, horse "racing," and Irish "beef" and "butter" have also become synonymous with its geography. Tourists pay handsome sums to gaze at the illuminated manuscripts in the Book of Kells, cathedral adornments, and ancient carved standing stones, all peppered with the likenesses of other animals. It would indeed be difficult to imagine Ireland without the presence and contributions of Nonhuman Animals.

These contemporary encounters with other animals, however, are but an extension of thousands of years of human-nonhuman relations. As with many premodern cultures, Nonhuman Animals were central to the ways of living and knowing in early Ireland. However, with the coming of the Celts and Christians, this relationship was magnified such that early Ireland can only be described as an animist society. Early historical accounts, mythology, and folklore absolutely teem with the exploits of Nonhuman Animals as they intersect with human activities and imaginations (Green 1992). Many place names derive from names given to other animals, especially Gaelic words for pig (*torc* and *muc*) (Mac Con Iomaire 2003) and cow (*bó*) (Mac Coitir

2010). The early Irish acknowledged other animals almost as equals. In fact, the traditional Irish diet was considerably plant-based until industrialization and modernization would make animal products cheaper, more accessible, and nearly unavoidable.

After the Celts, this entanglement persisted into the Middle Ages in perhaps a less forgiving manner. Famed historiographer Gerald of Wales, for instance, visited Ireland on behalf of the Norman colonizers with the task of documenting Irish culture, be it factual or fantastical. Gerald recorded many supernatural tales of human-nonhuman interactions in addition to his general anthropological and zoological observations. Courts in faraway medieval England gave ear to Gerald's accounts of pontificating werewolves, humanoid creatures produced by bestiality, and men who could take the form of fishes. He certainly embellished for the purposes of entertainment, but the medieval Irish themselves boast a rich history of animal-centric folklore. Supernatural beings who traverse the human-nonhuman boundary, such as banshees and faeries, abound in old tales, as do more familiar species such as hares, ravens, and horses. Nonhuman Animals, in other words, permeate the physical and cultural landscapes of Ireland, both then and now. For this reason, at least, it makes sense to acknowledge Nonhuman Animals as active and ever-present contributors to Irish society.

Food and Protest

Although the special role that Nonhuman Animals held in the Irish imagination clearly persists into modern times, Christian expansion, Norman conquest, and British colonization would ensure that relationships with other animals would become exceedingly human supremacist in nature. *Colonization* refers to the control or settlement of a region for the purposes of economic expansion and exploitation. Britain, in particular, relied on the exploitation of other animals (as well as the animalization of marginalized humans) to fuel and justify its global expansion and project of civilization (Thomas 1991). Perhaps most damaging for Nonhuman Animals, these cultural injections significantly increased "meat" and dairy production in Ireland and, as a consequence, their associated environmental tolls. The oppression of Nonhuman Animals, furthermore, was tightly linked with the increased oppression of the Irish under colonialism. The production of animal commodities swelled and did so primarily for the benefit of the British people and at the expense of the Irish peasantry. This process would famously push the Irish onto the potato, a vulnerability that would spell disaster when crops tragically failed. In several counties, food protests erupted as communities retaliated against threats of hunger and want. More than a means of procuring sustenance in a system that had failed so many, these campaigns challenged the legitimacy of the system itself (J. Kelly 2017).

Ireland was both bestialized and feminized under this colonization (O'Connor 2010); it was conceptualized as savage, wild, uncivilized, pagan, and in need of control and domestication. Sociologist Norbert Elias ([1939] 2000) has contended that the West's move to the modern nation-state system (a transition that consolidated power) was accompanied by a process of civilization. This *civilizing process* encouraged (and often mandated) greater control over bodies, emotions, and behaviors. Self-restraint and proper manners (defined by dominant classes and dominant nations) became markers of social superiority. In many ways, they also became markers of humanity itself, given that emotional excitability, basic bodily functions, sexual intercourse, and other "animal-like" behaviors were deemed uncivilized. Consequently, those who existed on society's margins, be they human or nonhuman, became vulnerable to all manner of violent mechanisms of control and discipline.

As republicanism came to a head at the end of the nineteenth century, many nationalists, particularly suffragettes, recognized this shared oppression at the intersection of sexism, colonialism, and speciesism. Vegetarianism came to be associated with the radical thinking of Irish liberation. A number of prominent nationalists and advocates of women's rights were vegetarian, such as Eva Gore-Booth, Charlotte Despard, and Annie Besant. More precariously, republicans would employ the old Gaelic tactic of hunger striking during the Troubles of the latter half of the twentieth century to protest ongoing British imperialism (O'Malley 1990). Food and consumption, this book aims to underscore, are always political in the shadow of colonialism.

Food memory in Ireland is compelling, and consumption patterns are deeply connected to the Irish identity. The Great Famine (*An Gorta Mór*), the most devastating of several agricultural collapses in the early nineteenth century, which resulted in the death of over a million Irish peasantry, was a watershed moment in Irish history. Its legacy created considerable bitterness, and, relatedly, it inspired a complete rethinking of Ireland's position in the United Kingdom. Land reformers later in the century, for instance, battled absentee landlords for fairer distribution of agricultural resources. One such landlord, Charles Boycott, who owned land in County Mayo, attempted to suppress protest with harsh penalties, but would himself be undermined as tenants and community members completely withdrew their cooperation. Indeed, the popular activist tactic of "boycott" derives from this early Irish campaign (Marlow 1973). Nonhuman Animals, especially those who are conceptualized as food, have thus been at the root of colonial oppression in Ireland. Yet, as this book will suggest, they have also been at the heart of resistance. The legacy of colonial-era speciesism informs development in today's sustainable and regional food production, as it is generally employed to attain Irish self-sufficiency and competitiveness in an international market.

Irish Animal Rights

In general, shifts in Ireland's agricultural economy have been especially harmful for Nonhuman Animals, as they have resulted in the institutionalization of speciesism and the large-scale violence it entails, but this sordid history has also supported the growth of Irish Nonhuman Animal advocacy. I suggest that a sort of prototypical vegan Irish ethic has shaped Irish society for thousands of years, fluctuating in relation to various economic conditions and political regimes. Here, I do not apply the dietary definition of veganism, but rather a more contentious variation. From the sociological perspective, *veganism* is a political resistance to speciesism that resists the exploitation and oppression of other animals (Cole and Morgan 2011a; Torres 2007; Wrenn 2016). It is both ideological and protest-oriented. Because the primary human behavior related to this oppression is consumptive, veganism necessarily challenges all aspects of humanity's Nonhuman Animal consumption, including eating them, wearing them, using them for entertainment, using them for product development (such as is done in scientific testing), and using their labor. Veganism involves more than food: it is a social justice theory that reimagines humanity's relationship to other species.

The use of other animals, I argue, takes place within a human supremacist order of relations. What I mean is that *use* is inherently exploitative and invariably causes harm to other animals, who have limited capacity to consent to their being used. Nonhumans the world over, whether directly or indirectly, are impacted by human economic activities, particularly so in today's state of environmental crisis. For these reasons, it is difficult to exaggerate the malevolence of anthropocentrism in human-nonhuman relations. Ireland's social structure is exceptional in this regard. It has been shaped by several projects of colonization across several hundred years, which have successively aggravated speciesism, but it has also harbored a penchant for egalitarianism harkening back to older Gaelic societies. I point to this dynamism as a tension from which a more equitable future Ireland can be realized. It may also provide a lesson for vegan efforts elsewhere in the postcolonial world. Indeed, analyses of Ireland in this context can be useful in "retrieving the different rhythms of historically marginalized cultures" and can deliver "alternative conceptions of culture and of social relations that account for their [marginalized cultures] virtual occlusion from written history" (Lloyd 2003, 62). What is more, this area of analysis offers a "different knowledge" with the potential to "convert the damage of history into the terms for future survival" (62). Perfect conditions are not necessary before meaningful efforts for social justice can begin; activists need only recognize and mobilize preexisting values and traditions that already align with their goal of an equitable and fair society. This repurposing of Irish values, new and old, is one aim of this book.

I argue that, as is true of many traditional societies, Ireland enjoys a comparatively egalitarian past, but this has been tested by the strains of colonization, which include intergroup divisiveness and entrenched speciesism. The spirit of Irish resistance is fierce, however, and new developments in social justice arenas may well release Ireland from the lingering burdens of colonialism, including those that are imposed on other animals. Although this book is one of the first to seriously examine this concept in the Irish context, animality has been pivotal to the maintenance of unequal relations in a number of other similarly situated regions. For instance, the Catholic Church brought to vote the humanness of Indigenous Americans in the sixteenth century, as their categorization as animals had been used to justify their subjugation (Stogre 1992). In parts of Africa, race was explicitly constructed vis-à-vis animalization by colonialists eager to insert divisiveness to facilitate control. In countries such as Zimbabwe, postcolonial land disputes would politicize Nonhuman Animals further as white settlers pushed for control and Indigenous Blacks strove for sovereignty. Nonhuman Animals were objectified as "livestock," tourism-attracting safari ingredients, and poaching victims (Suzuki 2017). Likewise, elephants were utilized in the colonization of Burma, made complicit in resource extraction and empire expansion (Saha 2017). In nearby India, scholars have examined how postcolonial politics maintained Indian dependence through the imposition of Western, animal-based foodways that displaced traditional systems, diminished health, and eroded identity (Gaard 2013). Gambert and Linné (2018) have noted this trend elsewhere in Asia, with stereotypes of effeminate plant-based eating used even today to maintain racialized colonial hierarchies. In such cases, Nonhuman Animals became collateral damage, suffering in droves to feed colonialist aims. The relationship between colonial domination, land grabbing, food conquest, animalization and racialization, and the exploitation of Nonhuman Animals is thus a well-documented one in the postcolonial world, positioning Ireland as another important case study in this larger narrative.

Vegan Intersectionality as a Guiding Perspective

These numerous intersections indicate that Nonhuman Animals have been pivotal to the Irish imagination and experience, but these are only a few examples from a much more complex entanglement. This book considers three areas of inquiry in pursuit of the story. First, I argue that Nonhuman Animals are an essential but underexamined component to the country's cultural, political, and economic infrastructure. Second, the oppression of Nonhuman Animals made necessary by this infrastructural reliance is tightly bound to the oppression of humans, be they colonial subjects, tenants, immigrants, women, Travellers, or postcolonialists struggling in the global arena. Third, there has been robust Irish resistance to the exploitation of other animals, and often this resistance intersects with civil rights efforts for humans as well. Irish studies have, for the most part, ignored these three points. Invisibilizing the struggles of Nonhuman Animals is not only an act of remarkable ignorance given the magnitude of their numbers and their suffering, but it is also a distortion of the human condition. For even the most anthropocentric of scholars, an honest incorporation of Nonhuman Animal studies is worth pursuing, given the connectivity between human and nonhuman experiences. One need not be vegan to appreciate the sociological importance of Nonhuman Animals in human society.

The *vegan feminist theory* I employ herein emphasizes that the relationship between humans and nonhumans in Ireland is a reciprocal, mutually influential one. *Black feminism* introduced this concept of *intersectionality*, which can be traced at least as far back as the early nineteenth century. Straddling the male space of the American abolitionist movement and the white-centric space of the budding feminist movement, Sojourner Truth, a former slave, pressed her audiences to consider how her experiences with sexism and her experiences with racism could not be separately understood. That is, systems of oppression do not operate fully independently. Laboring on a plantation while surviving on meager rations and lamenting the loss of multiple children to the slave trade, Truth faced tribulations that were bound to her female experience but foreign to the wealthy white women leading the feminist movement. A failure to recognize the interlocking nature of various systems of oppression offered a problematically incomplete analysis of social injustice. Finding herself excluded from both male-dominated abolitionist work and white-dominated feminism, an exasperated and invisibilized Truth famously queried in Akron, Ohio in 1851: "Ain't I a woman?"

More than a century of mobilization and scholarship would develop these early observations, culminating in the work of author bell hooks (1982) who would reignite Truth's question in her own contribution to intersectional feminist theory, *Ain't I a Woman: Black Women and Feminism*. For hooks, these layers of oppression were significantly more complicated. More than sexism and racism, hooks's interpretation of entwining marginalizations also included a critique of capitalist and colonial systems, what she termed the "imperialist white supremacist capitalist patriarchy." She was also deeply critical of the consumption practices of the dominant class that so characteristically undergird capitalist and colonial aims. Marginalized groups were vulnerable to figurative cultural consumption as well as the literal consumption of their bodies and labor (1992). This consumption not only entailed considerable violence against people of color, women, and colonized peoples, but it served the symbolic function of maintaining their status as "other."

Many other academics and activists were busily contributing to the dialogue, leading to a resurgence of topical interest in the 1990s highlighted by sociologist Patricia Hill Collins's "matrix of domination" theory (1990) and legal scholar Kimberlé Crenshaw's (1991) concept of "intersectionality." Scholar activists Angela Davis, Aph Ko (2019), and Breeze Harper (2010) would extend these frameworks even further to include the plight of Nonhuman Animals, while ecofeminists also introduced the exploitation of the environment as relevant (Gaard 1993). What is important to extract from these feminist contributions is the notion that no oppression stands alone, identity categories are manufactured and divisive, and that consumption practices are highly political. Both colonial studies and feminism have examined the trajectory of Ireland, but space remains to incorporate a nonhuman perspective. What might be uncovered if species and animality were granted relevance?

I subsequently apply intersectionality to this analysis, grounding the cultural, political, and economic developments of Ireland in the context of trans-species oppression. In doing so, I also utilize a critical vegan lens, with veganism applied in its political sense as a shorthand for species-inclusive intersectionality. More than a diet, I have argued that veganism is an ideology and praxis of species egalitarianism that is sharply critical of human supremacy and the institutionalized (as well as noninstitutionalized) exploitation of Nonhuman Animals. It is a radical epistemology, to be sure, but it is applied here as a means of demarcating attitudes, behaviors, systems, and histories that challenge the traditional anthropocentric treatment of other animals. And, more than a collection of theories and ideas, vegan feminist theory is backed by emerging social psychological research that presents quantified evidence as to the intersecting nature of human and nonhuman processes of dehumanization and its effects (Hodson, Dhont, and Earle 2020; Kasperbauer 2018).

Vegan feminist scholars such as Carol Adams (2000) have unpacked this species-inclusive intersectionality at length, but few have applied the aforementioned Marxist lens to develop a critique of the state and economic relations (Wrenn 2017). Nibert (2002) and Torres (2007) are two exceptions, advancing a *vegan socialist theory* that explicitly argues that the entanglement of human-nonhuman oppression emerges from a society's economic mode of production. Acknowledging this intersection and its material roots will be necessary to challenge and restructure these unequal and frequently violent relations. It is this sort of Marxian vegan feminism that I apply to the Irish case study, given how strongly the culture has been shaped by the state, its economic endeavors, and the resulting nature of human-nonhuman relations.

Despite these correlations, most modern societies have not opted to challenge the many intersecting oppressions fanned by nation-building. They have entered the fray and exacerbated them instead. In this vein, Laura Wright (2015) introduced the concept of *vegan studies* as a means of exploring both vegan practice and identity within the context of nationalism. As this book will demonstrate, the tensioned relationship between food and nationalism has been and continues to be relevant for Ireland. As Ireland's relationship to Britain fractured, the country might have utilized alternative, egalitarian economies to realize its dream for independence, healthy interdependence with other global players, and long-term sustainability. Should it have done so, it would have had a rich history of communal living and vegetarian farming in Ireland from which to draw inspiration. Although this book attempts to highlight some attempts to reimagine Ireland in this more affirming manner, it has generally been the case that Ireland has opted to remain complicit with an economic system and national identity that are harmful to vulnerable humans and other animals. In any case, Wright is correct to emphasize that food ethics shape the identity, aspirations, and embodied experiences of a nation state and its citizenry. I subsequently draw on Wright's concept of *animal nationalism* to examine the role of agrarianism, colonialism, capitalist competition, and environmental protection as particularly influential in shaping the identities and experiences of both humans and nonhumans over the millennia.

In light of these themes, this book will highlight ancient Ireland prior to its incorporation into the modern world system, Ireland under British colonization, and modern Ireland in the era of intensified globalization. This analytical choice is discipline specific. Many sociologists, particularly those of the Marxist persuasion, look to a society's economy to understand its social structure. Material arrangements, believed to be largely unequal due to power imbalances, dictate social arrangements and these arrangements generally foster conflict. In other words, it makes sense to examine the material arrangements of a society in order to understand its ideologies and the life outcomes of those living therein. As this analysis surveys Ireland over the millennia, I will examine systems of "hunting," "herding," colonialism, and capitalism as the primary modes of production. Archaeological evidence supports the theory that early human societies prior to the system of "hunting" were primarily egalitarian and vegetarian (Mason 1993). As a more recently inhabited area of the globe, Ireland's human inhabitants always relied on some system of speciesism, but I will argue that this reliance was far less oppressive than it would come to be under the colonial system. Speciesist economic systems, reliant as they are on the exploitation of Nonhuman Animals, are inherently hierarchical and oppressive. Recall that vegan feminist theory argues that these systems entangle human and nonhuman oppression. Speciesist systems create a spatial arrangement that not only oppresses Nonhuman Animals, but that also fosters a logic and framework useful for the oppression of vulnerable humans such as women, children, lower classed persons, disabled persons, older persons, and so on. Speciesist systems are predicated on the extraction of maximum benefit for a few at the expense of the many. Such a system has ramifications for humans and nonhumans alike.

Critical Animal Studies

I have taken care to explain the intersectional nature of human-nonhuman experiences to prepare the reader for the book's thesis, but it is also necessary because the notion that Nonhuman Animals play a pivotal role in human society is a relatively new and sometimes contested concept. This is not unrelated to my opening premise that knowledge is a social (and thus political) construction. Social science, as with any science, also entails some degree of bias. Nonhuman Animals are not excluded from inquiry due to their insignificance in social processes but due to the anthropocentrism of their researchers. *Critical Animal Studies* argues that a conscious application of intersectionality theory is necessary, bolstered by a strong, applied vegan ethic (Socha and Mitchell 2014).

Mainstream sociological and historical texts generally fail to extend this intersectionality praxis to include species. Susan Nance explores this disciplinary deficiency in *The Historical Animal* (2015), noting that the perspective of other animals is largely absent in official and cultural remembrance. Little record is kept, and what mention survives is invariably strained through the sieve of human supremacy. Vegan sociologists have emphasized the invisibility of Nonhuman Animals as a serious methodological failing, pointing to the validity of the nonhuman experience and the critical role they play in the human society that sociology prioritizes (Nibert 2003; Peggs 2012). My own research presented herein aims to combat this disciplinary resistance, offering evidence to the integral nature of human-nonhuman relations in the making, unmaking, and remaking of Irish society.

This book employs multiple complementary perspectives in pursuit of this goal, not only from sociology, but also from history, archaeology, feminism, and the interdisciplinary field of Critical Animal Studies. I make the somewhat provocative claim that the story of Irish humanity is more accurately conceived in the context of its relationship with Irish *animality*. Indeed, the boundary between "human" and "nonhuman" will itself be explored as a social construct. It is a derivative of human culture rather than the natural world, and it is made meaningful by its symbolic value. This boundary falsely classifies, categorizes, and reduces animal diversity. In this sense, it is a product of colonialism. Observes Ko, "*Animal* is a signifier that is always convenient and changing, and any group the dominant class deems unworthy is immediately branded with this label" (2019, 37). In examining the political manifestation of animality, we can better understand the mechanisms of colonialism and its impact on social relations and individual life chances.

Critical Animal Studies scholars are certainly not the first to identify these patterns. Once again, an Irish thinker can be credited for tackling this complexity early on. Literary satirist Jonathan Swift ([1726] 1900) famously explored modern boundary constructions in his eighteenth-century writings. Published in 1726, *Travels into Several Remote Nations of the World in Four Parts* (now colloquially known as *Gulliver's Travels*) grappled with the rapidly changing social relations of modern life, notably the changing boundary between humans and other animals, the violent divisions between social groups as they vied for power, and the ideological supports that both allowed for and explained widening social inequality. Some modern Irish thinkers, in other words, recognized that a transforming society was marked by its human and nonhuman inequalities and relations. Perhaps scholars today might take a cue from Gulliver and adopt an attitude of open-minded curiosity and adventure in the making of contemporary knowledge and meaning.

Swift may not have been vegetarian, but he clearly understood that the treatment of Nonhuman Animals was deeply connected to the treatment of marginalized humans, particularly those of colonial Ireland. As the protagonist of *Gulliver's Travels* discovers in his adventures to faraway cultures, the rationality and civility so frequently attributed to society's most privileged are characteristics that fall flat when institutions of domestication, slavery, and colonial oppression are examined. Humanity's distinction is undermined in places such as the Land of the Houyhnhnms, where horses, rather than humans, are found to be highly reasoned and virtuous. In this equine society, species constructions are reversed, and humans (known as "yahoos") are believed to be disgusting and irrational, suitable only for pet-keeping, draught, or butchery. The belief is so compelling that Gulliver begins to loathe his own humanity, allying with his equine hosts. As the metaphorical Land of Houyhnhnms demonstrates, the creation of animal difference brings order, logic, and hierarchy to humanity's social relations, but this separation is ultimately arbitrary. It is likely that Swift's own intimate relationships with Nonhuman Animals, particularly his horses, may have encouraged this critical examination of animality as a basis for social organization (A. C. Kelly 2007).

His work, contextualized within Britain's colonization of Ireland, submits that the boundaries constructed between humans and other animals and between culture and nature are fragile ones, but these are boundaries made necessary in the rationalization of inequality and oppression. Indeed, Marx recognized the divisive nature of class as instrumental in upholding capitalism. Without these divisions, exploited workers might recognize their shared oppression and revolt. Sociologist Pierre Bourdieu ([1984] 2010) likewise observed this boundary-making in the maintenance of power relations in modern society. Examining this boundary work in the context of speciesism can only serve to elucidate the mechanics of social conflict. In any case, I find Swift's examination of inequality and animality in the Irish context to be a fruitful jumping off point for a larger analysis of Ireland in the colonial and postcolonial context. Since Swift's death, the entanglement of human-nonhuman oppression would only grow more complex, adding urgency to the liberatory mission undertaken by vegan feminism, vegan studies, Critical Animal Studies, and Marxist sociology.

In the forthcoming pages, I introduce Nonhuman Animals to the discourse as legitimate social actors who are essential in the construction of the Irish state and its culture. This linkage is clearly evident in Ireland, but little has been published to illuminate it. Irish scholar Hilary Tovey (2003) is one of the few sociologists to question the wisdom of ignoring Nonhuman Animals in environmental and rural studies, given the role they play in "farmer" culture and identity as well as their ability to link rural and urban spaces. As she rightly identifies, sociology too often works in binaries by positioning human society against nature, and generally only recognizing communities of other animals in abstract environmental terms as "nature" or "biodiversity." Doing so not only marginalizes domesticated species who resist such categories, but it also overlooks the regular and complex interconnections and interactions between humans and other animals. Nonhuman Animals are not always distant and removed. Instead, they are woven throughout social life. The socially constructed, economically driven conditions that shape human systems, such as industrialization and rationalization, directly impact nonhumans as well, but this, too, is overlooked by sociological inquiry. Tovey envisioned a new societal paradigm in which Nonhuman Animals, as a distinct group, would be granted proper acknowledgment and not simply be reduced to tools and symbols for human ends. If sociological theories of social construction, inequality, and change are to hold weight, they must extend to the nonhuman condition.

Methodology

It is no small task to accommodate these radical ambitions of Critical Animal Studies, which include a reimagining and rewriting of historical and contemporary social narratives (often on a grand scale with little existing work to guide the way). Like Swift's Gulliver, I entered a great world of unknowns with a desire to explore uncharted territories and make sense of them with a critical lens focused on human-nonhuman relations. With so little place-specific research on which to base my species-inclusive Irish study, I found it necessary to undertake a rather haphazard approach to exploring the literature. I relied heavily on texts related to ancient, medieval, and modern Irish culture, farming, food, and environment, examining them for mention of human interactions with other animals, both benevolent and oppressive. Some digital archives were searched, such as the Letters of 1916 repository and the Bureau of Military History database. I also targeted works related to the oppression of humans and Irish protest with an eye for potential intersections, such as the diary of hunger striker Bobby Sands, reports on Victorian-era asylums, and books on Irish feminist mobilization. For more current information, I followed the *Irish Times* and other Irish newspapers, also watching for mention of human-animal interactions or conflicts. Helpfully, the *Irish Times* allows for a keyword search of its archives, which allowed me to search for mention of veganism, vegetarianism, "animal rights," and so on. I made use of the Vegan Society's back issues of its publication the *Vegan* as well, which reached back to its founding in 1944. Although the Vegan Society is a British organization and made only sparing mention of vegan activities in the Republic, copious reports can be found on vegan activities in the north of Ireland. Publications by Britain's Vegetarian Society archived online were likewise useful. Lastly, I did not hesitate to contact scholars and activists specializing in these areas for clues and suggestions, such as the aforementioned environmental sociologist Hilary Tovey. I otherwise relied heavily on publications in Critical Animal Studies to shape my analysis, looking for parallels that might be established in the Irish context.

As should be clear, my author positionality proved somewhat of a hindrance since, as of this writing, I am an American scholar based in Canterbury, England. Like many Americans, I can claim Irish heritage with my ancestors settling in Appalachia as part of the great wave of Scots-Irish immigration in the early eighteenth century. Also like many Americans, that Irish connection is distant and foreign. I lived in Cork for approximately a year and a half in the 2010s, but such a brief tenancy forces me to acknowledge that my familiarity with Irish culture and politics is still evolving and inherently vulnerable to misinterpretation. I inevitably run the risk of condensing and simplifying the great diversity of Irish societies, cultures, regions, and historical eras. Furthermore, as a practicing vegan, socialist, and feminist who is firmly positioned in the field of Critical Animal Studies, I cannot claim to have only a detached scholarly interest in these areas of Irish heritage. My sociological training also restricted my scope as to the relationships between humans and other animals—I generally avoid zoological examinations of the lives of other animals for instance.

There are additional methodological difficulties associated with my reliance on a historical record that normalizes speciesism and places little value on remembering Nonhuman Animals. The data that I have analyzed for this manuscript frequently objectified, belittled, or ignored the experiences of other animals, leaving me to reinterpret and reconstruct the record from time to time. Adding to this is the inherent bias attached to the human researcher, a bias that can easily inhibit said interpretation of the data. Therefore, the aim of this book is not to create an objective report, as any scientific endeavor entails some degree of professional spin. Nor will it presume to know the true, subjective experience of those nonhumans referenced herein. It can only offer a critical sociological perspective on the Irish nonhuman experience with the intention of lending legitimacy to the reality of society's most vulnerable, those who rarely warrant mention in the tomes of scientific and cultural dialogue. The intention is not to write *on behalf of* these individuals, for they were not and are not voiceless objects without agency. This book instead writes in their support.

Some other stylistic decisions warrant mention. "Ireland" will be used in reference to either Ireland the republic or Ireland the united colony where appropriate and unless otherwise indicated. With respect to the years following Partition, this book will focus primarily on Southern Ireland, although it will sometimes be fruitful to explore themes of economics, activism, and Irish Republicanism in the North. Neither do I intend to compress the diversity *within* these spaces, north or south, past or present, although some degree of generalization has been necessary, as I have intended this book to be an introductory glance at human-nonhuman relations in a region heretofore almost completely ignored by Critical Animal Studies scholars. Colonized people are not a homogenous group and obviously there will be significant diversity with regard to species, class, ethnicity, gender, age, ability, and so on.

Lastly, a note on language is pertinent. Sociology recognizes the symbolic power of language in normalizing attitudes and shaping culture. Sometimes this social function can be problematic, when that language helps to solidify inequality. Therefore, those terms and phrases that euphemize oppression (such as "meat" or "farming") are placed within quotation marks to denote their problematic nature, while objectifying mass terms, notably "sheep," "mice," and "fish" are modified. Finally, the term "Nonhuman Animals" is capitalized as a political measure of respect for the nonhuman diaspora in a human supremacist society. The popular, but otherizing term "animals" is avoided for similar reasons.

Conclusion

Although Nonhuman Animals have played a pivotal role in the development of Irish culture and nationhood, they have been largely erased from critical inquiries. Likewise, the experiences of Nonhuman Animals as they matter to nonhumans themselves are almost completely overlooked. Theories of intersectionality stemming from Black feminism emphasize that experiential analyses will be considerably lacking if deployed in singular dimensions. Instead, various identities often intersect at once. In the case of Ireland, identities based in species, gender, class, and colonialism have interlocked in support of a matrix of oppression, entwining the destinies of humans and other animals alike. Unfortunately, leading social science theory fails to extend this intersectional theory to the experience of Nonhuman Animals, but Critical Animal Studies has emerged to legitimize the study of speciesism and the liberatory promise of veganism.

Nonhuman Animals, if taken seriously as social actors in their own right, are well positioned to offer critical insight into the Irish experience. As such, this book examines the parallel narratives of oppression and resistance, arguing that a vegan feminist perspective holds potential in illuminating shared oppressions in colonial and postcolonial Ireland and envisioning a more equitable Irish future. I suggest that this can be accomplished by resurrecting a Gaelic vegan ethic that has been subsumed and adulterated by various oppressive economic systems and by constructing a new vegan ethic that incorporates egalitarian elements of Ireland's past with new developments in twentieth- and twenty-first-century Irish culture and economy.

This economic focus will also be examined from a Marxist perspective. Like vegan feminism, vegan socialist theory acknowledges the social constructedness of social difference and its political utility in sustaining unequal social relations. It further acknowledges that speciesism is a fundamental source of division as it undergirds most economic modes of production. The next chapter examines human relationships with other animals as they transfigure under various economies such as "hunting," "cattle" raiding, and stationary animal-based agriculture. Speciesist economies, I will document, dramatically influenced the trajectory of Nonhuman Animals, humans, and Ireland itself.

Chapter 1

Celticism, Christianity, and Animism in Gaelic Ireland

Sociologist Erika Cudworth (2011) has emphasized that the manufacture of difference between humans and other animals facilitates forms of social organization that are based in domination and hierarchy. One such system that relies on the domination of the "natural" world and the privileging of humans she terms an *anthroparchy*. Frequently, this domination is maintained through consumptive behaviors, and, for Nonhuman Animals, this materializes in economic systems that are predicated on the production of "meat," dairy, and other products made of their bodies and labor. Irish societies across the millennia are clearly anthroparchal, having depended heavily on Nonhuman Animals, both free-living and domesticated. Settlers arrived and quickly established agricultural systems with cows at the center of social organization (Cunningham 2015). The systematic exploitation of cows also guided ancient politics, and "cattle" raids between communities were a leading force of social and economic change. This society was also patriarchal; kings and chieftains proved their worthiness and right to rule through repeated raiding.

Early Irish peoples relied on Nonhuman Animal flesh and milk as a major source of calories (Green 1992; O'Kelly 2001). Indeed, human communities of this region were uniquely lactose tolerant, a place-specific genetic adaptation to the limiting climate. Between 73 percent and 95 percent of Irish humans are lactose tolerant, an occurrence that is much higher than regions beyond the British Isles and Scandinavia (Cunningham 2015). Irish humans and cows, archaeologists have argued, developed in relation to one another (Murphy and Stout 2015).

This chapter will not attempt to recount the entirety of early Ireland's greatly diversified relationship with other animals (strong catalogs are available in Miranda Green's *Animals in Celtic Life and Myth* [1992] and Fergus Kelly's *Early Irish Farming* [1997]), but I offer instead a very general overview of key elements to demonstrate the importance of other animals to Irish culture in the centuries prior to colonization. Rather than organize this analysis by particular eras of Gaelic Ireland, I instead examine various elements of human relations with other animals with an eye to the influence of animism, Christianity, and Gaelic folklore and how these relations are qualified by systems of class, gender, and other forms of human distinction.

David Nibert (2013) emphasizes that a society's economic mode of production will determine human relations with other animals, while vegan feminist theory (Adams 2000; Ko and Ko 2017) advances the notion that the social category of "species" is heavily dependent upon the construction of other social categories such as gender and class. Cudworth (2011), furthermore, argues that the economic exploitation of Nonhuman Animals is heavily gendered, given the clear gender divisions in food procurement and preparation as well as the gendered symbolic meanings ascribed to food and how it is consumed. Because Marxist vegan thought posits that these forms of social distinction emerged from humanity's shift to an animal-based mode of production ("hunting" and, later, domestication), it, like vegan feminism, acknowledges the entwined destinies shared by Nonhuman Animals, women, lower classed persons, ethnic minorities, and so forth. Both vegan Marxism and feminism reiterate that humanity's relationship with other animals will significantly influence the structural design of society as well as the status, access to resources, and life chances attributed to various human groups living therein. This relationship is never fixed, but shifts according to geographical changes, external influences, and cultural innovations. The story of Ireland spotlights this undulating process.

I suggest that, although Ireland today is stereotyped as deeply speciesist, traditional Irish peoples recognized a deep kinship with other sentients in their social world. Colonization would disrupt this solidarity and introduce a human-centric hierarchy that could be utilized to normalize its preferred system of oppression and disarm the Irish of an important form of social, political, and symbolic capital that might be found in their proximity to Nonhuman Animals. Indeed, humans and other animals shared many lived experiences prior to colonization's project of "civilization." The coevolution of humans and the other animals in their orbit with regard to ideologies, religion, food systems, family life, economic systems, and social stratification is the fundamental interest of Critical Animal Studies (Socha and Mitchell 2014), but structural sociologist Pierre Bourdieu ([1984] 2010) has also argued that the aforementioned creation of social distinction is key to the maintenance of social inequality. Thus, this chapter examines the negotiation of human distinction and the manifestation of difference in Gaelic Ireland prior to 1500. Colonialization would have a monumental impact on Irish speciesism, but, as I will catalog, the diversity of social arrangements that preexisted this shift also laid the groundwork for entangled oppression, particularly through the development of nonhuman domestication (Nibert 2013).

Irish societies of this time were certainly speciesist, but human relationships with the natural world were profoundly meaningful and often sacred. Anthropologists support modern sociological observations that Nonhuman Animals "contribute to the tapestry of everyday life" and were "much more than simple resources" (Pollard 2015, 135). They defined life, death, ancestry, economy, and other human social relations, thus resisting the sharp categorizations and boundaries that would be imposed in modern times. This *animism* was particularly marked with the arrival of Celtic culture in approximately 400 BC. The Celts lived amongst other animals and relied on them not just for sustenance, but also for guidance and spiritual support. Additionally, Celtic myths regularly featured zoomorphic human characters who could turn into nonhumans and back again, suggesting that the boundaries between humans and other animals was not so clear as it would later become under colonization.

This early way of life is partially recorded in the Irish heroic cycles, a mythology that blends knowledges, remembrances, and stories from prehistoric and Celtic Ireland. Comparable to that of the epic literature of ancient Greece, these heroic cycles focus on kings, the warrior elite, and their "cattle" raiding. As many of the heroic cycles primarily exist thanks to the efforts of medieval scribes, these stories were already several centuries in the telling by the time they were recorded and include a certain degree of embellishment. Nonetheless, they provide an important cultural dimension to the understanding of ancient Ireland that archaeology is limited in its capacity to uncover.

One thing is certain, Nonhuman Animals mattered immensely to the early Irish, as they feature prominently in the old texts. This suggests some recognition that other animals enjoyed a social status much closer to that of humans. Nonhuman Animals (usually native free-living species or mysterious species from faraway lands) were represented as metaphors for heroic behavior. Domesticated species surfaced most often in these tales in relation to their economic purpose (Mallory 2016). The use of other animals to explain the social as well as the natural world is a predictable technique, as folklorist Niall Mac Coitir explains:

> Animals are special to us because they are "flesh and blood" creatures like we are, with recognizable drives and motivations. Crucially we can see that many animals are unique individuals, with personalities of their own, just like us. For this reason it is inevitable that we should project our own fears and desires on to them, and ascribe human motives and characteristics to them. (2010, 236)

Thus, early Irish culture was both literally and figuratively constructed with nonhuman representations and relationships. The line that is today so clearly drawn between "human" and "animal" did not yet exist.

Perhaps the most compelling evidence to this permeable boundary between humans and other animals is the legend of mythological hero Cú Chulainn. Upon killing a chieftain's valuable guard dog, Cú Chulainn offered himself as a replacement. In doing so, he became a dog himself. His name Cú Chulainn (Hound of Chulainn) reflects this transformation. The great warrior would, after many successful exploits, eventually meet his demise after engaging in cannibalism when he broke taboo by accidentally consuming dog's flesh and killing an otter (known as a "water dog") before battle. He had a feline side as well, reportedly employing the "feat of the cat" as a combat skill in battle. Most gruesomely, Cú Chulainn and his warriors were said to enter a "warp spasm" in battle, literally morphing into the most disgusting and horrifying conglomeration of frightful features associated with a variety of species to terrify and intimidate the enemy (Cahill 1995; Larsen 2003).

The boundary between human and other animals was also tested in the epic tale of Fionn mac Cumhaill. Fionn kept two hounds, Bran and Sceolang, who were also his cousins. Born of a woman turned dog by magic, they had entered the world in the shape of dogs as well (Reinhard and Hull 1936). In fact, a number of hybrid beings inhabit Fionn's world. There is Beann Ghulban, a deformed boar born a human child, who does battle with him (S. Harvey 2000). There is also Fionn's wife Sadb and their son Oisin, who were both transfigured into deers. High King Labraid Loingseach was said to have ears like a horse, which he covered with his hair. His hair would be cut each year, but the unfortunate barber employed for the task was thereafter killed to protect the king's secret (Mac Coitir 2010).

As these examples illustrate, Nonhuman Animal imagery prominently appeared in war mythology, and predictably so, as early Ireland was a war-based society. This imagery could be utilized to instill fear, or to evoke prediction and protection in combat. Liath Macha (the Grey of Macha), a chariot horse from the tale of Cú Chulainn, was for instance thought to possess clairvoyance and was a fierce warrior. This was also true of the Badbh Catha, the battlefield ravens who could take human form (Sjoestedt 2000). Ravens were assigned particular importance in this regard, given their habit of feasting on the corpses of those who died in combat. As such, they were seen as harbingers of death. The Morrígan, a phantom queen, could become one such bird, flying across battlefields foretelling their outcome. When a crow lands on the shoulder of Cú Chulainn (who had already been weakened by eating dog's flesh) following his mortal wounding, it signals the death of the seemingly indestructible great hero. Given this intense symbolism, it is not surprising that surviving artifacts of Celtic battle accoutrements regularly depict Nonhuman Animals.

The elevated status granted to some Nonhuman Animals in their association with gods and heroes, however, would not protect them from human oppression, as Nonhuman Animals were regularly subject to violence to suit human interests. The general inability for Nonhuman Animals to become human in Irish tales (for the most part, only humans could transfigure) indicates a recognition of human supremacy despite the high regard nonhumans were granted. Indeed, these tales often feature human-to-nonhuman shape-shifting as a form of punishment (as was the case with King Labraid and his shameful horse ears) or as a means of serving the interests of humans in some way (as was the case with Cú Chulainn's battle skills) (Green 1992). This animist culture, in other words, was still anthropocentric.

Relationships with Free-Living Animals

As remains the case today (Cole and Morgan 2011a), early humans interacted with each species differently based on their assigned purpose in society. Domesticated animals were most often consumed as food, as were free-living animals (albeit less frequently). This differential treatment is reflected in mythological remembrance. The economic commodification and domestication of Nonhuman Animals necessitates a level of objectification and disassociation that free-living species could avoid to some extent. More often, "hunting" was engaged for ritual purposes, attaining skins, to reassert male and human supremacy, or for the entertainment of the nobility (Green 1992). In era of the "cattle" raids, "hunting" was also engaged as practice for battles. Archaeological evidence suggests that Iron Age communities before the arrival of the Celts were even less interested in "hunting."

Nonetheless, free-living species like wolves, brown bears, lynxes, "wild" boars and cats, and red squirrels would eventually be driven to near or complete extinction,[1] if not from "hunting" for human consumption or to reduce competition, then by human encroachment and habitat destruction necessitated by the keeping of domesticated animals (Yalden 1999).[2] The experiences of wolves exemplify the precariousness of existence for free-living animals living amid an animist human society that paradoxically both valorized and otherized them. Although wolves featured regularly in Celtic mythology as references to war and shapeshifted warriors, they were ruthlessly persecuted given their threat to the "livestock"-based economy and the perceived threat to human lives. The fall of Celticism and the establishment of colonial rule brought heavier persecution. A commodification of their skin and hair and the English bounty placed on their heads sealed their extinction in the eighteenth century (Kieran Hickey 2013).

The killing of free-living animals sometimes required the assistance of oppressed domesticated animals such as horses, hawks, and dogs. Irish Wolfhounds, Ireland's only native dog species, were kept for the killing of these wolves, a sort of canine extension of human oppression (although dogs were themselves eaten as food in the late Bronze Age and through the Iron Age) (Mallory 2016). In fact, following the extinction of wolves, wolfhounds, too, nearly disappeared as their utility to humans waned. For commoners who could not afford these nonhuman accomplices, snares, traps, and spears were popular killing instruments. Medieval records indicate that nonhumans were also "hunted" with leg traps or driven into nets, spikes, or pits. Others were held captive on private Anglo-Norman lands and parks for easy "harvesting" (Beglane 2015). More than an act of speciesist terrorism, "hunting" illustrates the intersecting nature of human and nonhuman oppression. Recall that "hunting" was used in the development of battle skills. It sharpened participants' knowledge of the landscape as would be useful in raids and war.

"Hunting" was not always engaged for such practical purposes. It was highly symbolic as well. For instance, the gifting of nonhuman bodies or the right to "hunt" them was a common means of political maneuvering, as was the cooking and serving of these bodies at great feasts, the networking events of the day. The gruesome ritual of "breaking" deers killed in "hunts" sustained social stratification with precise rules regarding the divvying of body parts to various parties involved in the killing (Beglane 2016). The Normans had strong restrictions on "hunting," and archaeological evidence would support a theory that these were successful, as the remains of deers, rabbits, and other "hunted" animals are infrequently found outside of castles and other buildings occupied by the ruling class. Given that they were heavily managed, they were more accurately categorized as "livestock" than "game." Medieval manor houses frequently contained dovecots and warrens for the regular supplying of doves and rabbits (Murphy and Stout 2015). Rabbits, having been introduced by the Normans, were killed in huge numbers by nets and ferrets. The middling classes attempted to emulate this status by purchasing and serving "game" when they could afford it. Lower classes may have participated in "hunting" (either legally or illegally) as a means of supplementing their income, given the high value placed on "meat," but evidence does not support the inference that they were high consumers of "game" themselves.

As would also be the case under colonial British rule, early "hunts" were displays of status and wealth, helping to preserve power structures. Furthermore, the intertwining of humans, assistant nonhumans, and nonhuman victims in the ritual of the "hunt" had important cultural ramifications. Violence against free-living animals could be romanticized in a blurring of the human-nonhuman boundary. "Hunters" sometimes recorded a sense of solidarity with the nonhuman world by taking on the animalistic role of predator and also by connecting with the "prey" through the ritual of the chase. Vegan feminist Marti Kheel (1995) supposes that this process is further functional in its ability to naturalize men's oppressive behaviors toward other animals. Indeed, the exaltation of human relationships with free-living animals and the symbolic importance of the "hunt" surfaces regularly in Irish mythology, given the persistence of anthroparchy. A number of these tales, notably that of Fionn mac Cumhaill, feature stags and boars who act as emissaries to the supernatural. These tales served to normalize the role of domination in the human social order by figuratively subordinating vulnerable humans and other animals, but also by exploiting the admired qualities of other animals to achieve and maintain hierarchies of power. In other words, Nonhuman Animals would become the vessels of human efforts for social control.

Relationships with Domesticated Animals

Domesticated animals were also integral to Celtic life, if less ostentatiously so. Horses, sheeps, pigs, and especially cows represented wealth, and this economic function would aggravate their vulnerability to human violence and exploitation (Nibert 2013). Most of these species are thought to have been introduced to Ireland with human settlers (van Wijngaarden-Bakker 1974). As prized possessions, they are heavily referenced in historical narratives, myths, pottery and cooking utensils, jewelry, and art (Green 1992; Mac Coitir 2010). Like free-living animals, domesticates were also used as political currency and were given as tribute to early clan leaders, as is fabled of the famous Brian Boru of Munster (otherwise known as Brian of the "Cattle" Tributes) (Newman 2011). Much of Ireland's precolonial economy was firmly based in the trade of "livestock."

Again, the vegan Marxist position posits that this economic reliance will direct social arrangements and the ideologies that sustain them. Pig myths, for example, dominate Irish mythology, demonstrating their importance to the culture. Morality lessons and creation stories for landscape features could be found in these tales. Two pig "herders" in Munster, for instance, were fabled to regularly cast pagan spells upon one another's herds to prevent them from growing. Ulster's Black Pig's Dyke (massive earthworks that date to the last century BC) is named for the belief that a magician turned himself into a pig and angrily rooted across the countryside (another tale attributes a different ancient ditch to the dying antics of Donn Cúailnge, the Brown Bull of Cooley, who was wounded in battle). Many warrior heroes were likened to boars as well.

Along with cows and pigs, horses were absolutely integral to early Irish society, exploited as they were for plowing, transportation, and war. Archeological evidence suggests that horses came to Ireland only as recently as 1,000 BC, with horseback riding beginning in approximately the third century BC (Mallory 2016). Old Irish texts copiously discuss horse-drawn chariots as conveyors of elites and warriors, but archaeological evidence offers only limited support for chariot use. Riding horses was less frequently depicted, yet ample bridle bits have surfaced in excavations. Horses were not just ridden; they were also eaten. Pre-Christian Irish peoples (and English Anglo-Saxons) ate horse flesh to the horror of outsiders. Gerald of Wales, for example, reported a gruesome Celtic kingship ritual that involved raping a mare before killing and eating her. Stories of this nature would prove useful rationales for the "civilizing" merits of colonization.

Although exploitation varied by species, most nonhuman communities were vulnerable in one way or another. Lough Gur in County Limerick, a popular living and worshiping site for Neolithic peoples, where Ireland's oldest and largest stone circle is located, was found to contain the bones of a wide variety of both domesticated and undomesticated animals (Grogan et al. 1987; Ó Ríordáin and MacDermott 1949), as was Newgrange in County Meath (van Wijngaarden-Bakker 1974). The precious nature of domesticated animals would account for their regular use in ritual killings. Dogs, cats, sheeps, cows, pigs, and other animals (or their body parts) were regularly deposited in ritual pits, grain stores, and graves. With fates no less precarious than their sister cows, bulls were also slaughtered ritualistically for purposes of divination and kingship (S. Harvey 2000). Given the androcentrism of many early Irish religious beliefs, this overlay of spirituality with dominion over other animals lends further evidence to the vegan feminist interpretation of human-nonhuman relations. Here, male leaders seek control and order in a newly expanding society with ritualized violence over feminized bodies, in this case, subjugated Nonhuman Animals.

Precolonial Food Systems

As the ancient texts indicate, early Ireland was a war-based society, due in large part to its "cattle" economy. It is useful to reiterate the Marxian observation that the economic base of society dictates its superstructure (its law, politics, culture, and ideologies) (Craib 1997). That is certainly the case in Gaelic Ireland, the fourth most "bovine nation" in the world (Cunningham 2015). Countless myths and folklores center cows, for instance, most of which concern the well-being and protection of these precious commodities (Mac Coitir 2010). Nibert (2013) extends this observation and argues that the reliance on animal-based economies eventually pushes societies to war as resources become scarce and raiding becomes necessary. Animal-based economies are extremely resource intensive and require considerable water, grain, and land to be sustained and expanded. As some scholars have indicated (J. Mason 1993; Nibert 2013), plant-based societies may be more sustainable and efficient, but they have been vulnerable to marauding animal exploiters seeking evermore resources to support their herds. Raids may have also been necessary to reduce inbreeding among humans and "livestock" in societies where travel was difficult, isolation was considerable, and stationary animal-based agriculture made mobilization impractical. Recall that "hunting" was one measure of preparation for these raids, meaning that Ireland's "cattle" culture aggravated speciesism against free-living nonhuman communities as well. The oppression of cows necessitated violence against neighboring human communities, which, in turn, necessitated the oppression of free-living animals to hone skills needed to survive regular skirmishes, or at least in the maintenance of alliances through shared "hunting" or feasting.

A speciesist economy also breeds classism and sexism. Indeed, women slaves were often taken alongside cows and other animals in raids, and then relegated to "milking" these cows and churning their "butter" (F. Kelly 1997). In parts of Ireland, monetary worth was measured in relation to accruements of bovine and female property (Davies 2010). Inequality and domination calcify in such an economy as the most appropriate form of social organization. The exploitative degradation of Nonhuman Animals was bound to that of other women such that their identities frequently intertwined. Bourdieu ([1984] 2010) notes that categories of social distinction are often maintained through language, suggesting that a critical examination of language can illuminate the values of a society. Indeed, just as the Inuit are famous for using over a hundred different words for snow, demonstrating the influence of their material conditions in an arctic environment, so did the ancient Irish have a large vocabulary for the description of cows, which evidences the importance of other animals to daily life (Mallory 2016). More than a reflection of social arrangements, Bourdieu complements this observation by pointing out that language is a conduit for power and domination. From a vegan feminist perspective, furthermore, language frequently demonstrates the entangled oppression of lower status humans and other animals (Dunayer 2004). Women, for instance, were often described in bovine terms in ancient Irish records. Not all depictions of cows and women were acquiescent in nature, though; they also represented virility and strength in mythology (Mac Coitir 2010). More than passive subjects of raids, cows and bulls could be warriors themselves. The same was true of women, who also feature prominently as warriors, queens, and chariot drivers in the ancient Irish texts. However, the human supremacist and patriarchal structure of this society remained paramount. The economic reliance on the exploitation of women and other animals limited their potential for status attainment.

Beyond the predominance of "cattle" raids, pigs appear to have been the most victimized (Mac Con Iomaire 2003). The Celts regularly killed both free-living and domesticated pigs, sometimes using them in harvesting rituals or sacrifice (Simoons 1994). By way of one example, a popular dinner for Samhain (the festival for autumn's end) was *banb samna* ("piglet of Samhain"). In later years, monasteries systematically exploited pigs, and many Irish saints began as pig "herders." In the Ulster tales, the consumption of pigs' bodies was considered a marker of high status (Mallory 2016). Sheeps and goats were of somewhat lesser importance than pigs, and the dominant sheep breed used in early Ireland went extinct some time ago. Before the institutionalization of "meat" and dairy for European markets, cloaks made of sheeps' hair were a primary export in the late medieval years, as were "hides" made of their preserved skin (Cunningham 2015). Waterford's primary export was "wool," in fact, a trading privilege protected by the English monarchy until the 1400s.

"Meat"

Despite the prominence of violence against Nonhuman Animals in Irish culture with regard to "hunting," cattle "raiding," and war, the Irish diet prior to British colonization was rather low on "meat." Anthropologist Marvin Harris (1989) notes that human relations with other animals often reflect material conditions. As a relatively small island, Ireland could be said to be somewhat limited in space and resources, such that living cows become more useful than slaughtered cows in their ability to provide breastmilk, blood, labor, and future generations of cows. This is only amplified by the country's northerly location, which made grain and vegetable harvest more difficult in colder months.

Thus, it is perhaps more accurate to describe ancient Ireland as agrarian, with "meat" consumption reserved for the wealthy (Cowan and Sexton 1997). Cows were exploited primarily for dairy production and plowing, while sheeps were used for their hair and breastmilk. It was primarily older, unproductive animals who would be killed to procure their flesh (Green 1992; Kate Hickey 2019; Lucas 1960). This was also the case for cows' male children, who could not produce prized breastmilk. The inhospitable nature of Ireland's geography has ensured that few remains of flesh and bone from human inhabitances have survived to the present, but analysis of storage and cooking vessel potsherds show that "meat" was no staple of the early Irish diet. This recent research into the material conditions of the Neolithic era has prompted archaeologists to "reevaluate our assumptions about how much meat was consumed on a day-to-day basis" (Smyth and Evershed 2015, 44). That said, legal records relating to food allotments dating to the 700s give indication that commoners did supplement their grain- and dairy-based diets with small-scale "hunting" and "fishing," where permitted by nobles and church leaders (Peters 2015).

All manner of species were tormented for this purpose. Ancient Irish culture created taboos against the exploitation of some animals, while it encouraged the mass slaughter of others. Killing seems to have been committed by throat-cutting and corpses were generally cooked in large cauldrons. Their remaining body parts would be formed into clothing, bedding, utensils, tools, and other items of use. Likewise, Nonhuman Animals were killed for a number of other purposes outside of the food system as well. For instance, the cocoons of silkworms were used from the eighth century onward in the construction of shoes and clothing, while birds' feathers were used in mattress making for those privileged enough to enjoy an upgrade from beds of straw (Mallory 2016).

Although "hunting" has thus far been discussed as a terrestrial pursuit, it is relevant that seals, porpoises, and whales were not exempt from human violence (Mac Coitir 2010). Archeological evidence indicates that sea inhabitants were a part of the early Irish diet, as would be expected for an island with considerable coastline, marshes, and rivers (Lucas 1960). There are certainly heavy references to "fishing" in ancient Irish texts (F. Kelly 1997). Recent analysis of cooking sites (Smyth and Evershed 2015) and skeletal remains (Peters 2015) finds that fishes did not comprise a major part of the diet, however. Other research finds that medieval Dubliners were dining on the corpses of pigs, cows, sheeps, gooses, ravens, seabirds, and shellfishes. In fact, a lively "meat" (and slave) trade flourished under Viking rule in Dublin (McCormick 1983). Consumption patterns not only reflected the material and geographic positionality of early Irish inhabitants, but also their location in social hierarchies. The privilege to consume the bodies of other animals, vegan feminists observe, is both a physical and symbolic act of domination and subsequently practiced more frequently by higher classed adult males (Adams 2000).

DAIRY

Dairy (or what would later be referred to as "white meat/food" or *ban bhia*) was another staple that was drunk both fresh and sour. It was also eaten as "cheese," "butter" on bread, milk in porridge, and so on. Forgotten stores and ritual deposits of dairy "butter" are still found in naturally preserving bogs today (Earwood 1997). The concentration of lactose persistence in modern Ireland lends further evidence to the coevolution of the Irish people and dairying. Dairying easily reaches back to Neolithic times alongside the introduction of farming, as pottery from the era has been found to contain remnants of milk lipids (Smyth and Evershed 2015). Landscape archaeology, too, indicates an economy that relied heavily on the oppression of cows (Caulfield 2013). The deforestation, spread of pasturage, and remaining rubble of many thousands of stone ringforts that were likely built to protect cows from "cattle" raiding all recollect a dairy-dependent society (McCormick 1983). So does the generic Gaelic word for boy, *buachaill*, which derives from a word for cow, *bó*, and may harken to boys' early role tending to herds (P. W. Joyce 1906) (*chaill*, for instance, translates to "lost"). Similarly, a term used for a successful "farmer" is *bóaire* (F. Kelly 1997) (which translates to "cowherd" today, but literally means to "to take care of cows").

Although cows and their milk were central to the early Irish economy, historian J. P. Mallory (2016) contends that there is very little mention of milk drinking in the early texts. This is likely because it was such common practice among the populace, but also because elites (whose stories were more likely to be chronicled) had access to more precious ale. It was also possible that milk was thought better fit for children and too infantile for the great heroes. Several mythical stories, however, dispute this observation. Cú Chulainn was sometimes likened to a "herder" of cows in his relationship with his Ulster warriors, and their blood was described as milk (Larsen 2003). Upon the death of Cú Chulainn's son, all the calves of Ulster province were prevented from going to their mothers as a ritual of mourning, suggesting that milk production did have symbolic meaning. In another story, the aforementioned Morrígan, who could take many forms, changed into the body of an old woman and tricked Cú Chulainn into healing her battle wounds by bartering a drink from her milk cow. Dairy even played a role in the demise of the great Queen Maebh, who was killed by a vengeful enemy with a piece of "cheese" flung at her by slingshot. Many Celtic festivals, specifically Beltane, Lunasagh, and Samhain, stipulated various rituals related to protecting and using dairy animals. They were also especially fortuitous times to sell Nonhuman Animals at market (F. Kelly 1997). Beltane, for instance, coincided with the usual time for sending cows up to higher pastures for the summer. Lastly, saints and high-status children were said to have been "baptized" in cow's milk, lending further evidence to its sacred quality.

Plants, Grains, and Forage

Early Irish texts employed the expression "corn and milk" to describe basic sustenance, sometimes extending it to include flowers, mast, and fruit (Mallory 2016). In Celtic legends, a kingdom's success was marked by bountiful fruit and vegetable harvest, indicating the cultural importance of plant foods (Sexton 1995). This was a seminomadic culture, and foods consumed by Mesolithic humans reflected this lifestyle. Hazelnuts, easy to harvest and store, were heavily used. Their cooked shells are found in many settlement sites (McComb and Simpson 1999). Later diets were more cereal-based and heavy in barley, flax, and oats (Monk 2013; Salaman 1985), and many homes were equipped with small milling stones or *querns*. These grains (and more rarely wheat) were regularly made into bread or porridge (Lucas 1960). By the 800s, industrial milling was introduced, spurring considerable economic growth. Cereal production greatly expanded, and, for a time, competed with animal-based agriculture (Davies 2010). Legumes were also a staple in the average diet (Lyons 2015).

Reliance on "meat" and dairy may be familiar to modern Ireland, but the even greater reliance on grains, vegetables, and wild-growing plants is a less remembered consumption pattern. Indigenous vegetation, nuts, crab apples, berries, and fungi were gathered and sometimes managed, though fruit and vegetables were not widely cultivated until the late Middle Ages (Kate Hickey 2019; Lucas 1960; Monk 2013). Beans, peas, cabbage, and innovative horticultural techniques appear to have been introduced with the establishment of monasteries, but also through Norman development in the area (Sexton 2013). Figs, grapes, and nuts were also imported. Excavations of rubbish heaps in medieval Dublin uncovered strawberries, apples, cherries, plums, and other berries and nuts (Harbison 1976), while cesspit analysis finds a huge variety of wild-growing herbs and other plants that are now lost to modern cuisine (Lyons 2015). Just how accessible this varied diet would have been to the average medieval Dubliner is unclear. An analysis of a grave occupied by a girl who died in the 900s, for instance, found that her last meal had been a simple porridge of goosefoot and knotweed. Other archaeological evidence from the medieval era finds that between one fourth and one third of skeletons show sign of starvation and nutritional deficiency (Stout 2015). There is ample record, however, that fruits and nuts were provided to poorer communities. Early medieval law tracts dictating food allocations in hospitality also indicate that the Irish peasantry had access to a variety of foods, including dairy, and, to a lesser extent, the bodies of birds, fishes, and sometimes other animals. Law permitted the snaring of birds and fishes, although part of their quarry would have to be forfeited in payment to the landlord. These tracts indicate that the distribution of food as well as access to it were key to the maintenance of class hierarchy (Peters 2015).

Food Magic

Social relations are also maintained through religious or spiritual beliefs, and food is often central to these. Analyses of Ireland's famous bog mummies also show that the victim's last meal was vegan or vegetarian. This could indicate the time of death was in warmer seasons when Nonhuman Animals were not usually slaughtered and would not be available to eat, or it could be that the plant-based meal held some sort of ritual significance (most bog bodies are victims of sacrifice) (Ahlstrom 2011; Lobell and Patel 2010). Indeed, a number of Irish plants were known to have medicinal properties or were thought to have spiritual or magical significance (Mac Coitir 2006). For instance, cabbages were used in fortunetelling, specifically for the prediction of future marital partners (Sexton 1995). This cultural meaning would continue into early Christian and even modern times. Monasteries practiced herbalism and native plants such as wood sorrel (shamrock was valued by the Druids for its healing and strengthening powers) became embedded within Christian theology (MacConnell 2016). St. Patrick is said to have referred to the shamrock with its three petals as a metaphor for the Holy Trinity. Likewise, seaweed (traditionally referred to as sea *fern*) was deeply integrated into Irish cuisine, custom, song, fable, and spirituality. Saint Cíarán took the plant with barley bread and water each supper, for instance (Rhatigan 2009), while seaweed gathering had ties with various holy days (Mac Coitir 2006). That said, many folk cures included ingredients sourced from the bodies or excretions of Nonhuman Animals, suggesting that some magical power could be derived from their consumption. Certainly, the consumption of "meat" was (as it still is) thought to empower strength and vitality, a belief that is heavily gendered and endemic to many hierarchal societies (Adams 2000).

The Impact of Christianity on Irish Human-Nonhuman Relationships

Old Irish tradition thus centered Nonhuman Animals in all levels of social life. Interactions with outside cultures in an age of protoglobalization would dramatically alter this relationship. Ireland may have avoided colonization by the Romans, but Irish traders and marauders did interact with Roman Britain, and missionaries were common beginning in the fifth century. Christian art and architecture frequently honor the relationship between humans, nonhumans, and the divine. Dublin's Saint Patrick's Cathedral has liberally utilized Nonhuman Animal imagery over the centuries to symbolize Christian narratives, particularly lions and sheeps. The many stone carvings of faces that overlook the nave include that of both human and nonhuman.[3] The famous Irish religious text, the Book of Kells (figure 1.1), teems with Nonhuman Animal characters who tell the story of Christianity (Mussetter 1977). As further testament to the interlocking of human and nonhuman, the book itself is made of Nonhuman Animal flesh. Medieval manuscripts were typically bound by the preserved skin of cows and the hair of other animals. The pages of the Book of Kells and other such texts were also constructed of calves' "vellum." The original binding was likely comprised of skin or hair, and even much of the ink was created through the rendering of insects. The same is true of the Book of the Dun Cow (Leabhar na hUidre), which is not only composed of cow remains but is also named after the remains of a cow who had belonged to St. Ciarán. This cow's skin, too, had been made relic. The oldest known manuscript written in Irish, the Book of the Dun Cow records a wealth of Irish history and mythology.

New Christian ideologies would worsen Nonhuman Animals' welfare overall. While animist Celts respected other animals as sacred, Roman thought would shift the Irish relationship with other animals to one of explicit anthropocentrism. Nonhuman Animals found themselves further subordinated under Christianity, and this oppression was entrenched by the belief that they existed as divinely sanctioned resources (Green 1992). The exceedingly patriarchal character of Christianity would only compound the patriarchal foundations already established by early Irish societies, creating a formidable social structure hostile to Nonhuman Animals and other feminized groups. Vegan feminist scholar Kim Socha's (2014) work on the intersection of religion and oppression supports this notion, arguing that the introduction of "God as creator" instills stratified thinking and rationalizes hierarchies of worth.

The transition to Christianity was not abrupt, however, and involved considerable intermingling, borrowing, and accommodation. This surfaces in trans-species mythology that depicts the cultural shifts of the era. The tale of the Children of Lir (figure 1.2), for instance, merged traditional Irish animism with emerging Christian values. In this story, a jealous mother transforms her stepchildren into swans who could only be freed after 900 years by

Celticism, Christianity, and Animism in Gaelic Ireland | 35

Figure 1.1. Page from the Book of Kells. Source: Wikimedia Commons, scanned from B. Meehan, *The Book of Kells: An Illustrated Introduction to the Manuscript in Trinity College Dublin* (London: Thames and Hudson, 1994).

the ringing bells of Christendom. Brendan the Navigator (Saint Brendan of Clonfert) was said to have traveled the open ocean with a crude boat compiled of cow's skin and softened with "butter" in search of the Garden

Figure 1.2. Children of Lir statue, Garden of Remembrance, Dublin. Source: Wikimedia Commons.

of Eden (Daly 1904). Here, the flesh of nonhumans served as the literal boundary between the known human world and the great unknown natural realm, filled as it was with astonishing creatures and dangerous monsters. Matron saint of milk and chicken "farmers," St. Brigit, meanwhile, could be relied upon for easing humanity's exploitation of other animals (Bitel 2004). She specialized in healing, which was demonstrated in her ability to cure deformities. Often these deformities resembled nonhuman features, such as horses' ears. One of her patients was the aforementioned Labraid

Loingseach, who rewarded her with the Curragh plain in Kildare for the grazing of her cows (Ó Briain 1991). Her link to Nonhuman Animals was also demonstrated by her ability to replenish "butter" and "bacon" reserves. All impoverished persons who came to her were graciously supplied with cow's milk. As with other saints, she had the ability to cross the boundary between human and nonhuman. For instance, she could cure disease and reduce the pain of childbirth, both afflictions that viscerally reminded patients of their animality and mortality. Likewise, her feast day is held on the first of February, aligning with the spring lactation of ewes, the traditional time that sheeps were moved into the hills for grazing, and the Celtic holiday Imbolc, which celebrates the stirring of renewed life.

As should be apparent, the Catholicism that would come to characterize much of Ireland is not especially dedicated to anti-speciesism. There are countless more examples. Saint Martin was believed to have miraculously produced pigs from a piece of fat to efficiently make use of grain waste. He also used his powers to create cats from his gloves to ward off the mouses who competed for human foodstuffs (Mac Con Iomaire 2003). Saint Patrick is famously fabled to have driven snakes from the island (snakes were likely a metaphorical representative of "sinful" paganism) (Owen 2014). To further demonstrate Christianity's inevitable triumph, he was also said to possess the ability to resurrect dead cows (Mac Coitir 2010). Reportedly, a chieftain sneakily gifted him a dangerous bull, who, instead of killing the saint as intended, went gently to slaughter (thus demonstrating Christianity's ability to subdue and control). Saint Patrick's Day eventually became the traditional time for the killing of pigs for human consumption as St. Patrick reportedly once ordered the killing of one pig for every monk and nun (Cowan and Sexton 1997; Mac Coitir 2010). Until only recently, pigs' heads were cooked and consumed by many Irish families as a favored dish on this holiday (Sexton 1995). Likewise, the feast of Michaelmas, which commemorates St. Patrick's prayers to Archangel Michael, called for the killing of sheeps and other animals to disperse among the poor. In many ways, early Christian rituals in their symbolic slaughtering of Nonhuman Animals were not much different from the pagan rituals they replaced.

Indeed, many Christian rituals in Ireland were quite violent. Saint Stephen's Day historically involved the killing of wrens. Also known as Wren's Day, the holiday is, like Christmas, a melding of Christian theology and pagan heritage (Spence 1999). Celebrations involved the capture of wrens who were paraded door-to-door through villages on sticks before being killed. Meanwhile, Saint Modomnoc doomed generations of bees to considerable suffering when he supposedly brought honey production to Ireland. Bees' wax was already in heavy use as a vessel sealant in the Neolithic era (Smyth and Evershed 2015), but bees' wax and honey would later become a religious staple in Christian ceremonies (Crónín 1995). Saint Gobnait, too, is heavily associated with bees and their ability to heal humans (Chaomhánach 2002). There is also Saint Martin's Eve (of the aforementioned Saint Martin who could manifest Nonhuman Animals for human use), which featured a sacrificial ritual that necessitated the killing of a sheep, chicken, or goose, who's freshly spilling blood was sprinkled in the corners of homes and applied to doorposts (Morris 1939).

Days of the saints were frequently occasions for a nonhuman sacrifice for feasting. The ritual killing was a spectacle well into the early twentieth century, with special butchers called in for the purpose in many cases. When pigs were to be slaughtered, households watched and applauded while the victim screamed in terror as a blade was shoved down their throat through to their heart. Recollects one observer, "The screeching during this performance was something awful" (Sharkey 1987, 165). While their flesh was, of course, consumed, hair would be used for household items and their bladders for children's kickballs. Free-living animals, too, were ritually killed. The slaughtering of red deers, for instance, came to symbolize the shedding of virgin blood or even Christ's blood (Beglane 2016). This is thought to explain why red deers appear frequently in early Christian art.

Gruesome rituals aside, some concern for other animals does emerge from the new faith. Although monks' diets waivered with regard to vegetarianism, depending on the region, several saints were said to be vegetarian or even vegan, such as Tigernach of Clúain Eois and Cíarán of Saiger (F. Kelly 1997). By the ninth century, the church was penalizing the pagan practice of consuming horse flesh. Poole (2013) suggests that church leaders penalized hippophagy due to its religious importance in pagan rituals and customs, and, consequently, its threat to newly establishing Christian orthodoxy. But this may not have been the case. After all, pagan culture was regularly incorporated into Christian practice. Meens (2002) counters that dogs were eaten just as were horses, but no penance had been constructed to prohibit their consumption. It is possible that the penalty against horse consumption was due to its stigmatizing association with severe poverty, as horses were only eaten by those most in need (laws against their consumption relaxed during times of agricultural crisis). Perhaps, like dogs, horses were more valuable to humans alive as laborers, supporting Harris's (1989) theory that food taboos reflect limitations of a region's material conditions.

The Christian fixation on hippophagy may also relate to the uncertain status of horses. As they were both domesticated and free-living, they resisted categorization in a modernizing society that was increasingly interested in cementing hierarchies of control. Meens (2002) supposes that the horse's resistance to clear categorization made laws necessary to enforce their inferior position in the social world given their potential to breach the "natural" order of human supremacy. Other nonhumans saved by taboo were those known to have consumed human flesh, such as any pigs or crows who were suspected of dining on a human corpse. Culturally imposed dietary restrictions were a means of maintaining hierarchy and exclusion. Poor Irish subjects who broke taboos were liable to be animalized as well, eating as they did in manners deemed uncivilized and inhuman. That monks, as privileged elites, had access to much cleaner, greener, and socially acceptable diets helped to elevate them from heathen horse-eaters.

In fact, medieval peasants were routinely animalized, and not always as a reaction to their diets of necessity (Freedman 2002). Animalizing the rural poor was a powerful means of naturalizing extreme class oppression. The physical characteristics of peasants were frequently highlighted as they were described as possessing bodily disfigurements and different skin colors. This may have been true, given their hard, laborious existence out of doors. In some parts of medieval Europe, peasants could be bought and sold the same as "livestock." Animalization intensified when the peasantry entered a state of rebelliousness or otherwise became a threat in numbers, prompting those in power to frame them as "savage." As with Nonhuman Animals, "domesticated" peasants were seen as docile, but *defiant* peasants were "wild." The degree to which they were controlled was the key determinant in their treatment and portrayal. Animality was leveraged by elites to rationalize a peasant's suitability to a life of toil as well as the necessity of forcing them into submission for the task (Freedman 2002). Few were seen to be more "wild" or "savage" as those living in England's westernmost colony.

Witches, Faeries, and Other Boundary-Crossers

Nonhuman Animals play an important role in human society in representing the "other," with animality standing as a category made applicable for all sorts of marginalized persons, be they biologically nonhuman *or* human. In this way, animality offers a powerful conduit for boundary constructions. This chapter has thus far examined human relations with other animals in

Neolithic, Celtic, and medieval Christian eras with regard to myths, legends, economic activities, and foodscapes, yet the persistent representation of Nonhuman Animals in traditional Irish folklore provides further evidence to the cultural importance of animality in early Irish social systems.

That so many nonhumans have been associated with bad omen, illness, and death in folklore suggests that Nonhuman Animals were feared as much as they were admired, if not more. With the process of civilization came the sanctifying of humanness and the otherizing vilification of other animals (J. Mason 1993). This dangerousness may have added to the allure of wielding nonhuman magic for good luck. The feet of rabbits were kept as charms, as were the bodies of butterflies, the preserved skin of stoats, and the hearts of little robins. Likewise, many Nonhuman Animals were killed and rendered for pharmaceutical uses, such as corncrakes and bitterns (D'Arcy 1999), suggesting that this magic extended to healing qualities and the ability to deter death. Bees and ladybugs could be lucky but could also warn of coming death. The Celts saw bees as healers with strong connections to the afterlife, an association that manifested in folklore with the practices of fortunetelling with bees' wax candles, "telling the bees" (a ritual of announcing news to resident beehives), and covering hives with black cloth when a human of the household expired (Chaomhánach 2002). It is also telling that so many nonhumans were presumed to carry the souls of the dead, most often children and infants. This association demonstrates the categorical similarity between Nonhuman Animals and vulnerable humans (Cole and Stewart 2014). The majority of Irish folktales, furthermore, seems to involve a mysterious Nonhuman Animal or a woman, if not both. That so many also warned audiences to steer clear of the dangerous spaces that magical women and other animals inhabit suggests that these stories reflected and reinforced segregation and otherization.

Many Irish communities certainly believed in magic (although, curiously, the witch trials of Europe largely escaped the island) (Sneddon 2012). An Irish witch (*cailleach*) is believed to inhabit and transfigure the landscape (perhaps most famously in County Sligo) (Byrne 2020). Witches transgressed the human-nonhuman boundary, given their supernatural powers, and, more specifically, their ability to project into nonhuman familiars (Murrin 2002). Less a force of malevolence, Irish witchery was thought mostly to manifest in the interference with cows' milk and "butter" production. Witches and the hares they transfigured into were most suspect (although *butter*flies were also targeted), such that farmers routinely killed hares that wandered into pastures as they were believed to be "butter witches" out for sorcery and thievery. Indeed, some claimed to have personally witnessed women transform from these hares. Farmers were said to maim them by breaking one of their limbs to deter them from suckling the cows, only to be surprised when the human witch later appeared with the same broken limb—proof, as it were, that the hares were evil shape-shifters. As one folklorist explains, hares were "beasts of ill-omen, universally to be regarded with grave suspicion" (Read 1916). That hares behaved in a confused, bewitched manner when "hunted" by dogs only reinforced this notion of sorcery. There was no end to the cruelty enacted on the bedeviled hares. They were to be stoned on May Day (Beltane), for example, the day of faeries and mischief.

In fact, quite a few superstitions emerged from this belief in witchcraft, explicitly evoking the perceived intersections of femininity, animality, and otherness. Many of these relate to cows and their breastmilk and thus underscore the economic importance of cow exploitation. Many folks refused to consume dairy on May Day under the belief that the luck of the year's production would be squandered as a consequence, although some cows' milk would be splashed at the doors to repel fairies (Mac Coitir 2010). Some families covered their home's walls with "butter" for the same reason and built "dairies" well away from fairy forts according to the Cork Butter Museum. In the seventeenth century, this was also a day to protect milking cows, whose udders and living quarters would be adorned with mountain ash to ward off attack. St. Brigit's cross was often hung in cows' living quarters, while "butter" churns might be guarded with a horse's shoe or even, as was documented in County Mayo, a human infant's hand. Cows (and human children) were also thought susceptible to the evil eye when befallen with sudden sickness. Cows swollen and suffering from gastric troubles would require the aid of a wise cow doctor, who might declare her to be "elf-shot." As a cure, he would set a charm by brewing a potion with fairy stones used to "baptize" the cow (Saunderson 1961). Thus, Irish witches interfered with humanity's relationship with other animals by way of food adulteration, but also by disrupting the controlled reliability of cows and other animals in the production of foodstuffs. These legends suggest a feminist resistance to male domination, but their ability to transform into Nonhuman Animals also underscored the permeable barrier between human and animal and thus threatened the legitimacy of human supremacy.

Perhaps the most feared of the feminized boundary-crossers are the faeries. To many outsiders, faeries (or *fairies*) are thought to be tiny, airborne friendly sprites. Not always so in Ireland. Here, faeries are similar in stature to humans, and, like other boundary-crossers, they were (and, for some, still are) frequently feared as tricksters and social menaces (banshees being perhaps the most terrifying variant). That faeries could also take the form of Nonhuman Animals, such as horses and cats, only underscored their contrariety to humans. In Gaelic Ireland, faery faith was strong, far surpassing the concern with witches that otherwise transfixed mainland Europe (Kramer 2010). Like "butter" witches, faeries were believed to threaten "livestock," and could famously spirit away babes, replacing them with changelings. Consistent with the premises of vegan feminism, lumping women, children, and other animals in this way served to elevate men as the civilized dominant group by comparison.

As was the case for unfortunate hares, this belief in supernatural malevolence meant trouble for society's vulnerable. As comparatively powerless groups, both women and children were more likely to be labeled faery abductees. Children thought to be faery changelings were sometimes abandoned in forests. Or, they may be held to the fire in hopes of driving the faery out. Not surprisingly, this custom could have fatal consequences, most famously so in the case of Bridget Cleary in the late nineteenth century (Hoff and Yeates 2000). An ill woman, she had been killed by her distraught husband who believed her to be, as a result of her out of the ordinary behavior, a changeling. Women who expressed too much independence, it seems, were in danger of being accused of faery mischief. Although the witchcraft trials did not reach Ireland, a similar pattern could be found in the mass imprisonment and execution of "deviant" women in the United States and Europe. In an anthroparchal system, both women and other animals are expected to practice obedience, docility, and submission to male leadership.

Conclusion

The tales of zoomorphic legendries, heroes, and saints are too numerous to recount here. That Nonhuman Animals are so prolific in this mythology is a testament to their importance to centuries of Irish culture. Indeed, as this chapter has argued, they shaped what it meant to be human. However, despite their frequency in Celtic and Christian mythology and their obvious importance, Nonhuman Animals would not be protected from human violence. As Ireland moved increasingly into an agricultural economy and adopted institutionalized religion, there came a growing disregard for the interests of Nonhuman Animals. The systemization of speciesism and hardening of hierarchy in human society sealed the once permeable boundaries between the world of humans and that of other animals. Indeed, permeability became problematic as the logic of anthroparchy requires control and clear categorization. Ireland's history demonstrates that what it means to be human is ultimately socially constructed, and the development of "humanity" as a symbolic category necessitates that other animals and their environment be relegated to an outgroup for purposes of comparison. This divisive otherization of vulnerable human and nonhuman groups, fortified by political strategies of feminization and animalization, provides a powerful rationale for a system predicated on oppression and exploitation.

The loss of communal egalitarian economic structures in the centuries preceding modernization created the need to buttress the species divide to ideologically justify growing inequality between humans and other animals. Recall that, in the Marxian tradition, a society's economic mode of production will determine the structure of a society and the social relations therein. Some historians have agreed, proclaiming of ancient Ireland, "Marx could not have devised better evidence in support of his theory that the economic base determined the superstructures of society and its institutions" (Murphy and Stout 2015, xxix). From a vegan socialist perspective, the anthroparchal economies that persisted for most of Gaelic Ireland's past have ensured considerable violence against Nonhuman Animals and some degree of anthropocentrism. Landscape, politics, laws, tastes, myths, and more revolve around Nonhuman Animals, who are integrated into Irish society as comrades, commodities, and cultural symbols.

When also applying the lens of vegan feminism, it is clear that these economies also encouraged a variety of other social distinctions beyond that of "species," namely, gender and class. Furthermore, marginalized groups were apt to be both feminized *and* animalized in anthroparchal systems, underscoring the shared symbolic meaning of "female" and "animal" in predominantly male-led and human-serving hierarchical societies. The gradual institutionalization of religion in Ireland only amplified these consequences. Dominion over Nonhuman Animals, women, and peasants was not only protected as natural, but, increasingly, it came to be understood as divinely sanctioned.

The adoption of Christianity would significantly alter the Irish relationship with other animals, but this shift was at least congruent with pre-existing pagan values. The role of colonialism and Ireland's introduction into the modern world system would arguably have a more dramatic impact on the island's nonhumans. Under British rule, Ireland's meadows, farms, and pastures were increasingly placed under the jurisdiction of absentee British landlords who were especially interested in producing "beef" for export. The indigenous Irish population would soon find itself without political representation, land rights, or food security. This meant that "meat" would become, for them, an item of luxury and privilege like never before. In a time of increased agricultural sophistication, the products of Nonhuman Animals would ironically become less accessible to the overwhelming majority of Ireland's populace. Having moved from an animist society to a colonialist one, the economic position of Nonhuman Animals would remain a driving force in shaping the human condition.

Chapter 2

Human and Nonhuman Relationships under British Colonization

As the previous chapter has highlighted, Irish relationships with other animals are heavily determined by the region's economic mode of production, and this has ramifications for social stratification and foodways. In addition to early tensions with Viking invaders in the Dark Ages, Ireland was occupied by the Normans in the twelfth century. The result was that many native Irish lost control of their land and were rendered highly exploitable (these changes varied by region and differential exposure to colonization). Most of the Norman "innovations" in Ireland related to agriculture, and the country was transformed by subsequent development of urban centers, markets, ports, roads, farming practices, and diversified animal-based agriculture (F. Kelly 1997). After the Normans, the English kept up the pressure with regular attempts to conquer Ireland, particularly under the reign of Richard II in the 1300s.

While these earlier incursions are certainly relevant to Ireland's trajectory, historians generally divide Irish history at the much later point of English colonization in the 1500s, following the monarchy's split from the Catholic Church and its commitment to creating a Protestant kingdom inclusive of Ireland. This is also a time when European trade was greatly expanding into what would become a world commerce system (Halley 2012). England's renewed interest in subduing the Irish in tandem with Ireland's newly vulnerable position on the periphery of a burgeoning global economy would significantly transform traditional ways of life on the island. Some of the most consequential shifts related to heavy taxation, a stunting of technological advancements in agriculture, and the rapid growth in Ireland's population that had been made possible by the introduction of the potato

(Kate Hickey 2019). The majority of the human population experienced impoverishment well into the twentieth century as a result of this troubled incorporation into Britain's orbit (Salaman 1985). The fate of Nonhuman Animals, meanwhile, would prove even more heinous.

A number of tactics were employed to provide both structural and ideological support to this oppression. This chapter brings a vegan socialist critique to examine the relationship between an exploitative colonial economy based in speciesism and the institutionalization of slavery, incarceration, eugenics, and even varieties of entertainment, all of which normalized extreme social inequality and oppressive relations. Perhaps the most critical mechanism of normalization was the demarcation of the "human" as a class category that privileged British colonizers and otherized Irish humans and other animals. Vegan feminists Aph and Syl Ko (Ko and Ko 2017) have argued that colonial oppressors strategically amplified the cultural concepts of "human" and "animal" to naturalize social hierarchy whereby "humanness" came to embody cultural ideals of worth and superiority well beyond the biological distinctiveness of homo sapiens.

Practices of consumption, as vegan feminism reminds us, is a primary means by which this colonial oppression is enacted upon animalized others. Thus, British colonization created a potent challenge to species relations. Whereas precolonial Irish culture was more likely to conceptualize humans and other animals as connected and kindred in the positive sense, colonial Ireland was imbued with the decidedly *negative* notion that colonized humans and nonhumans were both animals in their shared exclusion, lesser social worth, and consumability. This chapter examines the ways in which colonialism introduced a new system of production and consumption within which the oppression of humans and other animals became increasingly entangled. In doing so, I also demonstrate that colonialism's campaign of *animalization* (reducing persons, regardless of biological identity, into the cultural category of "animal") effectively buttressed grossly unequal social relations by naturalizing hierarchal and often violent control over vulnerable groups.

Changing Diets and Identity under Imperialism

Food for the Empire

One of the driving forces behind British imperialism was the acquisition of wealth through the strategic establishment of new food systems. The accessibility of products that had been rare commodities prior to the 1500s was regularized by colonialism, while the establishment of colonial markets greatly benefited elites and tradespersons. In Ireland's case, its subjugation allowed for "meat" and dairy to become a more accessible commodity to Britain through the displacement of humans, usurpation of land, and diversion of labor and resources. The production of cows, while intermittent and relatively modest in previous centuries, veritably exploded under pressure to provide for English markets. Cork, which boasts one of the world's best natural harbors, became a critical provisionary point between Britain and its far-reaching colonies. By the end of the eighteenth century, Cork's "butter" market had become the largest in the world. Ireland's "cattle" economy (which had waned somewhat after the 800s) was reignited and expanded. In truth, few species were spared. By way of some examples, billions of silkworms were boiled alive to release their cocoons for shipment to Ireland, where a booming silk weaving industry dominated the eighteenth century (Webb 1913). Rabbits were systematically killed so that their flesh and hair could be exported, thereby supporting an Irish industry that thrived until the late nineteenth century. Squirrels were also killed in huge numbers for this reason up until the eighteenth century (Mac Coitir 2010).

Britain would not be contented with Ireland's nonhuman "livestock," and quickly moved to exploit the human "livestock" as well. A mass exodus of Irish laborers to the Americas and Australia was necessitated by the British usurpation of their homeland. The process of colonization makes peasants out of many by disrupting traditional foodways, turning landowners into land-renters, and increasing unemployment. Many truly struggled to survive as a result, and millions were given little choice but to emigrate. In America, Irish immigrants were employed in the production of tobacco in what would become the United States, but many were directed further south to the Caribbean plantations. The rise of sugar as a cash crop hastened this migration, as the demand for sugar in England became so great that elites determined that forced labor would be necessitated to meet it.

For some years, in tandem with the enslavement of Africans, Britain relied on the importation of forced laborers and indentured servants from its own isles. Ireland would also provide a convenient market for these goods, with a good portion of the sugar produced by servants and slaves finding its way into Irish rum production and supporting Irish consumers' growing fondness for tea (a taste cultivated by British imperialism). By the 1770s, three quarters of exported sugar made its way to Ireland, where refineries for British markets were based (Sheridan 1994). Nonhuman Animals completed this linkage. The bodies of Ireland's cows (along with "butter" and "pork") were exported back to the Caribbean in return, and, in effect, fed the newly established slave system there (Nibert 2013). The colonial system presents an extreme variation of Marx's observation regarding the divisive nature of exploitative economic relations. Vulnerable groups were often separated by more than categories of species, gender, and class; they were also separated by vast distances. Thus, despite the heavy linkages between various oppressions within this extensive trade network, consciousness to this shared experience was less likely to materialize among the oppressed. Undoubtedly, this disempowering ignorance benefited the dominant class.

Constructing Racial Difference

While not fully slaves themselves, Irish servants experienced extreme oppression within this food system. In exchange for room, board, and passage across the ocean, Irish servants who were shipped to other colonies were bound to seven years labor. The production of cane sugar in the West Indies was difficult and dangerous work. The likelihood of extreme hardship and even death was high, but it was a gamble worth taking when prospects for making a living at home in Ireland were so dim (Beckles 1990). For many, this semblance of "choice" was not even granted, as the British government exiled them into servitude. Political prisoners, for instance, were sent directly to Barbados. Forced servitude served two purposes. It provided a highly exploitable and convenient workforce as well as a measure of social control on the home front. Irish colonial subjects could be subdued through enslavement or even just the threat of it. Any person, regardless of age or gender, who was thought to be burdensome could be sent to the Indies, Australia, or the like to be made "useful." This included society's most vulnerable, such as vagrants, homeless persons, prisoners, and inmates of hospitals and workhouses.

Those who did survive their servant contract to become free persons faced extreme anti-Irish sentiment designed to maintain their bondage and inferior status (O'Callaghan 2000). Oftentimes, free Irish immigrants were ordered to either take on another contract with an English master or vacate the colonies. This sanction resulted from what the dominant class perceived to be Ireland's cultural penchant for defying authority, as it was feared it would threaten the plantation power structure and its ability to subdue its large and involuntary workforce. The Barbados government ultimately had little interest in permitting the Irish to become free citizens, as this privilege would recognize their humanness and thus threaten the rigid social stratification system there. With the Irish thus animalized and otherized, it was critical that they maintain their role as subordinated colonial resources.

To be clear, the Irish were not slaves in the way their African counterparts were, but their social position and treatment were initially rather similar. Racial difference was manufactured by planters hoping to lure Irish laborers to the colonies, where they might experience upward mobility, as they were promised eventual freedom and opportunity, but this soon backfired, as Irish workers began to recognize that their condition and social status placed them much closer to slaves in the colonial hierarchy. As African slaves eventually replaced Irish laborers and Irish free persons began to own slaves themselves, ideologies of racial difference based on "whiteness" and "blackness" found firmer footing. Although the British believed Irish persons to be somewhat more evolved (sometimes describing them as the "missing link" between whites and Blacks), the Irish were frequently described as Africanized and Black as well. This might seem farfetched to the modern reader, given that the native Irish are today stereotyped for freckled paleness, but, indeed, British imperialists interpreted Irish complexion as physically dark and a marker of inferiority (Curtis 1971). This racial identification had less to do with biological reality than with the colonial illusion of natural power structures based on difference. Ko and Ko (2017) have emphasized that this racial construction is based firmly on the process of animalization. That is, as I have previously alluded to, to be nonwhite is to be nonhuman in the colonial imagination. The Irish experienced for some time both racialization and animalization as mutually reinforcing processes in their subjugation. It would only be after Irish persons became assimilated into the white dominant class that their Blackness and animality would dissipate.

In the end, the forced labor of Irish servants fell out of favor with British trade interests, prompting the full-scale switch to African slavery. Although the Irish were not yet considered fully white at this time, the construction of racial categories according to "whiteness" and "blackness" necessitated the large-scale dismissal of Irish servants, since they constituted a visible disruption to the desired conflation of slavery with skin color. To prevent intergroup solidarity (the very sort that Marx predicted was essential for fueling revolution), racial difference was injected to squash any potential that oppressed groups (who greatly outnumbered colonial and capitalist elites) might recognize similarities in their condition and mobilize. A divided work force is one that is more easily controlled. The tendency for Irish servants to revolt in arms against their masters, and, more alarmingly, to collude with slave rebellions made the need for ideological coercion all the greater. It was this fear of Irish alliance with Africans in revolt that finally encouraged the Barbados government to refuse further Irish servants at the end of the seventeenth century. The temptation of assimilation and the privileges it could offer encouraged the remaining Irish in the region to demonstrate their humanness by brutalizing African slaves as chattel (Ignatiev 2009).

The construction of Irishness in early colonial years demonstrates a complex interplay between species, race, and class in the defining of privilege and powerlessness. For Nonhuman Animals, a similar process occurs. Species difference, another modern construction, is a product of capitalist and colonial epistemology, just as race is. After all, *racialization* is only a human-specific variant of animalization, as it seeks to categorize sentient beings based on perceived physical and mental attributes (or lack thereof). I have argued that, rather than allow for oppressed humans to find solidarity in the shared suffering of other animals, oppressed humans may be tempted to align with the elite class as a measure of affirming that they are, in fact, "human." This biological connection, if successfully recognized, serves as one of the few privileges afforded to them. By this logic, it is not surprising that the Celtic tradition of animism that embraced inter-species kindredness was dislodged to make room for speciesist ideologies under colonialism. If the white Irish were to have recognized the shared condition of African slaves and Nonhuman Animals under British imperialism, it would have likely empowered them and certainly would have threatened dominant interests. It is difficult to justify the subjugation of millions for the benefit of a few, making social hierarchies of race, class, gender, and species valuable for the maintenance of an unequal system.

Foodways in Colonial Ireland

Because the colonial system is one that prioritizes the extraction and concentration of wealth for the dominant class, all others are animalized as a measure of justifiably reducing them to the status of resources. However, colonial subjects, both human and nonhuman, are not only themselves consumed by the dominant class, but their own consumption patterns will be manipulated in the service of the system. Considerable wealth is produced under colonialism, but this is an extractive, rather than a redistributive process. Most of the Irish (aside from the middling and ruling classes in alliance with the British) lacked the rights and privileges afforded to the people of England regarding food accessibility. In fact, colonialism ensured that many of Ireland's poor ate plant-based diets as a result of their class position (Cotter 1996), while the English population's diet would become much more varied (Clarkson and Crawford 2001). Monocultural diets that rely heavily on too few foods create considerable vulnerability for a society should those crops fail. There were actually about a dozen instances of extreme dearth or famine in the eighteenth century, well before the disastrous Great Famine (*Gorta Mór*). British market decisions aggravated by spells of bad weather frequently left Ireland's poor and working classes in the lurch. With poor relief unreliable, food riots erupted periodically in which desperate peasants confiscated potatoes, oats, and other foodstuffs destined for England (J. Kelly 1992). Thousands of cows, sheeps, and other animals simply starved to death because farmers, unable to feed themselves and their families, had no resources to spare for their "livestock."

Workhouse records predating the Great Famine show that meals consisted primarily of potatoes, bread, and oats supplemented with some cows' milk (Higginbotham 2008). Medical practitioners pointed to the potato as a source of disease in and of itself, as potatoes were frequently consumed undercooked and unripe. Irish peasantry outside the workhouse could scarcely afford the luxury of milk with their potatoes either. Cows' milk would become precious as industrialization increased demand in larger cities and inflated prices (Wiley 2011). Any "butter" or eggs produced on the farm were frequently sold by cash-strapped families rather than consumed (Langan-Egan 1999). Not surprisingly, malnutrition was rife in the eighteenth and nineteenth centuries, weakening constitutions and increasing susceptibility to disease.

To supplement their meager diet, cows were regularly bled, providing a renewable source of protein (Clarkson and Crawford 2001),[1] and blood sausages and puddings remain moderately popular in Irish cuisine today. Animal products were considered precious, and generally reserved for special occasions such as holidays, weddings, and wakes (Sexton 2002), although the pre-Famine proliferation of potatoes meant that many more families could afford to keep pigs for eventual consumption, since pigs could be cheaply fed on potatoes as well (Sexton 1995). Despite this austerity, "meat" and dairy production was lively in the sixteenth, seventeenth, eighteenth, and nineteenth centuries. Most of it would be exported or otherwise consumed by wealthier classes and landowners in Ireland. From the sixteenth century, Ireland heavily exported "hides" as well as living "cattle," their flesh, and their "butter" (Cunningham 2015). Later, the Irish "butter" industry dominated agricultural export, most of which, again, headed to Britain (J.

S. Donnelly 1971). The more perishable organs and entrails of nonhuman victims were unsuitable for export and subsequently found an expanded place in Irish diets, particularly so for the lower classes (Sexton 1995). It is fair to say, then, that Nonhuman Animals, as the most animalized of those suffering under colonization, were the most vulnerable in a system of extreme conflict and inequality.

As Nibert (2003) has emphasized, the economic reliance on speciesism manifested intersecting oppression for humans and other animals. Indeed, it is clear that the dislodging of traditional social arrangements in Ireland and the imposition of large-scale animal-based agriculture initiated a significant increase in suffering and discord. Recall Wright's (2015) argument that explicitly draws attention to the buttressing of speciesist agriculture and villainization of plant-based consumption in the project of nation-building. The British elite, willfully ignorant to their own culpability for any negative consequences related to colonization, pointed to the vegetarianism of Irish, Indians, and other colonial subjects as an explanation for their inferiority and need for rule (Adams 2000). The consumption of "meat" and dairy, a privilege that necessitates considerable social power, served as a means to enact one's humanness.

Conversely, plant-based diets were thought to reflect primitive, nonhuman, submissive behavior. Vegetarian reformers countered this by presenting medical reports that found Irish vegetarians to be taller and more physically fit than their carnivorous British counterparts.[2] The ability for Irish women and men to labor intensely on naught but vegetables, cornmeal, and milk was regarded as a testament to the utility of vegetarianism:

> Our vegetable-fed population in Ireland enjoy a higher state of healthfulness and vigour than the same class of people in England, who have the advantages of a stimulating flesh regimen, which makes them poor, weakly creatures in comparison, having none of the animation which is the happy lot of their compeers in old Ireland, who are robust, and merry, and laughter-loving, during their whole life. (Haughton 1864, 124)

This counterframing was only minimally impactful, however, as the association of vegetarianism with cultural weakness and subhumanity was potent. The exceedingly dramatic inequality between Britain and Ireland all the more easily served as evidence of the inferiority of Irish humans. This dietary polarization between the classes continued into the nineteenth century, with about 90 percent of the Irish population eventually coming to depend singularly on the potato (Salaman 1985). With a growing population and less available land (due to both British imperialism and the shift away from communal inheritance practices in Ireland), potatoes were affordable and adaptable. The nutritional sufficiency of a diet so heavily based on one root vegetable, is, of course, questionable, but its association with impoverished and dependent Irish consumers could only lend credence to the relatedness of vegetable-eating with a lack of civilization or humanness in the colonial imagination.

The Problematic Potato

In the context of political powerlessness and landlessness under British exploitation, the dependency on the potato would famously prove disastrous. The very same conditions that helped potatoes to thrive in Ireland's wet and cool climate would also welcome blight. By this time, traditional methods of food production that may have buffered vulnerable persons from agricultural crises had been largely lost, long since subsumed by potato production (Lucas 1960). By the nineteenth century, a large peasant population was subsisting on small landholdings with severe restrictions on what they could grow as tenants. This vulnerability was compounded by the introduction of British Corn Laws that would restrict Irish trade to the benefit of Britain, balloon grain prices in Ireland, and leave potatoes as the only recourse.

Following the blight, a quarter of a million humans would be evicted from their homes and over a million would perish from hunger or disease. Many more would leave the country if they had the means to do so. A considerable number of these refugees would not survive the journey on overcrowded vessels known as "coffin ships" (Coogan 2013). The Great Famine of the 1840s would have a lasting impact on the country's population, reducing it from 8.2 million to 6.6 million. In the half century following this decline, the population would further reduce to 4.6 million, mainly due to continued emigration and changes in family structure (Public Record Office of Northern Ireland n.d.).[3] To be clear, this was primarily an experience of the poor. Receipt books surviving from the eighteenth and nineteenth centuries indicate that the middle and upper classes enjoyed a sumptuous diet rich in sheeps, cows, birds, rabbits, lobsters, oysters, fishes, eels, sugar, dairy, and other luxury items (Sexton 2015).

Acknowledgment and assistance from the British dominant class were minimal and inadequate (to be fair, a large portion of England's populace was also experiencing considerable poverty and malnutrition). English reports from the time minimized the extent of the damage or even suggested that Irish diets were nutritionally sufficient (Clarkson and Crawford 2001). Malthusian philosophy that placed its trust in laissez-faire market ideology also influenced this ambivalence. By this reasoning, poverty and overpopulation were natural evolutionary processes of eradicating weaker elements of society, but, paradoxically, the Irish themselves were also to blame for the disaster. This interpretation reinforced the larger colonial narrative that the British were more evolutionarily advanced and thus human. Furthermore, British landowners recognized the crisis as an opportunity to exploit Irish powerlessness and subsequently intensified exploitative agricultural practices to dramatically increase "meat" production (Ross 1987), underscoring their humanness through more species domination.

Given widespread British callousness and exploitation in this time of crisis, historian Tim Pat Coogan (2013) goes so far as to describe the event as an act of deliberate genocide. It is certainly difficult to describe it as a famine, given that food production was ample. Jonathan Swift had previously extended this British indifference to its extreme in his famous essay *A Modest Proposal* (1729) in which he suggested that the Irish peasantry, perceived as burdensome and animal-like by colonial rulers, be made into food for British consumers, as were cows and pigs (in a terribly irony, cannibalism is known to have been practiced by famine victims a century later). As Ko and Ko (2017) argue, colonial consumption is perhaps the most significant way that the dominant class maintains power over the subjugated. Published over a century before the Great Famine of the 1840s, Swift's polemical work indicates that colonial attitudes to Irish suffering under British-constructed economic relations had already been marked by logics of speciesism, racism, and capitalist liberalism. The literal and figurative consumption of Irish humans and other animals seems to have been recognized in the cultural imagination, if only implicitly. Here, a vegan epistemology that is critical of state economic manipulations that entrench speciesism and ensure systemic suffering becomes especially relevant for explaining this tragedy. It also offers an explanation as to why the animalization of the Irish people was particularly poignant during this era, since the attitudes and behaviors supporting class, ethnic, and species oppression are so similar in their expression. As one poignant example, vessels used for feeding farmed animals were reused for humans as soup pots for community relief during famine times. Irish peasants were literally fed as "livestock."

In addition to its predictive and explanatory power, however, the vegan perspective may also serve as a map for resistance. For example, famine survival strategies and relief efforts were largely plant-based. Parsley, nettles, sorrel, charlock, leeks, and other native herbs and wild-growing plants were gathered and eaten. Cabbage could often be relied upon as an emergency foodstuff, especially valuable in the mid-summer months when other crops could not yet be harvested (Cowan and Sexton 1997). Indeed, cabbage was so heavily consumed in what was known as *Iúil an Chabáiste* (July of the Cabbage) (more commonly remembered as "Hungry July"), the skin of the populace was said to be tinted green (Kinmonth 2006). Likewise, seaweed was vital to coastal communities, serving not only as a direct foodstuff, but also as a fertilizer for potatoes. Seaweed had been traditionally used for agricultural purposes, but it was especially critical under colonization, when so few could afford to keep Nonhuman Animals or have access to their manure. In the years of the Great Famine, legal battles and physical skirmishes erupted over the farmers' right to access the resource (Dowd-Smith 2020). Land enclosure had privatized land such that even the "weeds" of the sea were no longer freely accessible to the people.

Corn, rice, and other nonindigenous provisions were supplied from abroad, with mixed success. Many of the foods offered as relief were foreign to the Irish poor, and improper cooking due to ignorance or lack of proper instruments and fuel aggravated their condition (Hatton 1993). Some charities offered assistance that was vegetarian. The Quakers provided a number of grains and staple goods in addition to monetary relief. Oatmeal in particular would enjoy a resurgence as a result of their efforts (Cowan and Sexton 1997). It should be noted that the Quakers were heavily involved in cereal and corn production, and the Irish disaster may have presented an opportunity for profiteering. If so, this would explain why these particular goods were pushed so heavily (Wells 1994). Although the Quakers often offered vegetarian fare and seeds for vegetable gardening, another important part of their relief strategy involved the development of Ireland's "fishing" industry (Hatton 1993). The Quakers also operated soup kitchens, and contemporary reports of their fare suggest that "meat" was thought to be an essential ingredient for achieving quality. Devout Irish Catholics would refuse this nonvegetarian soup on Fridays, even when facing starvation. Protestant Asenath Nicholson, an American philanthropist who worked with Irish immigrants in the United States, also traveled to Ireland during famine times to report on conditions, rally for relief, and offer assistance. She was a dietary reformer who published on plant-based living and operated a vegetarian boardinghouse in the slums of New York City (M. Murphy 2015).[4] She, too, offered soup and other vegetarian forms of sustenance to the suffering survivors.

The role that plants played in relief is not to negate the suffering of Nonhuman Animals marked as food. In times of starvation and natural disaster, Nonhuman Animals become especially vulnerable in anthropocentric communities. They are often the last to eat and are very likely to be eaten themselves. For instance, there are contemporary observations of starving dogs who had resorted to consuming the corpses of human victims, while these dogs were themselves targeted by starving humans (Hatton 1993). Families dying of illness or want of food prepared for the possibility of being eaten, and it would be the duty of the last survivor to blockade the door to deter famished nonhuman scavengers (Langan-Egan 1999). "Livestock" rustling increased by tenfold during this time as well, and presumably these kidnapped animals met lethal fates. The populations of pigs and birds categorized as "poultry" plummeted, as they, too, depended on the potato for food (Turner 1996). Communities of sea dwellers, such as fishes and cockles, were heavily exploited by the hungry. Because the disease was windborne, the potato blight was worse near the sea and in the lowlands, but starvation levels were lower in areas where humans could exploit inhabitants of rivers and oceans. Eels, at least, would be spared in later generations, as consuming their bodies became stigmatized by the poverty and desperation associated with the practice during famine times (Cowan and Sexton 1997). In the best of circumstances, Nonhuman Animals suffer greatly in human-dominant societies, but routine economic disruption heightened their vulnerability. On the heels of the Great Famine came two additional depressions in the nineteenth century (1859–64 and 1879–82), which would create further dips in nonhuman populations, as many were killed due to a lack of resources and want of quick profit (Turner 1996).

Animality and the Legacy of Famine

Additional potato blights would attack crops throughout the remainder of the century, but the Irish peasantry had greater ability to improve their land following the 1870 Landlord and Tenant Act and the Land Law Act of 1881. They also enjoyed higher wages and had access to a greater variety of foodstuffs, thereby staving off the catastrophic conditions of earlier years (Salaman 1985). Poor Law Unions attempted to discourage Ireland's reliance on the potato with the promotion of turnips and cereals (Friel and Nolan 1996), but potatoes would stubbornly remain a staple. Consumption after the Great Famine became increasingly plant-based as Ireland continued to export expensive animal products (Clarkson and Crawford 2001). "Cheese" making declined significantly, and few could afford to eat "butter." Meanwhile, the increasing availability of processed foods and sugar would have a deleterious effect on the population (Friel and Nolan 1996). Ireland was seeing some improvements in its agriculture, but Britain's hold over its patterns of production and consumption was still quite strong. There were, however, pockets of Irish mobilization seeking to attain some degree of self-sufficiency and self-governance. Indeed, this uneasy relationship with food in the shadow of the Great Famine and its legacy of shame and trauma would ultimately lead to a renewed push for independence (Rice and Benson 2005).

One of the first such responses was the collective push for land reform. The Land League, for instance, instituted regular boycotts under which workers would refuse to work without fair wage. There was a pressing desire for acknowledgment of tenure in occupancy of land as well, with the intention that this could introduce some degree of security in hard times. These tribulations were certainly not gender-neutral, as the economy following the Great Famine significantly altered the status of women (Beale 1987). Furthermore, this shift in sexual politics lends evidence to vegan feminist theory, given that women's relationship with other animals in particular featured so prominently. First, as the tenant system eroded, Nonhuman Animals took over tillage responsibilities and displaced women, who became increasingly confined to the home as men became primary earners (TeBrake 1992). Second, as the Irish textile industry (which was particularly strong in the north) faltered, the need for sheeps' hair and the female laborers who spun it also diminished. Third, the aforementioned changes in inheritance laws placed greater emphasis on the patriarchal line, weakening women's position even further, as they could not be eligible for inheritance. Inheritance laws also imperiled young men from lower class families. With land now passed through to the first son, younger sons had little to offer by way of marriage prospects. Men could at least enter religious work or take up occupations outside the farm, but, for women, the available options were scant. They could either marry or emigrate. Like unproductive "livestock," women became burdens to families, many of whom could not afford a dowry. Marriage was frequently arranged by matchmakers who sought out women of suitable stock and breed to maintain the farm, and it was not uncommon for fathers of both families to haggle over the arrangement not unlike barterers over the acquisition of horses. Women often had no say in the arrangement. Within the institution of marriage, all the farm and property would belong to the man of the house, herself included (McCarthy 2004).

Underscoring their subhuman status, women were relegated to the world of nonhumans throughout the day, given the gender segregation of farm life and the expectation that they would tend to the cows and chickens. Like "livestock," women were the last to eat, subsisting primarily on leftovers, a practice that led to widespread malnutrition of women and girls (Kennedy 1972). The animalization of these women was so severe that the female-favoring mortality gap between women and men that exists across the world was absent in Ireland. This situation would not improve until the 1940s and 1950s with urbanization and modern conveniences that reduced the hardships of women's work.

Contested Humanity in Asylums

For those women who would not find themselves absorbed into the institution of marriage, they could easily find themselves hidden away in asylums installed under colonialism for people with disabilities, essentially transferring the family's burden onto the state (McCarthy 2004). Unmarried women were especially likely to be committed, particularly those who had children out of wedlock, those who were believed to be sexually promiscuous, and those who were in any way deemed to be defiant within households that were increasingly patriarchal. Indeed, the hierarchy-building of colonialism only aggravated that of androcentrism in Ireland (Moane 2011). Institutionalization in asylums, meanwhile, reinforced the notion that women who resisted strict gender roles were in some way less than human. Many admittances related to problems concerning women's menstruation and childbirth, processes that undoubtedly highlighted their animality further.

Persons categorized as disabled in some way have been animalized over the past two or three centuries as a justification for their oppression and segregation from society. This ableism has been concurrently utilized to justify speciesism (Taylor 2017). The denigration of bodies and minds labeled different and inferior is at the root of inequality for both human and nonhumans in Ireland. Food, once again, was entangled in this boundary work. A 1901 report in the *Irish Times* cited poor nutrition resulting from colonial violence in Ireland as a cause for increased levels of insanity (as well as the practices of intermarrying, alcohol and drug use, and other markers of uncivilized animality) (Ní Chríodáin 2018). Institutional offerings were not much better, however. The standard asylum diet was based on porridge, bread, soup, and cows' milk; most institutions did not serve "meat," and, if they did, it was diluted in soup (Finnane 1981). Those women incarcerated in Irish "lunatic asylums" subsisted on a simple diet of bread and potatoes and were assigned to the maintenance of the institution's vegetable gardens (McCarthy 2004). Vegetable gardening, incidentally, was also assigned to farmers' wives as a general cultural practice in Ireland (Kennedy 1972). Plant-based consumption and vegetable gardening are behaviors that reflect the intersecting identities of these oppressed groups, specifically in their ability to feminize and animalize. Gardening and veganism have also been used as means of resistance (Alkon 2007; Harper 2010), but when imposed by patriarchal family and state institutions, this forced association with plant-based foodways is more indicative of control, austerity, and oppression.

Women, of course, were not the only group to be targeted for institutionalization. Sociologist Erving Goffman (1961) took particular interest in prisons and asylums as evidence of what he termed *total institutions*. In these insular spaces, segregated from larger society, individuals are deindividualized as they are banded together and treated alike. All aspects of their social lives are heavily managed under a single authority to serve the aims of that institution. These conditions (whereby individuality is stifled and persons are caged, disciplined, and controlled) facilitate dehumanization and mimic anthroparchal relations between humans and other animals. All varieties of Ireland's indigents who were easily animalized and deemed unfit or unsafe could be subject to asylums, and this included men as much as it did women. Mental disability and animalistic savagery became united concepts in the nineteenth century with the introduction of the Dangerous Lunatics Act, which provided that anyone whose behavior appeared unruly in any way could be admitted (Walsh 2004).

Ironically, Irish colonial subjects would themselves compound this system with relative cooperation. Poverty forced many to consider incarceration in asylums for themselves or their burdensome family members; admittance under the label of "dangerous," while frequently baseless, ensured police escort and guaranteed acceptance (Prior 2003). Adopting "dangerousness" was a strategy of bureaucratic circumvention and survival for those strapped of resources, but it strengthened the association between disability, poverty, and animality. For instance, the economic depression following the Great Famine decreased access to nutritional foodstuffs, which was, as I have previously noted, sometimes suspected to cause "lunacy" among the poor. This same depression, however, *also* stoked British fears of Irish revolution (recall that famine and extreme vulnerability had sparked considerable protest and demands for redistributed power). Animalization served to maintain ideological control. Vagrant, ill-fed, or riotous Irish subjects who were committed to asylums were sometimes described as wretched creatures, pests, and monsters (Mauger 2017; Prior 2003). Paying inmates (who were more likely to be of a wealthier background), conversely, were more likely to be provided with luxuries of "civilization" and refinement, such as finer foods and accommodation, even though they were more likely to be living with an *actual* disability (and presumably would be more vulnerable to discrimination).

The extraction of those deemed "idiots" from society for containment and treatment in asylums was part of Britain's larger project of colonial control over Ireland (Finnane 1981). Recall that the project of colonization is itself a mechanism of animalization and feminization (O'Connor 2010). Irish persons discontented with their life station were frequently portrayed as mentally unstable and emotionally volatile in a manner intended to characterize them as wild beasts (figure 2.1). Rising rates of schizophrenia and other mental illnesses became stereotypical explanations for the malaise and melancholia Irish persons experienced under extreme structural oppression (Clarke 1998). The very humanity of inmates was contingent upon the paternal care of British institutions, and many of the efforts to "cure" were actually attempts to rectify patients' moral failings. Premature death from disease, self-harm, and lack of stimulation was common, as was abuse. Scientific diagnoses and state institutionalization added substance to the human-nonhuman binary that colonial oppression sought to cultivate between oppressors and the oppressed. British colonization indirectly worsened these conditions in providing fodder to nationalists who were provoked by the horrors of the asylums (Finnane 1981). To the nationalists, the perceived increase in mental illness became evidence of Ireland's suffering under Great Britain. As a result, they would direct attention (and resources) to independence rather than social services, creating even greater vulnerability for those susceptible to institutionalization.

Animalizing the Irish

As has been demonstrated, Britain's oppression of the Irish was intimately tied to the oppression of other animals. Indeed, the colonial system is built on violence against domesticated animals, which, in turn, also requires systemic violence against human subjects (Nibert 2013). The exploitation of vulnerable peripheries like Ireland provided the wealth and resources necessary to increase "meat" and dairy production. The colonization of

Human and Nonhuman Relationships under British Colonization | 61

Figure 2.1. Wild and beastly depiction of Irish rebels by Thomas Nast. Source: *Harper's Weekly*, March 18, 1867.

Ireland not only harmed humans and nonhumans of the island in order to increase "meat" production for Britain, but this "meat" and dairy industry was also necessary for supporting the aforementioned British slave trade in the Caribbean (Ross 1987) and the bloody Napoleonic wars (Cowan and Sexton 1997). One source reports that, in 1880, over half of the island and two-thirds of its wealth were tied up in the "cattle" industry alone (Ross 1987). Ireland had essentially become an outsourced "cattle" farm, providing the English with luxurious animal products while millions of Irish were food insecure, undernourished, or forced to emigrate. The suffering of the Irish people, therefore, cannot be fully appreciated or understood without also acknowledging the suffering of cows, pigs, sheeps, fishes, and other animals living (and dying) alongside them. While I have argued that the process of animalizing Irish humans began with colonization, the massive disruption caused by the Great Famine majorly exacerbated this process. Animalization was regularly employed to resist Irish disorderliness as it manifested in rebellions, mass immigration, and petitions for independence.

Portrayals of the Irish as wild, untamable, and barbaric helped to justify English colonization as a sort of philanthropic effort. They also shaped the English identity of superiority in the process (Laurence 1988; Noonan 1998; O'Connor 2010). The Irish were described as savage, "wolf-like," and lacking in pedigree. Women in particular were likened to "livestock" in their supposed ability to give birth frequently and painlessly without need for assistance or recovery. Likewise, the British Crown transported Irish women in great numbers to Australia as "breeding stock" in its attempt to instill order in Ireland and strengthen its foothold in Oceania (BBC Alba 2016). Irish people were also animalized by the English based on their tendency to live and work closely with sheeps and cows. For instance, the typical cottage included a ground-level enclosure for Nonhuman Animals, who lived inside with the family for practical purposes of warmth and security. It was also common for families to follow their cows into summer pastures and take up temporary residence in crude huts amid them in a practice known as creaghting. This survivalist practice harkened back to the communal arrangements that existed prior to colonization and predictably spiked in times of economic hardships. Nomadic communities resisted settlement as well as colonial control, much to the irritation of the dominant class (Duffy 1982/1983). Britain subsequently enacted orders to discourage creaghting and disparaged Irish peasants heavily for their close association with nonhumans. Creaghting had also spiked in the medieval era as plague decimated the peasantry. With more land thus available and significantly fewer people to work it, nomadic animal-based agriculture became a more profitable system. The resistance to colonial control, however, branded Irish persons involved in the industry as barbarous and violent (Simms 1986).

Swift's aforementioned *Modest Proposal* famously indicates the level to which animalization had been applied to the Irish people who struggled horrendously under the colonial "meat" and dairy trade in the eighteenth century, but the entangled subordination of Irish peoples and Nonhuman Animals is further evidenced in English nineteenth- and early twentieth-century depictions of "Paddy." These depictions animalized Irish subjects as ape-like in appearance and behavior as a means to subvert Ireland's post-famine nationalist organizing (Curtis 1971) (figure 2.2). So, too, were the Irish associated with pigs based on their shared agricultural connection and supposed filthiness (O'Connor 2010). This animalization transpired in the colonies as well. Irish Americans had a propensity for keeping pigs in urban spaces to help make ends meet. These porcine residents roamed freely in the streets and caused considerable nuisance. Further, the collecting of "meat"

Figure 2.2. Simian depiction of Irish rebels by Ó. John Tenniel. Source: *Punch*, December 14, 1861.

scraps and other animal-based refuse for rendering (a practice undertaken by the working class, many of whom were of Irish origin) also tightened the association between Irish humans and other animals (McNeur 2011).

In New York City, tensions mounted as the city expanded and higher class citizens were pushed into closer proximity to the Irish working poor and their roaming pigs and stinking rendering pots. Municipal arbiters were met with violent confrontation, as Irish citizens took up arms to protect their property. As was the case in Ireland, Irish defiance against ethnic persecution in America was primarily interpreted by the ruling class as evidence of their animal nature. After at least three decades of resistance, the Irish finally relinquished their pigs when a small army of police officers brandishing weapons stormed the tenements and shantytowns to dismantle piggeries and boilers, impounding thousands of pigs. Out of desperation, some pigs were kept inside tenement houses to live among the human occupants, a "husbandry" practice that only deepened the cultural association between Irish immigrants and Nonhuman Animals. Many were even hidden in dank and miserable basements that served as makeshift pigpens.

The Irish were likened to dogs as well, a consequence of their perceived susceptibility for disease, especially rabies. This stereotype of uncleanliness derived from the English concern for purity in morals, class, and race in its civilization project. The stereotype also emerged from a general fear of foreign invasion (Pemberton and Worboys 2007). The Crown desired to civilize and control the presence of "mongrels" in the empire, an intent that endangered humans and dogs alike. For instance, suspicious dogs were preemptively killed in all manner of gruesome executions, particularly in the hot "dog days" of summer when rabies was thought to proliferate (B. Griffin 1994). America, too, animalized and otherized Irish immigrants over similar concerns with disease, cramped as they were in tenements, shanties, and basements (Kraut 1994).

Beyond sanitation efforts, welfare reforms of the nineteenth century would mark the Irish as animalistic in other ways. Early Nonhuman Animal welfare advocates regularly targeted Irish immigrants in urban areas for their proximity to working animals (J. M. Davis 2016). As exploited laborers themselves, avoiding the cruel treatment of Nonhuman Animals was generally impossible as their jobs required speed, heavy loads, and extreme weather for horses and other animals used in coaches, cabs, and construction. Regardless, the practices associated with working-class Irish persons would be scrutinized or judged more harshly than that of the English ascendency (Collins 2015). Imperialist Britain romanticized noble British traditions such as fox and stag "hunting" as a symbol of its supremacy, while it simultaneously identified cock "fighting" and other customs associated with the lower classes and colonies as evidence of their need for rule (Deckha 2013). Even in medieval Ireland, Anglo-Normans and church leaders who sought to control and reform Ireland would propagandize their ill treatment of other animals to demonstrate Irish barbarism (M. Connolly 2011). Beyond pagan rituals, the Irish were thought negligent in their "farming" practices as well. For instance, uninformed Irish farmers reportedly allowed their cows to graze to the point of exploding (here the cows are also portrayed as incompetent in being unable to feed themselves, but this likely refers to extreme bloat resulting from the practice of releasing them suddenly into fresh pasture in the spring) (Freeman 2001). Such imaginings of cruelty and ignorance toward Nonhuman Animals, whether true or not, served as further justification for colonialism, with the Irish depicted as less than human, given their failed domination of other animals. Although the Irish were portrayed as barbaric, they were also believed to be capable of improvement with proper "civilization" (Carroll 2003).

The Importation of New Speciesisms

I have conceded that it would be inaccurate to suggest that humans and other animals lived in a state of harmony prior to British colonization, but it is the case that the colonial system, built as it is on inequality and exploitation, introduced new horrors. The capitalist ideologies that fed the logic of colonial expansion reinforced the notion that no person or thing need be without commercial use to the ruling elite. With Ireland's lifeworld thus commodified, Nonhuman Animals were, and still are, deemed as worthy of existence only if they could be put to work, sale, or slaughter. The following section examines several forms of speciesism that were introduced to colonial Ireland and had the effect of normalizing discriminatory attitudes toward the vulnerable. "Breeding," "zookeeping," "hunting," "racing," and other such practices are thought to be crucial components of Irish culture and tradition, but they were recent introductions (or significant alterations of existing customs) that served to standardize inequality. These examples illustrate Gramsci's assertion that dominant classes will actively manipulate the prevailing culture to facilitate a self-serving power structure (Adamson 2014). In the case of Ireland, colonialism's institutionalization of speciesism was a profoundly effective means of socializing Irish subjects.

Irish Breeding

The "breeding" of dogs that popularized in and around Ireland under colonialism is one such speciesist practice that illustrates the entangled cultural construction of colonized humans and other animals. National identity, for one, is commonly associated with the dogs a country "breeds," as "breeding" reflects cultural values and economy (Weaver 2013). That many of Ireland's treasured dogs are "bred" to maintain farms and to "hunt" reflects the centrality of Ireland's agrarianism as well as its colonial past. Ireland is a leader in dog "ownership" in Europe (European Pet Food Industry 2018), but historically the right to "own" and "breed" dogs has wavered under successive rulerships. Consider the Irish wolfhound, perhaps the most iconic of Irish breeds. As was explored in the previous chapter, hounds had been bred for "hunting" purposes, but the Irish wolfhounds of prehistory are only partially related to today's descendants. Under Norman colonization, wolfhound "ownership" was restricted to the nobility, and, until the late nineteenth century, the "ownership" of hounds remained restricted to elites, as taxes were enacted on those who kept more than two dogs. This tax identified dog "ownership" as a mark of distinction, so much so that wolfhounds came to symbolize colonial oppression as Ireland moved toward independence. Indeed, this tarnishing association induced nationalists to instead advocate for the Kerry blue terrier as the official dog of Ireland (Knox 2017).

Given the historical bond between the two species, separating the Irish from their dogs was undoubtedly part of the British plan to divide and conquer. Indeed, sociologists have since identified that dogs can be symbolically leveraged to maintain racial boundaries. For instance, dominant classes have been known to surveille minority groups according to suspicions that they may mistreat their dogs (Weaver 2013). Or, dogs may simply be treated as extensions of the dominant class as though "white by proxy" to the extent that they (and the white spaces they occupy) become unapproachable by others (Mayorga-Gallo 2018; Parker 2019) (the political leveraging of dogs and other animals will be explored in the next chapter). For Nonhuman Animals themselves, this politicized status can be harmful. As was true of cows, sheeps, and other animals under colonization, new markets and new rules also meant greater suffering for dogs. The objectification and exoticization of wolfhounds, for instance, led to heavy exportation. Trade with Romans in the Iron Age sentenced several Irish wolfhounds to Rome for combat in the coliseums. By the nineteenth century, the export to Europe had increased such that Irish wolfhound populations became perilously low. A Scottish-led "breeding" initiative that incorporated bloodlines from a variety of other dog species led to the creation of a Victorian version of the traditional Irish animal. Of course, Irish wolfhounds had been shaped by humans for centuries, but colonization introduced another level of control and manipulation.

The toll on dogs increased considerably as restrictions on dog "ownership" relaxed in the nineteenth century and scientific advancements introduced the notion that animals could be genetically manipulated for the supposed betterment of the species. Aggravating this, the introduction of dog "shows" in England greatly popularized dog "breeding." The breedism involved in this practice entailed serious consequences for canines. Any dog deemed inferior was immediately vulnerable to "culling," and genetic manipulation made many dogs susceptible to inbreeding and genetic disorders that were frequently painful or fatal. It was no accident that "breeding" came of age alongside the eugenics movement (Fiala 2013; Ritvo 1989). The effort to purify canine bloodlines and delineate clear breed categories mirrored exactly white supremacist British and American efforts to manage the racial bloodlines that were threatened by integrating immigrants. No differently than wolfhounds and terriers, the "Celts" were quickly delineated in the racial imagination. The practice of manipulating the bodies and behaviors of dogs for the benefit of the socially privileged subsists within a larger logic that allowed the manipulation of Irish colonial subjects. Frequently, this manipulation was framed as a means of species or racial betterment with the effect of masking the interests of the dominant class.

Both domestication and colonization, I would argue, actively shaped subjugated bodies and minds with the aim of (whether successfully or not) inducing physical dependency and placid temperament. The aforementioned poverty and malnutrition of colonial Ireland is evidence enough of the deleterious effect that hegemonic manipulation can have on the human condition, but, for Nonhuman Animals, the effects can be even more insidious. Irish wolfhounds, for example, have been genetically manipulated such that their bodies begin to fail at an early age. The wolfhound's lifespan averages only seven years (some sources report it to be less than five years) (Urfer, Gaillard, and Steiger 2011). In their short lives, they are prone to a wide array of debilitating diseases, including, but not limited to, bone cancer, epilepsy, heart disease, and disorders of the digestive system. Prior to nineteenth-century "breeding" initiatives, Irish wolfhounds were more medium in size, similar to modern German Shepherds (McCormick 1991). Presumably, this less adulterated constitution and smaller stature would enable a longer and healthier lifespan. Tuan (2009) has observed this prioritization of aesthetics over health not only in the making of "pets," but in other relationships of dominance seen in gender, class, and ability politics. In the Irish case, it seems that entire communities of humans and nonhumans were made susceptible to chronic illness and dependency, a state of being which conveniently lends to their controllability.

Emboldened by the rising institution of science, which introduced the possibility of interfering with the natural design of animal specimens, Britain cast a calculating eye on the subjects of its empire, both human and nonhuman. Either unable or unwilling to acknowledge culpability for tension in Ireland, Victorians drew on post-Darwinian theories to suggest that Irish troubles emerged from racial difference. The English emphasized that the Irish were a subspecies, too irrational and animal-like to govern themselves. During parliamentary debate, Lord Salisbury infamously animalized *and* Africanized the Irish, describing them as Hottentots living amid "wild beasts" (Fox 1887, 181). This ideology was not restricted to nineteenth-century Britain. In the 1930s, American researchers from Harvard University spent two years surveying Ireland, measuring and observing samples of women and men from all over the country in their bid to scientifically define the Irish race (Hooton and Dupertuis 1955). As recently as mid-twentieth century, homes for rent in Britain were said to have brandished signs warning potential applicants, "No Irish; No Blacks; No Dogs" (Lonergan 2018), thus leaving no question as to the intersecting nature of race, ethnicity, and species in the British imagination.

British Exhibitions

The project of scientific otherization and categorization was not restricted to dog "breeding." Opened in 1831 at the height of colonization, the Dublin "Zoo" introduced the new Victorian trend of entrapping and displaying "exotic" Nonhuman Animals for purposes of entertainment and scientific inquiry. At the behest of English and Irish elites and with the patronage of William IV, the "zoological gardens" were established following the swift eviction of laborers who lived on the property (Went 1971). Initially, admission costs were prohibitive, reserving access to the middle to upper classes. This changed in 1840, when Dublin's working classes were granted Sunday entry for the cost of a penny, as the "zoo" was experiencing financial difficulty due to lack of interest (Went 1971). As with many "zoos," the costs of upkeep were considerable. During the years of the Great Famine, only foods unfit for human consumption were accorded to the inmates. World War I was especially disruptive, necessitating a fervent membership drive (Moore and Dixon 1921). Irish independence efforts of the same era also inhibited operations, leading the institution to kill some inhabitants for the sustenance of others (De Courcy 2009). Likewise, free-living deers and goats were killed for this purpose in World War II.

For the elite, a number of benefits served to offset the strain and cost of maintaining the facilities, the first of which emerged from the growing scientific discipline and its potent ability to shape the social imagination. "Zoos" emerged in a modernizing society, one that utilized species, race, class, and gender categorization to rationalize extreme social inequality. "Zoos" were essentially treated as outdoor laboratories, inviting visitors to examine and spectate, and these behaviors reinforced the relationship between human dominance and nonhuman submission. In fact, many of those elites responsible for the founding of the Dublin "Zoo" were part of the medical establishment. "Zoo" proponents thought of nonhuman inmates as living specimens for observation who could be easily retrieved for dissection upon their death (De Courcy 2009). Some brazenly supported the institution in hopes of procuring economically valuable "stocks" for their own property. Indeed, the Dublin "Zoo" frequently sold the bodies of nonhuman inmates, alive and dead, for the financial stability of the institution.

The importation of colonial "zoo" logic was useful in its ability to naturalize inequality, but it was also hoped to civilize the Irish by instilling humane sympathies. The Royal Zoological Society of Ireland (1929) hoped that the "zoo" would increase the public's love and knowledge of other animals, and the Zoological Society of London provided donations of Nonhuman Animals and much needed funds in support of this aim. Anti-cruelty activists hoped that visiting "zoos" would reduce the public's support for cruel "bloodsports" (such as "baiting" bears), but the reality was more complicated. Early reports of the inmates' living conditions reveal a dismal state of affairs. Nonhumans were kept in crowded enclosures. Some shelters were not large enough to meet the needs of bigger captives such as ostriches and giraffes, while carnivorous birds were simply chained to trees (De Courcy 2009). Feet became tender and nails overgrown from inappropriate cage floors. Many of the inmates died of disease, violence from other traumatized captives, and stress in general. Quite a few succumbed to the cold and damp Irish weather. By the 1880s, complaints about the well-being of Dublin "Zoo's" inhabitants were becoming frequent and annual visitor numbers dropped below 100,000.

Critical Animal Studies scholars have long been suspicious of the ideological narratives enshrouding "zoos" and other institutions that rely on the owning, corralling, and financial exploitation of other animals for civic development and the so-called public good (McDonald and Vandersommers 2019; Nibert 2002). Goffman's (1961) analysis of total institutions would certainly apply, given the encompassing nature of "zoos" and their ultimate function in controlling and confining nonhuman inmates under human authority. Others have acknowledged a shared carceral logic in "zoo" and prison spaces. Both sites, for example, regulate behaviors, discipline, and psychologically traumatize to the point at which the physical and emotional experiences of human and nonhuman inmates are comparable. Ultimately, this normalized incarceration supports the notion that certain groups of humans and other animals are disposable (Morin 2018).

Beyond the oppression experienced by the individual inmates, there would be a wider-reaching psychological impact on Irish society. "Zoos" were a manifestation of colonial oppression, and, perhaps unsurprisingly, they were installed across the globe. Germany also maintained "zoos" as an extension of its national dominance, for instance, while colonists in Africa introduced safaris for a similar purpose (Suzuki 2017). These institutions ritualistically upheld the legitimacy of hierarchy with a potent cocktail of white supremacy, speciesism, and conquest. They also aligned with the civilizing process by neatly containing Nonhuman Animals in sterile, restricted spaces where humans could safely and calmly "interact" with them. The confinement of "zoos" restrained Nonhuman Animals both physically, with bars, cages, and leashes, and psychologically, through domestication and mental numbing. As Elias ([1939] 2000) might understand it, this intensive control facilitated "civilized" mannerisms and squelched "animalistic" ones.

As inventions of imperial Britain, "zoos" do not simply serve in the education of anthropocentrism, but also in a national project of British superiority and Irish subservience. At a time when race, class, gender, and other social identities were reconstructed through scientific imaginations, the exhibition of other animals, many of whom were sourced from the far reaches of the Empire, acted as a display of colonial conquest (Cowie 2014). The scientific and rational undercurrent to "zoo" logic reflected that of colonialism in naturalizing the inferiority of those under British control. It must be wondered, then, what cultural impact the introduction of the Dublin "Zoo" had upon the Irish populace in the nineteenth and early twentieth centuries. Indeed, Britain cited "national honor" as justification for the initial funding of the facilities in Dublin and the injection of its specimens, many of whom had previously lived at the Tower of London.

The story of Sita, an elephant inmate of the Dublin "Zoo" in the early 1900s, exemplifies the role that "zoos" played in the maintenance of social control in colonized spaces. An import from British India and thus a spoil of imperial conquest, Sita lived in Dublin until the stress of imprisonment led to an injury to her foot. In her pain and confusion, she killed her "keeper" by crushing his head as he treated her. Any pretense of the "zoo's" desire to nurture "natural" behavior was subsumed under the more pressing desire to control. Plans were immediately put in place to execute Sita by Royal Irish Constabulary firing squad after an attempt to poison her with a cyanide-laced apple had failed. Some humans did object to her punishment, including the reporting staff of the *Irish Times*, but the sentence was upheld (Pope 2016). Colonial subjects, whether in the confines of imperial empire or "zoological gardens," face serious repercussions should they express rebelliousness, as this resistance disrupts the ideological construct of consensual, desirable, and beneficial subjectification and hierarchy. Sita's destruction was a display of British might, a warning to Irish onlookers as to the consequences of resistance. As a gruesome token, her foot which had killed her "keeper" was preserved as an umbrella container for the "zoo" cafeteria throughout most of the twentieth century until it was moved to the director's office where it presumably remains today (Keenan 2012; Went 1971).

Sita was promptly replaced by another unfortunate elephant named Padmahati, who was forced give rides to visitors before perishing from disease just a few years later (De Courcy 2009). Other elephants took after Sita in resisting their condition, only to meet with the same violent retaliation. In 1940, two "temperamental" elephants who were deemed too expensive to care for were shot. In 1962, Sarah, an elephant who had been forced to give rides to visitors despite years of disability in her feet was finally ridden to the point of lameness and killed as well. Komali, also deemed too resistant to her subjugation, was killed in 1966. Although colonialism was lifted with independence in the early twentieth century, these affronts to Dublin's pachyderms exemplified the shallowness of colonial ideology and its legacy. Paternalistic care and control are presented as being in the best interest of colonial subjects, but this "interest" is ultimately dependent on the whims of colonial rulers. As with the humans of Ireland, these nonhumans experienced a marked loss of autonomy and quality of life, as the colonial relationship is, of course, never an equal one.

Attitudes toward "zoos" are changing, however. The unhappy condition of the Dublin "Zoo's" inmates was eventually picked up by the Irish media, and the 1980s saw another dip in visitation. Indeed, Dublin's concern over the ethics of "zookeeping" was draining the institution's support (Keenan 2012). Tayto Park, a popular amusement park north of Dublin, has even attempted to block the government from releasing information on inmate deaths at its "zoo" for fear of negative publicity and loss of custom. Official inspections of the facility have resulted in periodic bans on further acquisition of Nonhuman Animals in response to poor and often fatal living conditions (McDonagh 2017). The mythmaking of Western "zoos" as spaces maintained for the well-being of other animals detours considerably from the reality of daily psychological trauma imposed on inmates, the stress of irregular and often international transfers between facilities, and the industry standard of "culling" individuals who impede on the facility's carrying capacity in the constant endeavor to facilitate newborns to delight visitors (Malamud 2017). Little has changed in the basic structure and traumatizing potential of "zoos" since the days of colonialism, but modern frames of "education" and "conservation" are effective strategies for protecting profits. Present director Leo Oosterweghel, for instance, has credited himself with the resurgence of the Dublin "Zoo's" popularity. Describing it as a robust business, he solicited capitalist investments and corporate sponsorship to catapult the once struggling facility into a premiere entertainment venue, doubling attendance in the process.

Sport and Subjugation

As "zoos" have exemplified, institutionalized animal-based entertainment and spectacle can be employed as insidious measures of colonial socialization and control. The Dublin "Zoo" provides a compelling case, but perhaps no other entertainment industry has had a greater influence over the Irish psyche than that of animal-based "sports." Indeed, "racing" horses, "angling" fishes, "hunting" deers, foxes, and hares, "fighting" cocks and dogs, "throwing" cocks,[5] and "baiting" cows and bulls have predominated in Ireland throughout its period of colonization (J. Kelly 2014). Ritual violence against other animals was an important measure in the upholding of social hierarchy and the solidifying of class boundaries. Because the English had the power to determine acceptable sporting activity and the means to enforce their cultural values, sport can be said to represent more than recreation; it is also an exercise in societal maintenance.

"Hunting" was a primary activity utilized in this symbolic maintenance. Of course, "hunting" had existed in Ireland long before British rule; it was integral to the maintenance of Ireland's power structure for centuries. The Normans, for instance, constructed parks where fallow deers and "feral" cows could be kept to demonstrate Norman dominance over the land (Beglane 2015). Goshawks exploited in "falconry" were also associated with nobility. They were frequently pawned for political favor and could be used in payment of rent (G. D'Arcy 1999). Likewise, the restriction of "hunting" stags to the British aristocracy and the introduction of fox "hunting" ensured British distinction. With colonization came the closing of public lands, the erection of heavy fencing and hedgerows, and the devolvement of Irish landowners into tenants. British might was underscored by the generally invasive and destructive nature of the pursuit. Damage to the homes and fields of Irish tenants was common, and county courts were generally unwilling to hold elite "hunters" accountable. The repeated traipsing across Irish lands with horses and hounds in tow demonstrated the British desire to control nature and its nonhuman inhabitants, but it ultimately had the effect of controlling the human inhabitants as well through ritualistic displays of entitled access and legal impunity (Kirkpatrick 2015).

The regular insult of British "hunting" eventually led to heavy anti-"hunting" protest during the land wars of the late nineteenth century. This was an anthropocentric resistance that had nothing to do with the killing of foxes and other free-living animals. In fact, Nonhuman Animals were victimized by both sides, as tenant protestors engaged in retaliatory violence aimed at the dog packs of landlords. Some tenants, for instance, slit the throats of the elites' "hunting" hounds and baited "meat" was dotted across properties. Unfortunately, "hunting" as a practice was not ended, only inconvenienced. Nineteenth-century tanneries of the same era, in fact, credited to the huge "hunting" industry a boom in production of preserved cows' skin (Webb 1913). Nonetheless, the tenant protest was at least successful in disrupting landlord hegemony and made clear that "hunting" symbolized something more than just "sport" (Knox 2017).

"Racing" horses was another "sport" engaged in by the nobility that bore a number of latent functions. Although "racing" had been practiced by the Celts, it was institutionalized in Ireland by the English monarchy in the 1600s (MacLysaght 1979). In fact, "racing" was the first "sport" to be structured in early modern Ireland, and, as with "hunting," it became a means of distinguishing class and civilizing the colony (J. Kelly 2014). This is not confined only to the racetrack. Horses have also been exploited in plowing matches. Competitive plowing not only encouraged agricultural improvements, but it was one instance in which a paternalistic class alliance could be formed between tenants and landlords (Bell and Watson 2014). Following independence, competitions spread, becoming an important binding element for the new nation. It encouraged relationships between counties and the state and cemented Irish identity. As Ireland proceeded with its agricultural emphasis in its departure from Great Britain in the early part of the twentieth century, the plowers were elevated as symbols of traditional life and self-sufficiency. Such competitions were almost completely reserved for male contenders until the 1970s, suggesting that they also served to strengthen the nexus of patriarchal power with mastery over the earth, Nonhuman Animals, and nation.[6]

Independence

Ireland's story of colonialism is not entirely a story of defeat, but also of triumph and liberation. Repeated efforts for independence across the centuries would not only challenge the status of Nonhuman Animals but would also alter the human conceptualization of animality. Animality was deeply tied to understandings of Ireland's identity. Most noticeably, the racialization of the Irish that had begun with Norman conquest in the twelfth century intensified in the late nineteenth century as the question of Home Rule was forced on the British state. Historian L. P. Curtis discerns political undertones to this process: "So persistent has been this theme of English cultural and racial superiority over the Irish that one begins to suspect the existence among those who tried to subdue and rule the Irish of a deep-seated need to justify their confiscatory and homicidal habits in that country" (1968, 18). Simianization peaked in the British media coinciding with Irish resistances. Land Leaguers, Fenians, and the rebels of 1916 were heavily portrayed as monkeys and apes. Depicted as criminal apes, it only made sense to the viewer to advocate that the Irish be locked up and behind bars like any "zoo" animal.

In response to this discrimination, nationalists came to embrace the socially constructed racial divide via *Celticism*, a romantic reimagining of Celtic culture and history for the purposes of upholding Irish society. Rejecting the negative stereotypes of unruly, distempered Paddies, Celtic revivalists reframed the Irish race as pure, proud, strong, and noble. To counter simian representations, Irish media depicted its people with angelic qualities. British racialization and Irish counter-racialization persisted until the 1890s in England, not fully disappearing until independence was achieved (although Irish rebels were depicted in British political cartoons as "monsters," "creatures," and violent animals during the Troubles of the late twentieth century) (Douglas, Harte, and O'Hara 1998). Simian references lingered a bit longer in America, where the pressures of Irish immigration maintained the tactic's usefulness to nativists. Indeed, simianization was no less potent in the United States. Vaudeville regularly drew on Irish Americans for material, and invariably portrayed them as hairy, drunk, bumbling, and inferior (Mooney 2010). These ascribed subhuman qualities prohibited them from assimilation or social mobility well into the twentieth century.

The term "hooligan" (a garbling of an Irish surname), used disparagingly by the British to emphasize the uncivilizedness and un-Britishness of the Irish in the nineteenth century (Pearson 1983), is another example of animalization in the colonial lexicon. To be a hooligan was to be subhuman, wild, out of control, and animal-like. Likewise, itinerant prostituted women working in cramped, rundown brothels were said to live "like animals" by "nesting" amid the gorse and were also referred to as "wrens" (Luddy 1997). The heavy economic duress created by colonialization pushed many women into this industry, but colonizers viewed them primarily as contagious vermin and sought to control their perceived threat to public health through heavy arrests (Luddy 2007). Dublin gangs of the early twentieth century (originally composed of raucous newsboys) were even referred to as "animal gangs" (Fallon, McGrath, and Murray 2012). As far back as the Battle of the Boyne in 1690, the Irish resisters were animalized. The "Wild Geese" of Limerick were named so to mockingly describe their speedy escape from Ireland to the continent following their defeat. The adversarial William III (the "King of Orange"), who defeated the Catholic Jacobites, on the other hand, is frequently depicted astride a great white horse in a speciesist manner that underscores his mastery and power. Nonhuman Animal symbolism, in other words, works as a linguistic extension of colonial power but may also be adapted in resistance efforts, given its importance in determining humanness and right to citizenship.

Because animalization is fundamental to the process of otherization and domination, it was also frequently present in sectarian tensions. The war of independence frequently found women gang raped or "bobbed" (sheared across the scalp with blunt scissors). These forms of sexual humiliation and dehumanization were committed by British soldiers to terrorize, but they were sometimes also attributable to male Irish rebels acting in retaliation against women believed to have betrayed the cause (L. Connolly 2019). Indeed, Irish independence fighters certainly engaged in their share of violence. Given the relationship between animality and belonging, this violence sometimes included Nonhuman Animals as victims. One recent example is evidenced in the IRA bombing of Hyde Park in 1982 whereby several British soldiers and their horses were killed in the attack. One surviving horse, Sefton, became an honored celebrity, representing as he did the British resilience against terrorism (Altheide 1987).

Animality, in fact, was a recurrent theme in sectarian tension. In the streets of Northern Irish cities under twentieth century British occupation, citizens (particularly the women who were left behind to defend their homes as hundreds of men were interned) referred to the British paramilitary as "pigs." The soldiers' tendency to assemble and progress in line also inspired the occupied community to disparagingly refer to their presence as the "duck patrol" (Keenan-Thomson 2010). Occupied women developed several tactics to disrupt the troops and protect their community from arrest or harassment. They rattled bins and blew whistles to alert the neighborhood to the presence of the British, and sometimes even stalked their movements and confronted them. The women would adopt an animal persona, too, referring to their defensive strategy as the "hen patrol." This language challenged the gender dynamics of occupation, turning "hens" into heroes and armed officers into infantile ducklings (Wahidin 2016).

This said, I cannot claim that the freedom Ireland desired was expected to be intersectionally minded or universal in reach. In 1916, Thomas J. Clarke and other Home Rule protestors released a proclamation for the provisional government of the Irish Republic, declaring independence from Britain. This was a radical move for many reasons. The proclamation was addressed to Irishmen *and* Irishwomen, for one, explicitly recognizing women's role in the resistance and their right to civil liberties. The political turmoil of independence, however, brought a long period of suffering for many. Much of Irish society doubled down on its Catholic values as both a measure of survival and a means to distinguish itself from Britain. The once feminist spirit of the rebellion gave way to intense Marianism. The pressure on women to perform perfect femininity for "Mother Ireland" was extreme. Infanticide committed by mothers made pregnant out of wedlock with nowhere to turn became so common in the 1920s that newspapers barely felt them worth a mention (L. Ryan 2004). Juries were usually sympathetic to their plight and acquitted many, but the crude disposal of babies' corpses indicated that women and Nonhuman Animals are not the only marginalized groups to be stripped of personhood in societies wracked with economic inequality and political upheaval. The atrocities enacted upon rape survivors, unwed pregnant women and girls, and countless children and infants in "mother and baby homes" throughout the twentieth century only reiterates this intersection.

Glaringly, the new republic made no declaration with regard to nonhuman welfare. The proclamation of independence completely invisiblized Nonhuman Animals who had suffered greatly for Ireland's cause. Although the new republic guarantees "civil liberty, equal rights and equal opportunities to all its citizens, and declares its resolve to pursue the happiness and prosperity of the whole nation and all of its parts," Nonhumans Animals were clearly not considered worthy of said rights, opportunities, or recognition. This is a critical oversight, given the deeply intersecting nature of colonialism and speciesism outlined in this chapter. Consider that the new republic was also committed to "cherishing all the children of the nation equally, and oblivious of the differences carefully fostered by an alien government, which have divided a minority from the majority in the past" (Clarke et al. 1916). It may be unrealistic to expect that Nonhuman Animals would be considered citizens in a deeply speciesist era, but they are not even infantilized as the "children" or objectified as "parts." Although speciesism was intensified by British rule and this intensity had ramifications for Irish subjects, the discourse of nationalism was all but silent on the role of speciesism in upholding social inequality for humans as well as other animals.

Conclusion

Capitalism's reliance on ever-expanding markets and resources meant largescale political, social, and economic oppression for Ireland's inhabitants as Britain flexed its control over the island. Across its several centuries of operation, the colonial project in Ireland was predicated upon casting the Irish as wild, unruly, animalistic, and in need of control. The tendency for the Irish to live with and work with Nonhuman Animals in tandem with their subordinated status as colonial subjects fueled the animalization process. In America, Irish Americans were also animalized, depicted as infiltrating vermin as thousands of immigrants took up residence across the country fleeing British oppression. Vegan feminist theory predicts that various categories of distinction will be manufactured and wielded in service of oppressive social systems. This theory finds support in colonial Ireland. Processes of racialization, animalization, and nation-building worked simultaneously to categorize the Irish as "other" in the service of new social hierarchies. Both Britain and America animalized the Irish in illustration, literature, and political discourse. Categorized as such, they were not deemed worthy of full rights or independence.

Animalizing the Irish was an essential mechanism for the naturalization and maintenance of exploitative economic structures. Indeed, vegan socialist theory finds evidence in the story of Ireland as well. Colonialism's divisiveness reduced capacity for solidarity-building, yet, as Marx predicted, extreme economic exploitation can incite resistance under certain conditions. Irish servants, for instance, did sometimes collaborate with African slaves in the Caribbean, while tenants on Irish land pushed back against the British in various land and food protests in the nineteenth century. Furthermore, as will be elaborated upon in the succeeding chapter, some Irish nationalists recognized the role that Nonhuman Animal exploitation played in the destruction of Ireland. Vegetarianism, they conjectured, was not only good for Nonhuman Animals, but for the Republic as a whole.

Although speciesist economic relations were disastrous for the humans of Ireland, I do not wish to diminish the experiences of other animals. While Ireland had been involved in dairy, "meat," and skin production for thousands of years, the economic shift that came with colonization would dramatically alter production to the extreme disfavor of Nonhuman Animals. Communal lands were privatized, Irish persons were displaced, and Nonhuman Animals were commodified for considerable profit to the dominant class. This chapter has subsequently argued that colonialism is an exploitative economic arrangement that necessitates the manufacture of "animality" to rationalize its operations—as the most vulnerable group in the social system, Nonhuman Animals are without question the most affected by this animalization process. Speciesism reached new magnitudes, instilling a system-wide human dependency on violence against other animals. The institutionalization of Nonhuman Animals in projects of domestication, "zoos," and "hunting" helped to normalize speciesism, and, in doing so, furthered the British colonial agenda in Ireland. These various oppressions worked in harmony to protect extreme social inequality, producing ideologies that continue to shape the experiences of human and nonhuman persons in Ireland today.

Chapter 3

Activism for Other Animals in Ireland, Nineteenth and Early Twentieth Centuries

Irish Contributions to the Anti-cruelty Crusade

As was explored in the previous chapter, Ireland has a historical familiarity with plant-based consumption, as "meat"-eating was primarily associated with colonial expansion and most Irish persons could not afford such a luxury. Yet, as concern with Nonhuman Animal welfare began to root in Western culture, the Irish were not unaffected, and they also began to consider the politics of their diet.[1] Although social distinction can increase the controllability of vulnerable groups, vegan feminist theory suggests that alliance-building across these boundaries can destabilize oppressive social relations (Ko 2019). Vegan feminism also suggests that a radical reimagining of consumptive behaviors can achieve the same. Early efforts to highlight intersecting oppressions, opportunities for solidarity, and revolutionary diets do surface in Ireland under colonization.

Take poet and political essayist Percy Shelley (one of the most influential early vegetarian thinkers and advocates), who began his plant-based journey in Ireland. He and his partner took up vegetarianism while visiting Dublin, eagerly awaiting summer months for the variety of vegetables it promised (Ingpen and Peck 1965).[2] Shelley took to the diet well, thereafter publishing his famous essay *A Vindication of Natural Diet* in 1813. Framed in terms of morality, this type of vegetarianism also served as means of social distinction and enlightenment, although Irish vegetarians, coded as poor, were infrequently able to access these positive associations. British vegetarian romantics of Shelley's era instead categorized the Irish alongside the Indigenous communities of far off continents, suggesting that their close-to-nature plant-based lifestyles served as anthropological evidence of "primitive," and thus "natural," human behavior (Morton 2006). Instead of uplifting the Irish, Ireland's vegetarianism in some ways became another means of objectifying and animalizing them.

This paternalistic relationship extended even deeper for Shelley. His *Vindication* was written on the heels of *An Address to the Irish People*, published in Dublin in 1812. As the document revealed, Shelley was as incensed by cruelty to the Irish Catholics under British rule as he was by cruelty to other animals. Unfortunately, he made for an ineffective ally. Although he took care to make the pamphlet accessible to the poor in hopes of inspiring and mobilizing them, its content criticized both Catholicism and the militaristic response to colonialism as antagonistic. From the perspective of oppressed Catholics, this was a false equivalency. To his great frustration, *An Address to the Irish People* was an address unheeded (Rolleston 1890). Perhaps its failure to impact Irish politics was due to the loftiness of its construction. Shelley's interest in Ireland primarily reflected his abstract philosophical interests, and both vegetarianism and Irish republicanism provided test studies in this regard. Ireland's republicanism ultimately proved incompatible with his pacifist beliefs.

While Shelley's influence over Irish politics and foodways may have been limited, other Irish-born activists of the time found greater success. Indeed, the British Nonhuman Animal rights movement that emerged in the early nineteenth century was dependent on Irish agitation. Irish politician Richard Martin, for instance, succeeded in passing the 1822 Cruel Treatment of Cattle Act in the United Kingdom, considered one of the first substantial Nonhuman Animal rights laws in the West. Martin did not stop there. He further campaigned against a number of especially cruel forms of speciesism and was also partially responsible for the formation of the first Society for the Prevention of Cruelty to Animals (SPCA), as the 1822 "Martin's Act" placed the power of prosecution in the hands of the public, a responsibility that necessitated an organization in order to implement it (Phelps 2007). Martin was known as a flamboyant man with poor financial skills, which kept him in perpetual debt. His support for social reforms in the areas of Catholic suppression, capital punishment, and cruelty to other animals was unrelenting, underscoring his eccentricity and earning him the nickname "Humanity Dick" from friend King George IV (Ryder 1989). True to his name, he was hesitant to prosecute poorer persons who harmed Nonhuman Animals, often paying their fees in hopes of instead educating them to their wrongs.

Not all caricatures of Martin were good humored. Using a typical tactic leveraged to demean Irish political efforts, the British media frequently animalized Martin. This maneuver was particularly salient following a trial held over the abuse of a donkey (figure 3.1). Martin brought the victim into the courtroom to make their suffering viscerally evident, and the British press responded by illustrating him with a pair of donkey ears (Potts 2015). Animalization, after all, serves to disempower and dilute threats to the state. Despite this resistance, Martin continued to push, albeit unsuccessfully, for additional anti-cruelty legislation throughout his career. He lent his support to the SPCA for the remainder of his life, once bailing out the society's secretary Arthur Broome who had been sent to debtors' prison regarding arrears the vulnerable new organization had incurred. His continued love of "hunting," however, appears to have caused some internal discord, particularly with the radical vegan Lewis Gompertz, who would succeed Broome.

Although Martin's contributions in the early nineteenth century are generally referenced as the birth of anti-cruelty efforts in the West, Nonhuman Animal rights law actually extends even further into Irish history. Martin's Act was the first modern law against cruelty to other animals, but the first ever legislation of this kind occurred in Ireland two hundred years prior to that in 1635. This British legislation targeted Irish agricultural practices primarily with the intention of civilizing the country, not alleviating Nonhuman Animals (Ryder 1989). The practices targeted were those that entailed the painful plucking of hair from sheeps in an effort to

Figure 3.1. *The Trial of Bill Burns, under Martin's Act*, by P. Matthew. Source: Wikimedia Commons.

shear them and hitching plows to the tails of horses. Irish farmers defended their choice of draught on the basis that plowing by the tail encouraged horses to stop as soon as the plow struck an obstacle (a regular occurrence in the rocky terrain of the region), thus preventing damage to the gear (MacLysaght 1979). To the British, it was simply a heathen practice that proved Irish ignorance and barbarity (although the practice is not likely to have originated in Ireland) (Beirne 2009). Colonizers also took issue with the practice of "blowing" mother cows to induce more milk production (literally blowing air into their vaginas). Likewise, another custom that struck the interest of the English was the killing of calves in the winter to protect milk supplies. The unfortunate infant would be skinned, stuffed, and propped up with wooden legs. Irish farmers referred to this trick calf as a *pocán*, and the mother was said to wail and lick at the remains, continuing to produce milk, but without a calf to consume it. With Gaelic agricultural practices thus maligned, land enclosures and Irish disenfranchisement was more easily accomplished. The 1635 act, which fined these behaviors, was also a useful source of revenue for the English, what Beirne describes as a "use tax for giving them permission to engage in the practice" (2009, 31).

Many were also outspoken against the popularity of "cock throwing" in the eighteenth century, not simply because of its association with the plebian behavior of the working classes, but also on genuine welfare grounds (J. Kelly 2014). These outcries were published in newspapers across Ireland, and mayors of major towns intervened regularly, though it would persist for another hundred years. Concern about cruelty to other animals was by no means confined to modern times, but it is clear that much of this clamor was related to Britain's imperialist interests in civilizing its colonies (Deckha 2013). Here, colonialism's strategic construction of animality not only created social division between those demarked as humans, subhumans, and nonhumans; it also enhanced that division by politicizing Nonhuman Animals for the purposes of further subjugating their fellow humans who had been deemed animalistic. In other words, the kinship between Irish humans and other animals was strained under colonialism, but colonists could also leverage this strain as a rationale for colonial rule.

Early anti-cruelty laws were tied to the suppression of Irishness, but they did indicate that concern for other animals was becoming culturally relevant. Ireland was not simply the target of the first anti-cruelty efforts, but a source of them. Also in the eighteenth century, resistance poetry was penned to implore the public to consider the perspective of "hunted" victims (L. Collins 2015). Consider, for instance, Laetitia Pilkington's "The

Petition of the Birds," which implores of men, "What phrenzy has possest [sic] your mind, to be destructive of your kind?" (Carpenter 2013). In the 1600s, Irish physician Edmund O'Meara was vocal against the growing practice of vivisection, another practice associated with British colonizers. No results garnered, he insisted, were worth the injustice inflicted on other animals (Dewhurst 1983). More than morally repugnant, he also claimed it was scientifically invalid, as the pain and suffering experienced by the vivisectors' victims distorted experimental results.

Another outspoken Irishman who has been forgotten in the history-making of Western Nonhuman Animal rights efforts was William H. Drummond, author of *The Rights of Animals, and Man's Obligation to Treat Them with Humanity* (1838). Drummond was born in County Antrim but had useful social ties to England. He was a minister, a naturalist, and a prolific literary figure, writing several books and poems on Irish culture, history, and religion. An affiliate of the newly formed SPCA, he left London in 1829 to advocate the cause in Dublin. While there, he began incorporating messages of anti-speciesism in his ministerial work. One resulting essay, "Humanity to Animals the Christian's Duty," was printed and distributed in the community. Drummond was encouraged to submit it to a writing contest sponsored by the SPCA, but, having missed the deadline, had to seek publication elsewhere. The final product was the book-length 1838 rendition, *The Rights of Animals*.

Drummond's work represents some of the very first published philosophy on the subject of Nonhuman Animal rights. Like other anti-speciesists of the era, Drummond relied heavily on the belief that cruelty to other animals was a mark of sinfulness and corrupted morals. He was especially critical of "fighting" cocks and dogs and "baiting" bulls. "Bull baiting" was a notoriously difficult practice to stamp out in Britain, and Ireland was no exception (Collins 2015; Ryder 1989). It was originally considered "sport" by English kings and other aristocrats, helping to establish it in Ireland, where neighboring counties would be made to do battle for the entertainment of elites (MacLysaght 1979). Graphic accounts of the practice survive from the seventeenth century from all over the island. In fact, it was so rampant in Dublin that eighteenth-century reformers felt the need to compromise by simply working to confine it to Phoenix Park (J. Kelly 2014).

As it grew in popularity, elites began to fear that the bloodlust would have serious degenerative effects upon their communities. "Baiting" was an especially repugnant form of oppression. The unhappy victim would be secured by rope and set upon by dogs. They were often quite literally torn apart, and the dogs were invariably harmed as well. Sometimes the victims would be run through the streets, chased by humans who would harass and beat them before they finally met with the slaughterer. The practice was thought to tenderize the flesh of the intended victim, but it was also simply found to be good fun among the working classes. Indeed, this association with the poor would be a primary reason it was targeted for prohibition. Moving to ban blood "sports" was a measure of social control, with landlords concerned that the enterprises encouraged disorderly behavior, impudence, and aversion to work.

Although Drummond is not typically highlighted in humane histories, his work was impactful, even crossing the ocean to inspire other leaders. The president of Harvard University, for instance, held a copy of *The Rights of Animals* in his private collection.[3] American abolitionist William Lloyd Garrison was also influenced, having been exposed to Nonhuman Animal rights through a meeting with Drummond in Ireland in the 1840s. Some years later, Garrison recollected of this:

> I made the acquaintance of a most amiable and worthy gentleman—WILLIAM H. DRUMMOND, D. D., Honorary Member of the Belfast Natural History Society; and on taking leave of him, he kindly put into my hands a thin volume written by himself, entitled, "THE RIGHTS OF ANIMALS, AND MAN'S OBLIGATION TO TREAT THEM WITH HUMANITY." I read it with inexpressible delight, every page of it indicating a truly benevolent spirit, and inculcating, by apt illustrations and the most cogent reasoning, lessons of kindness to the whole animal creation. My heart actually leaped within me as I read the expressive title, "THE RIGHTS OF ANIMALS"! I was myself then, as now, engaged in vindicating "THE RIGHTS OF MAN [sic]"; but here was a claim even for animals, affirming the possession, on their part, of certain absolute and inherent rights, which could not be disregarded without great wrong, as well as positive suffering. (Merrill 1972, 13).

That Garrison, a legendary figure of nineteenth-century social justice agitation, should speak so highly of Drummond is a testament to Drummond's integrity and the potency of his anti-speciesist theory. Nonhuman Animal rights literature is not the only branch to ignore his contributions, the field of Irish studies does this as well. Despite his pioneering and influential work for other animals, Drummond's anti-speciesism is generally subsumed by his other literary efforts in Irish history, if mentioned at all.

This omission is as unfortunate as it is inaccurate. He held strong opinions on all leading issues of nineteenth-century speciesism. Drummond was deeply critical of vivisection, for example, recounting many gruesome experiments in *The Rights of Animals*. He also wrote critically against the torturing of horses, bears, monkeys, and other animals for gambling or entertainment purposes, given the propensity for vice and cruelty it unleashed. He was not, however, supportive of vegetarianism. Drawing on divine providence as justification for violence against other animals for dietary wants, Drummond employed the same logic that he used to admonish vivisection to also admonish vegetarianism. In fact, the wanton killing of Nonhuman Animals for food was perhaps the only form of violence against other animals that was not condemned. Animal flesh, he emphasized, was necessary for humans, and the tradition of drawing blood from cows for survival during famine times in Ireland was one such example he provided. In part, this rejection of vegetarianism emerged from his fear that he would repel audiences should his argument appear too extreme, an anxiety that continues to plague modern day activists, who disagree over the appropriateness of promoting total liberation or simply advocating welfare reform (Wrenn 2019).

Perhaps he had reason for concern. By way of an example, a vegetarian demonstration at Dublin's Rotunda Hospital in September of 1866 was disrupted by hecklers and facetious questioning (McGrath 2013). Evidently, the first wave of modern polar expeditions in the early nineteenth century had a hold over the Irish imagination and considerably informed its resistance to vegetarianism. Not only did the 1866 meeting become sidetracked by questions about the suitability of vegetarianism in the North Pole, but Drummond himself dedicated a considerable portion of his chapter against vegetarianism in *The Rights of Animals* by advocating the important role that flesh played in sustaining the health and vitality of the explorers. Arctic explorers of the nineteenth century were veritable heroes, a symbol of national pride and ambition. That several of them were Irish born undoubtedly made countering their heavy "meat" consumption throughout the course of their dangerous treks all the more difficult for vegetarian reformers. Vegetarianism of the nineteenth century celebrated the relationship between bloodless consumption and athleticism (Shprintzen 2013), but the ability for this frame to resonate was hampered by a cultural infatuation with polar expeditions and other "meat"-powered feats. As Ireland contemplated independence, the hypermasculinity of sportsmen was especially celebrated. Macho athleticism was essentially equated with Ireland's capacity for national strength beyond Britain's influence (Ward 2017).

That said, Drummond *was* quite critical of rearing and slaughtering methods deemed especially cruel, such as the butchering or cooking of Nonhuman Animals while still alive, or "tenderizing" practices such as the whipping of pigs to death and force-feeding of geese. "Can our kitchens, our larders, our festive boards testify nothing against us?" he pressed. "No; we take care to shut out from our eyes and our ears whatever would offend" (1838, 122–23). Ignorance, Drummond emphasized, was as much the root of human violence toward other animals as was sin. Having been greatly informed by his own studies as a naturalist, he believed that education was an important form of resistance to rampant cruelty.

Irish Vegetarianism

Drummond may have been inconsistent in his anti-speciesism, but other Irish reformers were very much involved with vegetarian advocacy. James Haughton of County Laois, for instance, made a living in the grain and flour trade, which was in the nineteenth century linked to the natural food movement (figure 3.2). In the 1840s, he added vegetarianism to his multifaceted reform work that already included anti-slavery efforts, temperance, sanitation, and resistance to capital punishment. Like Drummond, he caught the attention of American abolitionist William Lloyd Garrison, who remained a friend throughout his life. Haughton's (1849) advocacy incorporated his sanitation reform interests. He once boasted in Garrison's *The Liberator* that his vegetarian diet had protected him from cholera, insisting that vegetarianism had great potential to reduce outbreaks. Most fundamentally, however, he was morally opposed to violence against other animals (S. Haughton 1877). In his later years, he even served as president of Britain's Vegetarian Society. Of vegetarianism, he wrote:

> Among all these great works of human duty and human labour for the development of the highest civilisation of our race, I would give Vegetarianism a prominent and honoured place. It is not only a question of great importance to man [sic], but also of the highest interest in relation to our moral nature. . . . Benevolence requires a strict investigation of its principles; because if the supporters of this philosophy be right, her [sic] claims need be no longer outraged by the cruel slaughter, daily, of unnumbered living creatures. (1861, 21)

Figure 3.2. James Haughton. Source: Wikimedia Commons.

Vegetable diets indicated destitution and oppression to many, but Haughton thought them liberatory. He advocated temperance and vegetarianism for the health of Ireland's poor, pressuring medical practitioners to eliminate alcohol and flesh from their curative measures (J. Haughton 1865). By the late nineteenth century, city officials began to recognize the connection between Nonhuman Animal production, slaughtering, and selling and public health. Dozens of "dairies" and slaughterhouses operated in Dublin alone. Although few urban reformers advocated vegetarianism in the way Haughton did, they did push for considerable improvement in standards of operation and, at least partially, did so out of a concern for Nonhuman Animal suffering (Prunty 1998). More accurately, these efforts to standardize and "clean up" Nonhuman Animal "processing" reflected the colonial fascination with "civilizing" Ireland by controlling Nonhuman Animal bodies and human interactions with them.

Although the vegetarian movement today more often caters to the interests of the middle class (Harper 2010), nineteenth-century vegetarianism had a much greater appeal to common laborers, primarily due to its affordability and the tendency for food reformers to provide free meals (Shprintzen 2013). The relationship between diet and oppression was not lost on Haughton. Writing of post-famine suffering, he made clear that he regarded the British regime as an obstacle to healthful eating: "If Ireland, with her [sic] fruitful soil, was properly cultivated,—that is, if fruits and farinacae, instead of cattle—were the main objects of our farmers, three times her present population might be amply sustained in comfort and happiness; whereas misery is now the lot of multitudes of her people" (1863, 54). Indeed, the Great Famine assisted dietary reform efforts, as it heightened public awareness as to the political nature of food and the relationship between imperial interests and human suffering (Gregory 2007). Unfortunately, this claimsmaking failed to resonate widely. Haughton's regular publications on Nonhuman Animal rights and other social justice issues in Irish and British newspapers earned him the mocking nickname "Vegetable Haughton."

Haughton was ahead of his time in many ways, but his desire for peace and liberation did not extend equally to Nonhuman Animals. First, he denounced veganism, explicitly protecting cows' "butter," and birds' eggs as compatible with vegetarianism (J. Haughton 1861), although, these, too, are (and were) products of oppression. Second, like other Irish elites who supported the construction of the Dublin "Zoo," Haughton believed the institution could nurture a cultural love of other animals. In fact, it was Haughton who spearheaded the initiative to reduce admission on Sundays in order to open the facility to commoners, thus saving the "zoo" from closure (Delany 2007). In honor of his son Samuel, who would continue this patronage, the "zoo" opened the Haughton House in the late 1800s. The Haughton House presented tearooms for members upstairs and incarceration for nonhuman inmates below. The Haughton's intentions were certainly aligned with Nonhuman Animal rights, but their investment in the "zoo" achieved contrary aims.

Legendary Irish playwright George Bernard Shaw, of the same era, was also a vegetarian and an activist. Although personal recollections of Shaw from his friends, family, and other contemporaries regularly mention his vegetarianism and anti-speciesism (usually as a curiosity or an inconvenience) (Gibbs 1990), much of the biographical work on Shaw's life overlooks or downplays this aspect of his career. As typically happens in mythmaking, the hero is recast to suit the norms and values of those doing the retelling and remembering. For nonvegan historians, Shaw's anti-speciesist commitments may have appeared an inconsequential personality quirk. In any case, Shaw went vegetarian in 1880, citing easy access to affordable vegetarian restaurants and the writings of Shelley as his impetus. Shaw, a teetotaler, understood vegetarianism to be a matter of ethical consideration for Nonhuman Animals, but also of human vitality. In his words, "I flatly declare that a man [sic] fed on whiskey and dead bodies cannot do the finest work of which he is capable" ([1896] 1990, 27). For Shaw, this conclusion is a simple result of critical thinking: "The enormity of eating the scorched corpses of animals—cannibalism with its heroic dish omitted—becomes impossible the moment it becomes conscious instead of thoughtlessly habitual." Perhaps not surprisingly, then, both he and Shelley were socialist and atheist, as were several of the vegan activists of the mid-twentieth century who will be described in the next chapter. Shaw's vegetarianism was typical of the Victorian era, influenced as it was by a variety of reform movements. As a biographer summarizes, "Shaw's comments on his attitudes towards such subjects as vegetarianism, dress, female suffrage, religion, love and marriage, are drawn together by the common thread of opposition to the orthodoxies and conventional wisdom of his day" (Gibbs 1990, 399).

Shaw was heavily engaged with Nonhuman Animal rights activism in addition to his vegetarianism. His disdain for vivisection, which he objected to for both scientific and moral reasons, surfaced in his work quite a bit. As a socialist, he was suspicious of professionalized medicine and its tendency to exploit vulnerable humans and torture helpless nonhumans. For Shaw, vivisection was no practice of intellectual curiosity or discovery, but only cruelty. As was typical of other anti-vivisectionists of the late nineteenth century, he did not believe vivisection to be a harbinger of human liberation but thought it instead a conduit to eventual human experimentation and exploitation (Hill 1978). Writes one biographer, "No bland exponent of unchecked freedom of the laboratory in the name of the great modern conjure-word 'science' can dismiss the case against vivisection unless he [sic] has read and answered Shaw" (Fuller 1950). Shaw was not isolated in his protest and was well networked with the anti-cruelty movement. He was close friends with Henry Salt, a leading anti-speciesist author and activist who founded the Humanitarian League in Britain, and he frequently stayed with Salt and his wife in their country home in Tilford. Their relationship was a reciprocally influential one. Salt recollects of a visit they paid to the new home of one of Shaw's acquaintances, "The floors had just been stained by the ladies of the family with bullocks' blood. Shaw said nothing, until the question of a *name* for the house was mooted, when he suggested, with emphasis, 'Goreville'" ([n.d.] 1990).

Salt was amused by such antics, but others found Shaw's vegetarianism annoying, particularly as he had a habit of competing with others in various ways to highlight the superiority of his plant-based physical vigor over that of his flesh-consuming companions. In other instances, his morality simply caused discomfort in social situations. In an interview with women's suffrage activist Maud Braby, Shaw disrupted the conversation to comment on the repugnancy of a stole of sables' hair she wore, prompting her to remove it (Gibbs 1990). Shaw's partner Charlotte, only a vegetarian for a short time herself, reportedly kept George well fed on impressive vegetarian cuisine, but travel would test his commitment. One friend recollected that, upon their trip to Italy, hoteliers had to be told that the atheist Shaw was a devout Catholic under a vow of abstinence before vegetarian fare was finally served and he could eat (Okey [1930] 1990).

In his old age, he was plagued with anemia, which necessitated injections of extractions from nonhuman livers until a vegetarian substitute could be found. To his consternation, the news of this flesh-based treatment was immediately reported in mainstream news, as vegetarianism had become a defining characteristic of Shaw's public persona. Given his important role in representing and legitimizing the diet, his lapse was also sensationalized in the vegetarian media as well. The backlash he received from the vegetarian community was especially cruel and unwarranted. Shaw was never comfortable with his brief reliance on the liver extract. Neither did he waver on his vegetarian diet. In fact, he was relentless in researching plant-based treatments in pursuit of a nature cure (Holroyd 1997). However, the unrealistic and falsified claims made by the vegetarian movement that plant-based eating eliminated disease and staved off mortality were contrary to Shaw's rationalist leanings. His rejection of unrealistic vegetarian fancies of pure and perfect living would thereafter become to him a personal campaign. Certainly, this association between plant-based eating and physical superiority draws on patriarchal norms. Today, vegan feminists have pushed back against this movement's claim as contrary to feminist values of inclusivity, particularly as they can stigmatize feminized and disabled bodies (C. L. Hamilton 2019). Furthermore, this emphasis on extreme control runs the risk of reinforcing the problematic "civilizing process" of colonialism, as it so often serves to maintain social distinction and inequality.

Irish Vegetarians Organize

Vegan feminists advise caution with regard to the health claims made by vegetarian activists, as there are political ramifications. Ireland provided an important test case in the nineteenth century, however, clearly demonstrating that plant-based consumption was a viable but, given state interference, artificially impeded option. The peasantry's reliance on plant-based foods and cows' milk demonstrated that vegetarianism was sufficient for human sustenance, and unmistakably so given the laboriousness of Irish agricultural life. More importantly, it also underscored the role that exploitative political structures play in shaping food systems, a point that was easily exploited by the Vegetarian Society. As landlords evicted families and emptied towns in the northwest to make way for further animal-based agricultural production, a speech at the fourteenth annual meeting declared the inevitability of such tragedy "unless the consumption of animal food be diminished." The link between violence against humans and other animals in Ireland was duly highlighted by society secretary Reverend John Clark: "Vegetarianism provides a remedy for this conflict, and would not be a cause of it. There would certainly be no use for the enormous number of animals now in the country if we were all Vegetarians" (1862, 14–15).

The troubles brewing in the northwest would continue to be an inspiration to vegetarian reform. The Belfast Vegetarian and Food Reform Society and the Belfast Vegetarian Association coalesced in the 1870s, following a second wave of organized vegetarianism in the United Kingdom (J. Davis n.d.; Gregory 2007). Two decades later, the Irish Vegetarian Union of Belfast formed, as did societies in Lisburn and Londonderry, also in the north of Ireland. The Belfast union successfully applied for membership with the Vegetarian Federal Union in 1890, immediately following the formation of this international congress in 1889 (*Vegetarian* 1890). The creation and dissemination of vegetarian literature was a primary tactic for the Belfast organization, and it aligned itself with several religious leaders (although it met with considerable resistance from most). Belfast vegetarians worked among slum dwellers to improve their nutritional knowledge and cookery skills. They also gave lectures and magic lantern shows.

Activists remained frustrated by the limited resonance afforded by cultural attachments to "meat" and insufficient funds (Semple 1897), but other novel vegetarian experiments transpired that warrant mention. The Irish Village, a vegetarian soapmaking enterprise of Brown's Soapworks in Donaghmore, County Tyrone, was opened as a visitor's attraction and emphasized traditional, plant-based recipes. It reportedly maintained at one point a staff of two hundred vegetarians. The soap-making enterprise[4] helped make the vegetarian community sustainable, at least for a time. American vegetarian organizers looked on with envy, well aware that such vegetarian industries did wonders for the cause (*Vegetarian Magazine* 1909).

Further south, vegetarians organized in Dublin as well. The Dublin Vegetarian Society was in operation sometime prior to 1890, when it first appeared in British vegetarian subscriptions (J. Davis n.d.). Indeed, all organized vegetarian societies in Ireland closely collaborated with those in England. By 1910, the Irish Vegetarian Union (referred to as the Irish Vegetarian Society from 1911 on) was based in Dublin, applying the standard tactics of lecturing, cooking demonstrations, writing to the press, and spotlighting vegetarian athleticism. Despite Ireland's longstanding participation in regional vegetarianism, the years following independence saw a lapse until the end of the 1930s. A reincarnation of the Vegetarian Society of Ireland would not form until 1978. The Dublin Vegetarian Society faltered but would be resurrected in 1946, after the disruption of wartime. Membership was undoubtedly limited, as press coverage in the 1940s and early 1950s reported only about thirty to fifty affiliates (*Irish Press* 1949).

Ireland was not only entangled with British activism; there was a strong Irish influence on American anti-speciesism as well. A prestigious Belfast dermatologist and lecturer who advocated vegetarianism for the clearing of skin diseases (Purdon 1896) and had helped form Belfast's Irish Vegetarian Union was, for instance, invited to speak at the third International Vegetarian Congress in Chicago, as was J. S. Herron, secretary of the same Irish Vegetarian Union (*Vegetarian Messenger* 1893). Emarel Freshel, founder of the Boston-based Millennium Guild, the first American organization to advocate vegetarianism as a baseline requirement for anti-cruelty efforts, listed George Bernard Shaw as a significant influence on her politics (Shprintzen 2013). Likewise, Caroline Earl White, who founded some of the country's first and most powerful anti-speciesist organizations, had Irish influence to partially thank for her success. White cofounded the Pennsylvania Society for the Prevention of Cruelty to Animals (PSPCA) in 1867 and the American Anti-Vivisection Society in 1883. Due to the gender mores of the era, she chose to withdraw from her leadership role with the PSPCA, quickly founding an even more successful women's auxiliary two years later. Her partner, Richard P. White, was Irish born and Catholic (Caroline would convert upon marriage). A Philadelphia attorney, he supported his wife's activism, and he himself took a leadership role in the PSCPA (*Philadelphia*

Inquirer 1916; Unti 2002). Indeed, he would frequently speak on Caroline's behalf. In an era when women were effectively barred from politics, women's participation was often relegated to influencing sympathetic men. That said, some successfully repositioned advocacy for sanitation, children, other animals, and the environment as women's work, a strategy that granted them some entry into the public sphere.

Noticing Caroline's concern for other animals early in their partnership, it was apparently at Richard's urging that she began to support the British SPCA (Unti 2008). This support would blossom into a lifetime of organizing and lobbying on behalf of other animals. The two collected signatures for the formation of the PSCPA, having been emboldened by the establishment of the American SPCA by Henry Bergh in nearby New York City. Richard White was not just a mouthpiece for his wife in this collaboration. His legal competence was consistently useful, and he was also instrumental in drafting the first charter and bylaws. Richard was an anti-vivisectionist like his partner and served as counsellor to the AAVS. Caroline counted heavily on his expertise. The PSCPA faced considerable harassment from the scientific community, notably that of the University of Pennsylvania, determined as it was to seize dogs for medical experiments. In one such incident, scientists petitioned the city council for special permission to obtain "specimens" from Caroline's facility. Richard successfully requested access to the meeting with the intention of representing the Nonhuman Animals in question. Caroline remembers of her partner,

> With his well-known powers of debate and of setting all vexed questions in a clever and practical light, he soon convinced them that it would be at the height of inconsistency for an organization that had been formed to prevent cruelty, to aid in the very object it had been formed to prevent. Consequently, a reply in the negative was returned to the doctors. (White 1913, 36)

Unfortunately, the battle over pound seizure would continue to exasperate anti-cruelty activists throughout the twentieth century. At the height of scientific countermovement activity, Nonhuman Animals had at least one very dedicated Irishman on their side. On his death in 1905, the Women's PSCPA observes, "This Society and the American Anti-Vivisection Society owe much to Mr. White, for without his watchfulness each day would probably have sustained pecuniary loss and suffered injurious opposition" (*Zoophilist and Animals' Defender* 1905a).

The Irish Response to Vivisection

In Ireland as well, vivisection was a serious threat to activists and the nonhumans they represented. The struggles of the developing Irish colony became a bargaining point, with physicians requesting additional vivisection facilities to bring the country and its medicine up to speed.[5] By the turn of the twentieth century, there were a number of medical schools, veterinary schools, and scientific laboratories registered in major Irish cities that experimented on guinea pigs, mice, dogs, goats, calves, birds, sheeps, and oxes, most commonly in the study of pathology (*Zoophilist and Animals' Defender* 1905b). Great Britain's 1876 Cruelty to Animals Act, created under pressure from Nonhuman Animal activists who were horrified by the exploding popularity of painful and gratuitous experimentation on other animals, only resulted in adding a veneer of legitimization to the vivisection industry. Licensure for experimentation as required by the act was liberally granted, and Ireland was no exception.

Indeed, the act did little, if anything, to curtail the activities of scientists. Vivisection, which horrified the moral sensibilities of Victorians in a modernizing world, was effectively normalized. One such exasperated Victorian was the infamous anti-vivisection campaigner Frances Power Cobbe (O'Connor 2010) (figure 3.3). The Irish-born Cobbe was deeply invested in social reform and women's rights work, but she was especially horrified by violence against dogs and other such species. In addition to penning over two hundred pieces against vivisection, she founded the National Anti-vivisection Society (NAVS) and later the British Union for the Abolition of Vivisection (BUAV) when she determined that NAVS had lost its effectiveness and radical edge (Phelps 2007). Specifically, she was infuriated by the reformist outcome of the 1876 act and advocated nothing short of the total abolition of vivisection thereafter. Both of Cobbe's organizations are still in successful operation today. Despite this deep engagement with anti-cruelty campaigning, Cobbe was not a vegetarian. Indeed, she was hostile to the idea. She also failed to take a critical stance against "hunting." Both positions caused considerable friction with other activists, and Cobbe was frequently on the offensive.

Although she was not able to make the connection between Nonhuman Animals' oppression and the consumption of "meat," she did adopt a prototypical vegan feminist perspective in her explicit fear for the safety of women in a society that had normalized vivisection and celebrated

Activism for Other Animals in Ireland | 95

Figure 3.3. Frances Power Cobbe. Source: Wikimedia Commons.

patriarchal scientific authority (O'Connor 2010). It would be a fear well-founded. Gynecological vivisection on Irish women in the United States, for instance, was regular practice. The "father of gynecology" and former slave "owner" Dr. J. Marion Sims routinely denied Irish American and African American women anesthetics during surgery. To Sims, these women were only brutish animals. As such, they held a higher tolerance for pain and did not require the gentle treatment afforded to wealthy white women (Sartin 2004). These same speciesist beliefs, incidentally, made the need to employ anesthetics in nonhuman vivisection questionable. The destitution of Irish women in the nineteenth century made them especially vulnerable to consenting to experimental treatments. Like Nonhuman Animals, these women were frequently objectified for the purposes of spectacle as well. Many operations took place in front of an audience of all-male medical personnel (Owens 2008).

Beyond Cobbe, several Irish writers and activists were engaged in the battle against vivisection. In one instance, the egregious practices of French vivisectors at the 1874 congress of the British Medical Association were met with such persistent protest by two Dublin surgeons that the meeting was temporarily halted (Ryder 1989). In this horrific episode, dogs were to be injected with alcohol and absinthe for demonstrative purposes that held little scientific value. The procedures caused extreme anguish and seizing. One of the surgeons, Thomas Tufnell, then president of the Royal College of Surgeons in Ireland, reportedly interrupted the experiment on grounds of injustice: "The dog is struggling hard to get free. I am a sportsman as well as a surgeon, and I will never see a dog bullied" (*British Medical Journal* 1874).[6] He then cut the victim loose to demonstrate that the dog was fully aware, sentient, and liable to suffer from the impending procedure. The interference brought the membership to a vote as to whether or not the experiment should proceed, but the outcome of the impromptu election was not favorable, dooming the temporarily reprieved dog and his companions. However, the Irish protest was such that the SPCA caught wind and attempted, unsuccessfully, to prosecute the vivisector for the crime of unnecessary experimentation.

Elsewhere, the Irish would become involved in the most high-profile anti-vivisection protest of the era. In the first decade of the twentieth century, a number of Irish Home Rulers were present at the momentous demonstrations relating to a contentious South London memorial for dogs who had been killed in British vivisection (P. Mason 1997). Pro-vivisection university students tried to remove the offending monument, but were met with a band of anti-vivisectionists who hailed from a large number of social justice affinity movements, Irish nationalists included. Council meetings to debate the appropriateness of what came to be known as the Brown Dog Memorial were regularly disrupted by violent students. Irish stewards wearing ribbons of green for Ireland were necessitated to either quell or expel the university protestors. In fact, the Battersea location had intentionally been chosen, given its high population of leftist Irish immigrants who could be relied upon for support and solidarity. Anti-vivisectionists heavily intersected their activism with other social justice causes of the day, and easily found a home for the memorial in the area. This cooperation was perhaps aided most effectively by the involvement of Charlotte Despard (figure 3.4), an Irish nationalist and suffragette who gave stirring orations in defense of the Brown Dog. Despard had been active in poor relief and labor rights in Battersea. Both she and George Bernard Shaw were present at the memorial's unveiling.

Activism for Other Animals in Ireland | 97

Figure 3.4. Charlotte Despard. Source: A. Gardiner, *Pillars of Society* (New York: Dodd, Mead, 1914).

This nationalist Irish connection did come with a cost, as it had the effect of fueling the university student countermovement. To this privileged bunch, the memorial had come to represent the threatening encroachment of women's liberation, Irish independence, and anti-speciesism. Ireland on the eve of independence had a number of competing visions for its future, some conservative and others radically liberal (Ward 2017). Advocates of different alternatives battled in the press, but, as the turmoil over the Brown Dog demonstrates, the debate sometimes also spilled into the streets. This was more than a fight for the recognition of Nonhuman Animals; it was a struggle between proponents of a more equitable, democratic, and fair society and the protectors of the patriarchal, anthroparchal, and class-divided established order.

After great disturbance and protest, the memorial was finally removed. The city councilor had insisted that the community pay additional fees to offset the cost of police efforts necessary to quell persistent disturbances caused by detractors. Battersea at the time was little better than a slum and was unable to afford such costs. Community members were incensed that they would be made to pay for their own police protection, particularly as the troublemakers were arriving from outside the community. The density of poor Irish radicals in Battersea undoubtedly shaped the penalty. MP Hugh Law of West Donegal proposed, without success, that the Criminal Law and Procedure Act of 1887 (commonly known as the Irish Crimes Act) be extended to control the pro-vivisection protestors. Law was probably wasting his breath. This colonialist and ethnically driven enforcement act had been enacted in order to quash Irish land leaguers and boycotters and was never intended to provide equal protection. In any case, the ferocity with which the Irish defended the memorial is a testament to a consciousness of entangled oppression under Victorian rule. Britain's calculated and coldhearted institutionalized oppression of dogs and other animals in the name of national interest had come to represent the injustice also imposed on women, the poor, the Irish, and others. Anti-vivisectionism was one of the few campaigns from the nineteenth century that targeted the elite class rather than the working class (Kean 1995).

The leadership of the Anglo-Irish nationalist Charlotte Despard in the Brown Dog affair hints at the deeply intersectional nature of anti-speciesism and anti-oppression efforts of the nineteenth and early twentieth century. In addition to her socialist, feminist, and anti-prison work, Despard made time to advocate vegetarianism and anti-vivisectionism. She recognized that food and consumption were political. For a short time, she even ran a strawberry and raspberry jam operation on her property in the republican effort to employ Irish persons and break Ireland's reliance on Britain (Linklater 1980). In fact, a number of feminist activists of this era worked for Irish independence in addition to their Nonhuman Animal advocacy (Leneman 1997; O'Connor 2010). British-born but from an Irish family, Annie Besant supported home rule for both Ireland and India, meeting with Home Rule leaders and writing to newspapers in support of their cause. She was close with George Bernard Shaw and was influenced by his work. Like Shaw, she was also a member of the Anti-Vivisection League. She fiercely resisted oppression wherever it existed, crafting many impassioned speeches and publications against the exploitation of Nonhuman Animals. She, too, was present at the vegetarian summit at the Chicago World's Fair, demonstrating the global reach of Irish feminist vegetarianism. Irish nationalists and feminists Eva Gore-Booth (Leneman 1997) and Margaret Cousins

(O'Connor 2013) were also vegetarian protesters. Gore-Booth found that vegetarianism aligned with her abhorrence of the institution of marriage given its potential for reducing time spent in the kitchen, while Cousins' vegetarianism, like that of Besant, was inspired by Gandhi's theosophy and his country's resistance to British rule.

These activists understood speciesism, sexism, and colonialism to be deeply related systems of oppression, with vegetarianism acting as a form of resistance. Writes Besant:

> The misery that you cause is as it were mire that clings round your feet when you would ascend; for we have to rise together or to fall together, and all the misery we inflict on sentient beings slackens our human evolution and makes the progress of humanity slower towards the ideal that it is seeking to realize. (1908, 11)

This intersectional consciousness was particularly salient in the case of Ireland, which, like other British colonies, was feminized and denigrated as weak and inferior for its plant-based eating. Britain's "beef" eating, in contrast, was taken as evidence to its strength and superiority (Adams 2000; Kellogg 1923). Vegetarianism was simultaneously an act of defiance against imperialism and patriarchy. First-wave feminists viewed vegetarianism as a means of women's empowerment, and this sentiment emerged in conservative Ireland as well. For instance, a Dublin woman presenting at a British vegetarian conference was recorded as having emphasized the liberatory power of cooking plant-based meals for housewives (*Vegetarian Magazine* 1908). Of course, the feminist consciousness also applied to the welfare of Nonhuman Animals. Suffragettes sometimes took up Irish anti-speciesist campaigns. In addition to the attention they paid to the horrors of the scientists' laboratories, the export of "livestock" across the Irish Sea was a particular concern.

Irish Barbarians in Nineteenth Century America

Although Ireland made many important contributions to the formation of the Western Nonhuman Animal rights movement and modern vegetarianism, the history of Victorian advocacy tends to mention the Irish primarily as a bane to the well-being of other animals. Founder of the American movement for Nonhuman Animal rights and the American Society for the Prevention of Cruelty to Animals (ASPCA), Henry Bergh, for one, was positively disgusted by Irish immigrants in his city of New York. In the mid-nineteenth century, Irish immigration was at its peak, with Irish Americans comprising as much as one quarter of the city's population. As most left Ireland due to joblessness, landlessness, and poverty, they were primarily unskilled and disproportionately relegated to slum living and low wage labor. As such, Irish laborers were often in close proximity to working Nonhuman Animals. This inevitably put them under the scrutiny of humane advocates as working urban nonhumans were the primary population targeted by anti-cruelty efforts. Cab-driving, a notoriously grueling occupation in which drivers and their horses were exposed to long hours in all-weather, employed many Irish workers under steep competition that discouraged safe working practices. Horses died by the thousands each year in East Coast cities, and their Irish drivers often died under the strain as well. Many Irish also worked in construction and mining, which took a toll on the bodies of humans and nonhumans alike.

Although Irish workers were rarely in a position to control their working conditions and were under extreme employer pressure to overwork and endanger horses, mules, and other animals, anti-cruelty crusaders villainized the Irish for their complacency. Henry Bergh referred to Irish Americans as "foreign semi-barbarians" with "savage instincts," although their growing power in New York governance forced him to keep his anti-Irish sentiments under wraps. He viewed cruelty to other animals as a marker of decline in a civilized nation and the Irish were a threat as such. He was even said to have kept an official file on their misdeeds titled *The Crimes of the Celtic Race* (Unti 2002). One of the ASPCA's first successful campaigns targeted dog carts used by destitute Irish immigrants, who employed them in the procurement of garbage, swill, and rags in the 1860s. With regard to Irish shores at least, American opinions were more relaxed. The American Humane Association (1902), for instance, reported that Nonhuman Animals were treated relatively well in Ireland and found the RSPCA sufficient in its upholding of welfare laws.

As the American movement progressed, it began to concern itself more exclusively with dogs and cats. This would once again put the Irish under suspicion, as dog "fighting" rings were often run by Irish Americans. Dog "fighting" was especially disdained by social reformers, as the fights attracted gambling, drinking, and brawling. The Irish community's involvement with dog "fighting" operations only aggravated stereotypes of subhuman Irish brutality and its propensity for cruelty to other animals. Kit Burns, an immigrant who had come to New York City during the famine years, was a particular nuisance to welfare advocates (Kaufman and Kaufman 1972; Unti 2002). He had built a small industry running saloons and "fighting" rings where dogs and rats were matched against one another for bets. Burns claimed to be a passionate lover of dogs who accorded better treatment to his canine companions than most humans could afford, but this "love" and "treatment" included brutal training and violent coerced fights for profit, which frequently ended in death (figure 3.5). Training included prolonged running on rudimentary treadmills for hours at a time, and "mongrel" dogs would be sacrificed as bait to prized dogs in training. For those dogs who survived to be "fought," numbing ointments might be applied to improve their performance, while toxic substances could be added to undermine that of their opponent. Dogs were mangled in "fights," frequently experiencing broken bones and slashed faces. Dogs who did not meet the standards of the ring were, of course, unlikely to find loving, adopting homes in which to retire.

Thousands of rats were also killed for sport. One dog, Jack, was said to have killed 100 rats in under seven minutes in one exhibition, while

Figure 3.5. Kit Burns and his dog "fighting" ring. Source: J. McCabe, *Secrets of the Great City* (Philadelphia: Library Company, 1868).

another, Jocko, accomplished the same in under six. It is unlikely that these rats died instantly, and they were undoubtedly dehydrated, starved, and terrorized before meeting their end in the ring. Humans were also invited to "fight" rats for sport. After the dogs finished their rounds, spectators would descend into the pit to join the mayhem, kicking the remaining desperate victims. Sometimes humans also replicated the canine demonstrations in stunts that required the participant to quickly grab each rat, place the rat's head in his mouth, and bite the unfortunate victim's head off. The frightened rats, of course, would bite the faces and mouths of their attacker in a desperate bid for survival. The disgust elicited from spectators eventually convinced Burns to eliminate the practice from the program. A "pet" black bear was also forced to "fight" until he died. The skin was pulled from his corpse and preserved by Burns as a memento. It was indeed an all-around unpleasant establishment for Nonhuman Animals.

In the nineteenth century, the police were often hesitant to involve themselves with blood "sports," but Burns's activity was particularly noxious to crusaders. Societies for the protection of Nonhuman Animals usually hired their own officers, but they also relied on the municipal police for strength and credibility (Unti 2002). Although he was arrested several times, Burns proved a difficult case for the ASPCA to crack, given police hesitancy and Burns's ability to exploit legal loopholes. In one case, he masqueraded his establishment as a building of worship to avoid scrutiny. He also made a mockery of Henry Bergh's quarrel with the killing of rats, insisting that rats were not animals, but simply vermin. The belittling of cruelties that even an unenlightened audience would otherwise not support is a common tactic that abusers can wield to dismiss genuine ethical violations. Indeed, courtrooms unsympathetic to Nonhuman Animal welfare found Bergh's efforts humorous. For these reasons, the ASPCA was never quite successful in bringing Burns's enterprise to an end. The battle between Burns and Bergh only ceased with Burns's abrupt death at the age of 39 while awaiting trial.

The tension between early reformers and Irish immigrants highlights the sticky constructions of animality, race, and ethnicity in the age of industrialization. The role of "animal" was a fluctuating one, moving to encapsulate agendas of social control and reflecting the anxieties of a rapidly changing society. Burns may have animalized rats and objectified them as vermin, but Burns himself had been subjected to the same. Nineteenth-century nativist America certainly viewed the "swarms" of Irish immigrants enveloping the country as vermin as well. Stereotypes regarding their propensity to carry dirt and disease (exacerbated by their relegation to slums) supported this notion. For instance, the infamous New York Irish criminal organization, the Dead Rabbits, of which Burns was a member, married the Irish immigrant identity with the less than flattering rodent identity. The Dead Rabbits gang formed in the post-famine years and was identifiable by the red stripe affixed to the trousers of its members (T. J. English 2006). The term "dead rabbit" quickly became a pejorative label entrenched in the lexicon of the city's media, and its citizenry applied it in reference to any sort of Irish delinquency. In fact, the term "dead rabbit" is thought to be a distortion on the Gaelic word for "lout" (*ráibéad*), demonstrating the intersection of animality and violence in ethnic depictions.

One grim consequence of this Irish animalization process in America surfaced with the rise of medical science and its need for human cadavers. Nineteenth century scientific epistemology was deeply invested in the development of race, class, and gender categories. With science came the power to categorize, name, and otherize. Irish bodies (and the bodies of other marginalized groups) were subsequently targeted by physicians and their grave robbers for dissection purposes, a practice justified by the subhuman status allocated to these specimens (Sappol 2002). The 1854 Act to Promote Medical Science and Protect Burial Grounds (popularly known as the Bone Bill) aimed to requisition the bodies of "vagrants" for scientific study and struck fear in the Irish community due to its racial and ethnic connotations. This was compounded by Catholic beliefs regarding the sanctity of the body and the need for it to be interred intact. The procurement of Irish cadavers represented not only the oppression of Irish in the living world, but forevermore in the afterlife. Animalization made the wanton objectification of their bodies and their inhumane living conditions possible. The Irish were conscious of this, proclaiming that the Bone Bill treated them as dogs (Sappol 2002). In turn, they employed their own brand of animalization by describing proponents of the bill as predatory hyenas, ghouls, and vampires.

Consider also the cultural impact of nineteenth-century disease outbreaks and subsequent efforts to civilize urban areas through sanitation reforms. The rising hegemony of science was again poised to explain these calamities as researchers were beginning to understand the concept of contagion, but the science of pathology collaborated heavily with the science of race biology, and this would make scapegoats of the Irish. Irish American slums had long been a target of sanitation reformers, but their association with urban food production attracted criticism as well. Prior to the industrialization of animal-based agriculture, slaughterhouses and dairies were dotted throughout cities. These provided accessible occupations for many immigrants, although they were not without their risk to the community. Swill milk dairies, often operated by Irish Americans, recycled brewery slurry into food for cows who were kept in pitiful urban stables and coerced into eating the unpalatable swill through periodic starvation. Without access to fresh air, water, or pasture, the intense confinement further degraded the cows' mental and physical wellbeing. Fires frequently broke out, killing many, but the lifespan of a swill dairy cow who escaped such a fate was still only about one year.

Diseased cows in diseased conditions produced diseased milk, and many vulnerable infants and working-class persons were sickened or killed from drinking it (Egan 2005). This enraged reformers and fanned racial and ethnic tensions. Writes journalist Lambert A. Wilmer, "This foul and wicked trade is carried on chiefly by Irishmen; and Irishmen . . . are the special 'pets' of the newspaper press" (1859, 161–62). "Hundreds of lives," he imagines, "are probably lost every year, by means of the general consumption of this horrible article of food" (164). Although sanitation problems were acknowledged, consumers had little way of knowing the source of their purchases. Swill milk had a telltale blue hue, but this was masked with adulteration. Political elites also blocked attempts to reform or abolish the swill dairies, as the industry had become a profitable one for the Irish American bureaucrats who were gaining power and influence.

Irish Americans may have been heavily involved in swill milk production, but Irish American consumers were the hardest hit as well. Cholera outbreaks were tied to swill milk, and more than 40 percent of those who died in one such outbreak in 1832 were Irish. Some were uncomfortable with the ethnocentric element of swill milk denunciations, but fear of disease fed discriminatory fervor. Wilmer, for one, directly challenged the moral character and honesty of Irish swill milk producers: "Of the Irish people who come to America, I do not believe that one in fifty assists the productive industry of the country . . . and some of their favorite pursuits are eminently mischievous" (1859, 139). As with other nativists of the period, he subscribed to the belief that Irish immigrants were no better than animals themselves, accusing them of converting the "Home of Liberty into something resembling a stupendous PIG-STYE." He resented that citizenship was granted to these subhumans who were "morally and intellectually inferior to the negroes whom we hold in personal and political bondage" (136). Journalist Frank Leslie also animalized the Irish swill dairy keepers in illustrations for his paper. Several of his subjects were depicted as apelike in both feature and behavior (figure 3.6). To further demean them, swill workers (who were

Figure 3.6. Swill milk production as depicted by Frank Leslie. Source: *Illustrated Newspaper*, May 15, 1858.

predominantly men) were feminized as "milkmaids." Sensationalistic and effective, Leslie's images depict deplorable conditions for cows, intending to shock readers as to the dangers lurking in the milk supply and the corrupted nature of the Irish immigrants extracting it (McNeur 2014). Wright (2015), recall, has emphasized that constructions of animality, ethnicity, and class tightly comingle within symbolic understandings of foodways. As the swill milk industry demonstrates, this is particularly true of those foodways that are based on the exploitation of Irish immigrants and other animals.

The racist association of Irish immigrants with depravity and propensity for cruelty to other animals materialized in the humane education efforts of the day. In the nineteenth century, imprinting youngsters with messages of kindness to Nonhuman Animals was thought essential to their moral development. Racial and ethnic minorities, such as Blacks, poor whites in the American South, people of color in colonized territories, and Irish immigrants, were the recipients of much of this effort (J. M. Davis 2016). Native-born whites, meanwhile, were inadvertently encouraged to view Irish persons and Nonhuman Animals in the same category, as both were patronized as lowlier beings in need of care and compassion.[7] Early Sunday school curricula intersected the importance of charity to the Irish with charity to other animals. It was sermonized that the moral development of Irish persons was also bound to that of Nonhuman Animals. One American Sunday School Union (1845) reader told of Jack, a "deaf and dumb" Irish boy, who was literally animalized in his inability to speak or fully understand English. Like other domesticated animals, it was explained, Jack communicated with his caretakers through touch and body language. Thus, even charitable efforts to relieve Irish suffering relied on problematic structures of speciesism to protect a hierarchy of authority and worth.

Conclusion

Although the history of Nonhuman Animal rights in the West highlights the contributions of Great Britain and the United States, the movement has Ireland to thank for many important advancements in resistance to speciesism. In the first decades of the nineteenth century, Irishmen such as Martin, Drummond, and Haughton paved the way for Western anti-speciesist thought in the creation of groundbreaking and internationally influential legislation and literature. Later in the century, many powerful Irish women also incorporated vegetarianism and anti-vivisection activism into their feminist agendas. Irish activists also mobilized in Great Britain and the United States, with Irish immigrants populating the Brown Dog protests in London and helping to found major anti-cruelty nonprofit organizations in America. A prototypical vegan feminist ethic can thus be situated in the Irish imagination; many activists recognized that the condition of the Irish people was tied to the condition of Ireland's nonhumans. Some Irish activists, like Drummond and Besant, also recognized how the struggle for Nonhuman Animal rights related to other social injustices in the United States, India, and beyond. Opponents seem to have understood this intersectionality as well, as the Brown Dog affair, which targeted a simple anti-vivisection monument erected in a working class hub of radical activism, so vividly demonstrated. Anti-speciesism had come to represent defiance against patriarchal and colonial control.

In order for the Irish to achieve emancipation, Marx ([1867] 2000) prescribed nothing short of an agrarian revolution and the destruction of class inequality; he recognized the fundamental role that food production (and, if only indirectly, the reliance on Nonhuman Animals) played in Ireland's suffering. Marx also recognized that exploited English laborers would need to recognize their shared hardship and actively resist the antagonism between the Irish and English that was "artificially kept alive and intensified by the press, the pulpit, the comic papers, in short, by all the means at the disposal of the ruling classes" (640). This antagonism, he observed, was the "secret by which the capitalist class maintains its power" (640). Unfortunately, this strategy of resistance faced formidable challenges, particularly with regard to the relationship between Irish immigrants and other animals. Many entrepreneurial Irish folk had paved the way for advances in Nonhuman Animal liberation, but many more would serve as fodder for anti-cruelty campaigns.

The propensity for the Irish to be animalized and their close working and living relationship with other animals systematically subjected them to the punitive efforts of humane reform. Despite so many important Irish contributions to anti-speciesism, this discriminatory agenda has chronicled Irish cruelty to the effect of erasing a legacy of Irish solidarity with the cause (this historical portrayal, I suggest, continues to feed the stereotype of Irish backwardness and brutishness today). The Irish were not likely to find comradery with the laboring classes in America or Britain, as they were relentlessly harassed by political and cultural commentators, nativist legislation, police-enforced city policies, Nonhuman Animal welfare protection efforts, and so on. Underscoring this ethnic tension was the more fundamental division that colonialism had fostered between humans and other animals.

Marx recognized that capitalist exploitation essentially diminished the physical "species-being" of humans by reducing them to specialized, alienated cogs in the great machine of capitalist production. However, I suggest that Marx's theory might be strengthened should it also acknowledge that the ruling class actively encourages the *symbolic* animalization of exploited workers for the maintenance of unequal social relations. The predictive value of Marx's work might also be improved by more fully appreciating the injustice imposed on Nonhuman Animals themselves—Nonhuman Animals, too, are animalized for political purposes. The persistence of these divisions and unequal social relations impedes human-nonhuman cooperation, ultimately protecting the capitalist logic that some bodies may be acceptably and freely exploited for the benefit of more powerful groups.

That said, Irish mobilization on behalf of other animals would persist through the twentieth and twenty-first centuries (although British and American activism has come to dominate the annals). Ireland's unique political, social, and economic history would shape a vegan ethic that resists absorption into these larger historical narratives. Specifically, the civil rights struggles of the mid-twentieth century would unsettle the state's domineering relationship with other animals. Like their nineteenth-century counterparts, modern societal disrupters would find themselves animalized in the discourses of hegemony, but a greater consciousness to social inequality adapted from adjacent social movements would positively shape anti-speciesist campaigning as well.

Chapter 4

Modern Activism for Other Animals in Ireland

Irish Veganism of the Mid-Twentieth Century

The story of Ireland's human relations with other animals has thus far been monopolized by Britain's colonial violence, but I have emphasized that the intersecting oppression of humans and other animals has also offered a measure of resistance. Gramsci noted that hegemony could dominate through culture, but he also advocated the manufacture of counterculture to achieve social justice (Adamson 2014). Activists in a modernizing Ireland were keen to succeed in this regard. This chapter examines this direction as it is informed by postwar welfare ambitions in Europe and the contagiousness of neighboring social justice causes related to race and ethnicity, sex and gender, the environment, and so on. This formational period between the end of the world wars and the era of the professionalized anti-speciesism advocacy is most commonly analyzed as it transpired in Great Britain (Ryder 1989), the United States (Unti 2002), and even Australia (Villanueva 2018). These narratives rightly draw attention to important influences in the global effort to resist speciesism, but they can also reflect and replicate colonial control in invisiblizing the contributions of other regions that have been deeply manipulated and exploited by more powerful nations. Resistance efforts in Ireland have not simply mirrored the efforts of the imperialists. Much of Ireland's defiance has been culturally unique and, in many ways, specifically informed by its colonial experience. The modern anti-speciesist movement is subsequently indebted to this calamitous history. Colonial exploitation built the economic wealth of Britain and its contemporaries, but, as a form of structural violence (Galtung 1969), it also fueled an epistemology of resistance particular to Irish society.

Following a frenzy of activity in the nineteenth and early twentieth centuries, the Western Nonhuman Animal rights movement entered a period of abeyance after the World Wars and would not find its second wind until the civil rights era in the 1960s and 1970s (Wrenn 2019). This era of dormancy was not uninterrupted, as there were certainly individuals and groups advocating for nonhuman welfare and working to normalize lifestyles sans animal products. In some ways, war provoked critical thinking about humanity's relationship with food and other animals. The vegan movement, for instance, began with the launching of the Vegan Society in Great Britain in 1944 at the height of war. Born out of years of debate over the appropriateness of dairy products in the vegetarian diet, a number of vegans wished to form a subgroup within the British Vegetarian Society. Denied this, they were encouraged to form their own society, and so they did (Calvert 2014).

Vegans were primarily located in England, but, as the movement spread, vegans could be counted in Scotland and Ireland as well. In 1949, the *Irish Press* interviewed Moira Henry, whom it dubbed "the Only Vegan in Ireland." Henry had gone vegan in the 1940s and remained so until her death in 1997. The honorary secretary of the Dublin Vegetarian Society, she was also active with the Irish Vegetarian Society and the Irish Union against Vivisection. Her interview provides a rare glimpse into early vegan and vegetarian life in Ireland. In it, she speaks enviously of English advancements in plant-based alternatives, such as nut meat and nut butter, and worries over the increased cost of vegan staples following postwar rationing. Despite these hindrances, she does report some 120 to 130 vegetarians living in Ireland.

Henry likely facilitated collaboration between Irish groups and Britain's Vegan Society, as the society's journal the *Vegan* reported successful lectures being hosted there. Claims the editor following one such event, "Although Veganism is a new approach in Ireland, the audiences listened carefully to the speaker's frank opinions on the use of dairy produce. . . . The proverbial warmth of an Irish welcome was experienced both south and north of the border" (Henderson 1948, 2). Most activities took place within England, but Ireland was clearly part of the vegan scene. Interest in plant-based living was at least robust enough to support a small collective. Between 1953 and 1957, the *Vegan* advertised the Dublin New Health Group in Ballsbridge as an establishment catering to vegans. When the president of the newly founded American Vegan Society visited the United Kingdom in

1971, his speaking tour included Ireland. Likewise, the Veganic Association, which "promotes the growing of vegetables, fruits, cereals and nuts by the purest and easiest method," was active at least for a short period in Dun Laoghaire, County Dublin,[1] while Irish bed and breakfast holiday homes accommodating vegans were advertised from Counties Antrim and Kildare (Vegan Society 1971). This same publication reported as many as "a few dozen" Scottish and Irish members of the Vegan Society by 1970 (Sanderson 1970). The number of actual vegans was undoubtedly more, as the fledgling society regularly bemoaned low membership in the face of much higher vegan demographic estimates.

Several Irish members held influential positions in the organization and in the wider community. For example, Brian Gunn-King, had been appointed as senior planner for the Ministry of Development in the community of Ballymena, County Antrim, a position that granted him stewardship of several hundred miles of coastline, forests, and nature reserves (Vegan Society 1973). Brian's new leadership role greatly pleased the society, given that it promoted environmental sustainability as a core principle of veganism. Originally from Coventry, England, Brian and his partner Margaret were incredibly active vegans, regularly appearing in issues of the *Vegan* to report on their vegan family life and community work in the North of Ireland. Brian was also a general secretary (the first vegan to hold this post) and executive vice-president of the International Vegetarian Union, and, as part of his duties, hosted vegetarian spiritual leaders from Asian countries, sparking the interest of local papers (*Ballymena Guardian* 1974). He also served as chairman of the National Society for the Abolition of Factory Farming (*British Vegetarian* 1968a). Gunn-King's efforts would have a lasting impact on his community, with youth activists taking up his work following his death in 2013 (*Ballymena Times* 2013).

Not to be outdone, Margaret was also involved with the IVU and was elected to the committee of the Vegetarian Society. She volunteered service for anti-speciesist British organizations as well (*British Vegetarian* 1968b). Both she and Brian were official delegates for the Vegan Society (J. Davis 2012). The society was delighted by this connection to the IVU, given the networks and legitimacy it could grant to the burgeoning vegan movement. In 1975, the couple renovated an old school in Ballymena, which acted as IVU Headquarters, vegetarian center, and yoga studio (Margaret was a certified instructor). It housed educational materials, a working vegan organic garden, and Margaret's cooking demonstrations. Its grand opening entertained a crowd of fifty (Jannaway 1975). The Gunn-Kings must be considered two of Ireland's founding vegans, but their influence reached far beyond County Antrim. Also in 1975, they helped to organize the twenty-third World Vegan Congress in Maine (American Vegan Society 2013), and this meeting is recognized as the originator of the modern Nonhuman Animal rights movement in the United States (Farm Animal Rights Movement 2016). Ireland can thus be placed at the heart of Western activism both past and present.

Another pioneer of Irish veganism in the 1970s and 1980s was Irish-born Kathleen Jannaway, who served as honorary secretary to the Vegan Society and remained a highly influential leader with the organization for most of her life. She also founded the Movement for Compassionate Living in England in the late twentieth century (Main 2003). Christopher Fettes, another Irish representative, was a leader of the Esperantist Vegetarians. Esperanto was an artificially invented universal tongue promoted for some time as a way to overcome language barriers and facilitate international collaboration. While Esperanto may not have taken off as hoped, Fettes would go on to act as the European regional secretary for the IVU (J. Davis 2012). There was also Wilfried M. Capper, who served as assistant treasurer to the IVU from 1969 to 1982. He, too, hailed from Northern Ireland.

Service work of this nature was essential to the legitimization of the movement, but it was limited in its outsider appeal. To attract the interest of the wider public, an element of adventure and excitement would be necessary. One man who enthusiastically adopted this strategy was Jack McClelland of Belfast, one of the Vegan Society's dearest heroes and one of the world's first vegan celebrities. McClelland was a member of both the Vegan Society and Ulster Vegetarian Society for over thirty years and held leadership positions with both organizations. He was perhaps best known in Ireland for his athleticism, however. Fighting as the "Belfast Bulldog," he distinguished himself as an Irish light heavyweight champion, as well as taking part in wrestling and refereeing in the 1940s and 1950s (Historyo n.d.). He was also involved in cycling, international soccer, running, and weightlifting (*Vegan* 1963, 1969), but he would truly find his stride when he began long-distance swimming in the 1950s. His achievements were often record breaking and always perilously earned. In one failed attempt at the English Channel, he went missing for an hour, terrifying the rescue team and riveting the newspapers. In other swims, he met with severe cold, whirlpools, cross tides, submerged rocks, sharks, and dangerous jellyfishes. Stereotypes that characterized veganism as weakening and nutritionally inadequate had no traction in the wake of McClelland.

McClelland was a longtime vegan. He was said to have chewed dulse (red alga) "by the fist-full" (*Vegan* 1969), even forgoing the application of goose fat to protect his body during long swims, as was customary practice at the time (Batt 1965). Praises the president of the Vegan Society, "Very few can have done more for Vegetarianism and Veganism. . . . He is a man who is not just out for new long distance swimming records, but who is determined to demonstrate what non-flesh eating can do for all mankind [sic]" (Sanderson 1963, 1). McClelland was truly a vegan spectacle. Thousands witnessed his swims, and many more read of them. One report supposed that more folks showed up to greet McClelland after his swim across Galway Bay than to greet President Kennedy just a few weeks earlier (*Vegan* 1963). His efforts proved that veganism was not only healthful but could sustain a vigorous professional athlete. Even in today's health-conscious society, veganism is stereotyped as nutritionally insufficient (MacInnis and Hodson 2017), but in the 1960s, veganism was a relatively new concept and very little scientific evidence had been accumulated to demonstrate its safety. McClelland's exploits provided powerful anecdotal evidence. McClelland was acutely aware that his body had become a working experiment. He was genuinely interested in the capabilities of human endurance on the vegan diet, sometimes testing his abilities with different types of foods and issuing public challenges for races by land or water (Sanderson 1965; *Vegan* 1968).

Like other vegan activists of the 1960s, McClelland was an environmentalist and anti-speciesist. He campaigned against the "coursing" of hares and the "fighting" of bulls, and regularly traveled to England as a committee member to participate in the activities of the Vegan Society. The McClellands sometimes collaborated with the Gunn-Kings. For instance, Jack and Brian both appeared on a November 24 airing of *Gordon Burns Hour*, a live weekly talk show on Ulster Television in 1973 (*Vegan* 1974). Truly a Jack of all trades, he made a living managing a chain of health food stores in Ireland that he had developed with his partner Betty (Gunn-King 1996). These stores helped make plant-based living possible in Ireland and were an important extension of his activism.

Along with the Gunn-Kings, the McClellands were highly influential leaders in Ireland, and their efforts helped to energize collective action there. The Ulster Vegetarian Society, puttering along since 1932, seems to have been doing well by the 1970s with their help. Even at the end of his life, McClelland was sustaining the organization as president. Just a year after his death, the UVS secretary was reporting difficulty in obtaining membership despite heavy outreach efforts. "We have applied from time to time for help from trust and grants but without success," she writes to the IVU. "I think we are the least supported charity in N. Ireland, yet we have the practical answers to world's problems" (Gourley 1995). Unfortunately, the UVS disappears from record thereafter. The UVS surmised that its mobilization difficulties could have been cultural.

Animal Activism and Civil Rights

Many vegans were well aware of these attitudinal and structural relationships as barriers to animal equality. As was the case with first wave activism of the nineteenth century, twentieth century activists employed an intersectional lens and were allied with other social justice causes. For instance, McClelland also held top positions in the Ulster and Belfast humanist groups in addition to his work with the Ulster Vegetarian Society (UVS). He was disturbed by the sectarian turmoil in the North of Ireland and believed that violence in diet inspired violence in community. He regularly contributed to news outlets on the importance of bodily health in this regard, such as a letter published with a Belfast newspaper entitled "Years of 'Bad Food' Cause of Troubles?" (Batt 1969). He made repeated but unsuccessful attempts to pique the interest of the BBC on this correlation as well.

This belief that diet, environment, and health shapes the propensity for political violence in a community may have been commonly accepted in activist circles. Nineteenth century American vegetarians held vegetarianism to be the lynchpin of moral reforms of the era, convinced that a violent diet led to violent constitution (Shprintzen 2013). In Ireland, visiting vegetarian leaders from India made remarks of this kind in their observation of the sectarian Irish conflict (*Ballymena Guardian* 1974). Given the symbolic role that the Great Famine continued to play throughout rebellions and troubles of later years, poor nutrition has been explored by psychologists as a potential influence on Ireland's political behavior as well (Rice and Benson 2005). That is, observers surmised that the food presently consumed in Ireland could be influencing conflict but also that the food that was *not* consumed nearly two centuries ago was contributing to contemporary turmoil as well.

Recall that scholars of Critical Animal Studies have identified similar relationships between oppressive food systems and other forms of postcolonial systemic violence (Gambert and Linné 2018; Wiley 2011). Not all Irish persons necessarily recognized this intersection of course. Playwright

Oscar Wilde, for one, disagreed with this theory of "meat" and mayhem. Writing of nineteenth century republican discord, he observes on the subject of vegetarianism:

> It is strange that the most violent republicans I know are all vegetarians: Brussels sprouts seem to make people bloodthirsty, and those who live on lentils and artichokes are always calling for the gore of the aristocracy and for the severed heads of kings. . . . In the political sphere a diet of green beans seems dangerous. ([1887] 2000, 334)

As is Wilde's manner, he may have embellished a bit. After all, many of these vegetarian republicans were feminists and pacifists. Wilde himself recognized at times the relationship between social justice and the treatment of other animals. Some of his letters, for instance, reflect the Victorian interest in humane education for children:

> A lad [sic] who learns any simple art learns honesty, and truth-telling, and simplicity, in the most practical school of simple morals in the world, the school of art, learns too to love nature more . . . [and] learns too to be kind to animals and all living things, that most difficult of all lessons to teach a child (for I feel that when he sees how lovely the little leaping squirrel is on the beaten brass, or the bird arrested in marble flight on the carven stone, he will never be cruel to them again). ([1882] 2000, 170)

This logic was a popular one. Humane education was the leading and most successfully implemented tactic of the British and American anti-cruelty movements of the nineteenth century. More than a matter of protecting Nonhuman Animals, it was a campaign designed to protect the vulnerable character of children and, ultimately, the character of the country (J. M. Davis 2016). As social inequalities of the postwar era wrested the attentions of twentieth century anti-speciesists, this connectivity between peace and kindness to Nonhuman Animals and achieving the same in the broader society became a favored activist framework again. The status of Nonhuman Animals, in other words, often defined a nation. Recall that Wright (2015) has outlined this relationship between national identity and consumption, but vegan feminist theory, too, posits that violence against other animals provides a framework for other forms of social violence related to sexism, racism, classism, and more (Adams 2000; Ko 2019). Both early and contemporary thinkers, then, would support McClelland's theory that diet is political.

The Irish press may not have been buying McClelland's hypothesis that bad food was linked to social disorder, but radical food politics did find some resonance in the North of Ireland during the Troubles of the mid-century. In the early 1980s, Warzone, a volunteer organization that adhered to anarchical philosophies, prepared and served vegan food with a side helping of Nonhuman Animal rights philosophy (Stewart 2014). Prior to the Warzone initiative, the Belfast Anarchist Collective ran a center in Belfast that also served vegan food and hosted punk music, both of which presented a powerful political critique and nurtured a much-needed sense of community. The Warzone, with an anti-sectarian, pro-intersectionality, pay-as-you-go policy, continues to serve vegan food today in its volunteer-run Giro's Café. It is perhaps the first and certainly the longest running vegan restaurant on the island. It may seem improbable that such an ethical vegan project could emerge amid such turmoil, but the intersectional nature of human and nonhuman oppression can sometimes facilitate campaigning convergences of this kind. Indeed, it is this recognition of solidarity that inspired hope in Marx and his ilk, who felt certain that consciousness raised to shared oppression would ignite resistance.

CONFLICTS WITH TRAVELLERS IN SETTLED IRELAND

Irish morality was not the only focus of food justice efforts. Activists were also genuinely concerned with the suffering of Nonhuman Animals. One notable mid-twentieth century international campaign focusing on Nonhuman Animals in Ireland related to the live export of horses for slaughter and consumption in mainland Europe (Horses and Ponies Protection Society 1963). While limits on the legal age of slaughter were imposed in the 1960s, which restricted the practice somewhat, these did not apply to those categorized as "workhorses." This proved a serious loophole since "workhorses" were most likely to fall victim to the trade, given their displacement following agricultural industrialization. This live export of horses is a practice that continues today, and it remains a concern of the Irish Horse Welfare Trust and the Animal Rights Action Network (M. O'Reilly 2013). For activists, the exploitation of horses and the fight to relieve their distress presents a critical case study in the difficulties that a colonial legacy imposes on campaigners who resist nonhuman oppression that is deeply entangled with human injustices. In this instance, horse "trading" is a leading occupation of Ireland's Travelling community. Just how to relieve horses without burdening an already distressed ethnic minority group that is so heavily reliant on exploiting horses would not be especially apparent.

The transition to an industrialized society has long since been accomplished in Ireland, yet the violence enacted on horses rendered superfluous by modern technology has not diminished. The number of "spent" and retired equines killed for food actually increased by 25 percent between 2015 and 2016 to include nearly eight thousand individuals. This number jumped to an astounding twenty-four thousand during the desperate years of the recession, lending weight to the vegan socialist argument that economic stress will be disproportionately absorbed by Nonhuman Animals, given their status as disposable commodities (Nibert 2013). According to the Irish Society for the Prevention of Cruelty to Animals (ISPCA), this killing is a preferable solution, given high levels of horse homelessness and abandonment (Kelleher 2017). This justification, however, relegates the issue to an individual irresponsibility, overlooking the structural causes for horse production and disposal. Incredible state and community level support for professional "racing" in tandem with postcolonial economic inequality that presents "racing" as a possible means to get rich quick means that horse populations are unlikely to diminish to more sustainable levels. Here, Nonhuman Animals become casualties of an Ireland seeking equal status, another missed opportunity for solidarity in the face of colonial antagonism.

The economic viability of Travellers, too, is tied to "racing." Travellers are heavily involved in the knackering industry, as it remains one way of independently eking out a living. Most commonly, Traveller brokers have collected "spent" horses to turnover for slaughter, but another practice was to resell "spent" horses. Even older and disabled horses could tempt unsuspecting customers with an appearance of vigor after a cruel application of irritating spices to their rectum, which inflicted great pain and caused them to prance (Gmelch 1975). This association between Travellers and the pain and suffering of horses has aggravated ethnic stereotypes and makes for convenient scapegoating by welfare advocates who primarily hail from the dominant class in Ireland. While it may be difficult to sympathize with any group that makes a living from killing, by far the largest contributor to Nonhuman Animal suffering and death on the island is the settled community, given their control over speciesist social institutions, including the legal system, which relegates so many nonhumans to exploitative use and slaughter for consumption.

Indeed, the settled class's stereotypes against the Travellers ignores the fact that horses do play a more positive role in Traveller culture (Helleiner 2000). Horses represent the free-spiritedness and propensity to roam that Travellers ascribe to their own character. In years past, horses pulled their carts and wagon homes, and today their utility lies in their economic and entertainment value. For years, Travellers have relied on the "breeding" and sale of horses as an important means of livelihood. More than this, horse "trading," often in seasonal festivals, is a fundamental aspect of socializing, networking, and community building. Horses are also tied to the Travellers' machismo culture. Because "racing" is relevant to familial rituals and provides an expression of masculinity, young boys and men dominate sulky racing. Their mastery over ponies and horses and the speed and danger of open road contests (frequently amid traffic) provide opportunities for status attainment.

The frequent fatalities and injuries associated with Traveller racing has drawn heavy criticism from the settled community. Systematic violence against Nonhuman Animals is frequently a survival strategy made necessary by a long history of social exclusion (Li 2017). This is unlucky for Nonhuman Animals, but also for marginalized human groups who are more easily targeted by privileged groups seeking to locate (or construct) points of debasement for political purposes (J. M. Davis 2016). The charge of cruelty is a readily available grievance that the settled Irish may wield against ethnic minorities, but Travellers are also concerned about horse welfare. Indeed, this attention to welfare is strategically listed as a core principle of the Tipperary Traveller Horse Owners Association (TTHOA), which organized to counter stereotypes of Traveller cruelty (*Tipperary Star* 2014). That said, racialized debates over cruelty are apt to reflect the prejudices of the human groups in conflict and overlook the interests of the nonhumans caught in the crossfire. The primary goal of the TTHOA, for instance, is to *expand* rather than curtail horse ownership. Most humans do not "breed" and "own" horses for nefarious reasons and may genuinely care for and love the horses in their care, but it remains the case that domesticated animals are in a state of extreme dependency and are vulnerable to violence (Hall 2010). The existence of numerous horse welfare organizations in Ireland can attest to this. Even those horses who escape neglect are subject to slaughter once deemed to be useless to humans, while those used for sport and work are further susceptible to routine injury and undue stress.

That said, nonhuman exploitations associated with dominant groups are more likely to be accepted as appropriate and humane, while minority uses are likely to provoke moral panics and are subject to heavy policing (J.

M. Davis 2016). Sociologist Stanley Cohen (1972) introduced the concept of a *moral panic* to describe the process of ascribing extreme stigma and sanction to vulnerable groups that are marked as a threat to societal values. The ensuing "panic" is characteristically far out of proportion to the actual extent of the behavior deemed problematic, but the ensuing fervor can serve political aims at suppressing the targeted group. In Ireland, the extensive attention devoted to ending sulky "racing" (a practice that is proportionately miniscule in comparison to the larger scale forms of speciesism facing horses and other animals under the Irish state) might be said to exemplify Cohen's concept. Kilkenny, for example, banned Traveller sulky "racing" in a reaction to numerous accidents that left horses maimed or dead. Other regions, such as County Tipperary, have considered doing the same, due to the danger to inexperienced child drivers as well as to the public. The extreme brutality inflicted on many horses has only heightened the conflict (*Nationalist* 2013). Explains the Mayor of Kilkenny, "We were witnessing appalling scenes of horses left for dead by the roadside, horses being beaten, horses being raced on public roads risking the lives of road users and those involved and so on. It had to stop" (*Kilkenny People* 2016). The ISPCA agreed and offered its support to the campaign, calling for a national ban. Advocates and policymakers have been hesitant to promote reform over abolition given the level of suffering imposed on horses and ponies (Cusack 2014; Meagher 2013a), but the institutional killing of horses for food in the settled community's slaughterhouses remains perfectly legal.

The Travelling community has organized to resist the depiction of sulky "racing" as cruel and to protect its legalization (Tipp FM 2017), but the number of horses killed continues to horrify the settled public. Worse still, the magnitude of survivor numbers has overwhelmed the ISPCA and shelters, leading to the blanket "euthanasia" protocol for any horse seized in Kilkenny (McNulty 2015). The TTHOA counters that horses are integral to the economic survival of Travellers, as well as their mental health. Given high levels of unemployment and social exclusion, horses are often a young man's primary source of self-worth and community integration (Meagher 2013b). The astronomical rate of suicide among Travellers (the rate is seven times higher than that of the settled population, mostly afflicting boys and men) is a strong indication that this counterclaim holds weight:

> Looking after horses is time consuming, it involves handing down skills from one generation to the next, and there are fairs to look forward to, which in themselves are major social

events. For those without work, who have lost the traditions of travelling and keeping horses, there is nothing to do. They lack purpose in life, they have no reason to get up in the morning and nothing to look forward to. Particularly vulnerable are single young men. (Walker 2008, 102)

Without horses, researchers warn, Travellers are prone to social isolation, delinquency, and self-harm.

Again, the conflict between settled and travelling Irish is a manifestation of colonial interference and the class, race, and species hierarchies it constructed, making for difficult negotiations. Sulky "racing" is only a recent manifestation of equine-centered ethnic tensions in Ireland. Horses are not always portrayed as victims but are sometimes made guilty by association. The imposition of private property and the closing of common lands has burdened lower-class Irish and Nonhuman Animals alike. Not content to relegate their horses to often insufficient roadside grazing, it was not uncommon for itinerants to sneak them into privately owned fields under cover of night in hopes of granting them a good supper. These unfortunate horses were often maimed or even shot by retaliatory farmers (Gmelch 1975). Welfare campaigns designed to tend to the Nonhuman Animals belonging to Travellers did exist, but these were funded primarily by British donations and received little support from the Irish. Today, spaces that traveling horses may legally occupy have become even fewer and farther between. Some communities, such as Cork City, have worked in tandem with Travellers to create monitored communal horse grazing sites. In addition to improving the relationship between settled and nonsettled Irish groups, such projects hold promise with regard to improving the welfare of horses and reducing the burden on regional agencies (English 2017).

The minimal courtesy of considering Travellers in this decision-making is itself a marker of multicultural progress in modern Ireland. Ireland's Travellers were officially recognized as an ethnic minority only in 2017. Although slow in coming, this acknowledgment will be essential in granting the community legal protection and fair representation. It is an important first step in countering the extreme structural discrimination that Travellers have faced under the Irish state assimilation schemes. In a way, it offers admittance into the category of "human." In a settled society that favors law, order, and predictability, Travellers have been treated similarly to Nonhuman Animals in being systematically subjugated to the economic interests of the state. Under British rule, "gypsies" were persecuted and could be killed, and the closing of open lands on which they depended under English custom worsened their situation. This privatization of communal spaces, recall, has been a powerful strategy of oppression under capitalist endeavors. Privatization creates precariousness and vulnerability for those relying on the resources land provides, but it also erects physical barriers between dominant and oppressed classes. As has been the case with many nonhuman species under colonialism (Boom et al. 2012), Travellers were frequently depicted as violent, dangerous, dependent, and bothersome (Fanning 2002). In some cases, the dogs, horses, and other animals that lived with the Travellers were identified as health hazards, while, in other cases, the Travellers themselves were identified as such (Helleiner 2000). For free-roaming Nonhuman Animal communities, humanity assumed control by either domestication or extermination (Nibert 2013), and the reality for Travellers in a settled world was not much different. The voices and interests of Nonhuman Animals and Travellers alike have historically been dismissed in decision-making that shapes their lifeworlds.

Although there have been signs of improvement, as I have already mentioned, state restrictions on human-nonhuman relationships continue to target the Traveller way of life. Designed to control wandering horses and curtail sulky "racing," the 1996 Control of Horses Act greatly impacted the Travellers (Pavee Point Traveller and Roma Centre 2014; Walker 2008). The act emerged from concerns about public safety and horse welfare, but Travellers had not been consulted. This was a significant oversight given that Travellers' ability to use horses is already constrained by their limited land ownership and itinerary. Landlords can complicate matters by imposing additional restrictions on the number of Nonhuman Animals allowed on leasing properties, if any at all. The vagabond lifestyle that was once a means of survival in the economic uncertainty of an earlier Ireland has subsequently become a liability in a society that mandates law, order, and conformity. The civilizing process, again, shows itself to be a cover for structural violence with regard to vulnerable groups deemed "animal-like." The failure to include the Travellers community in the development of welfare laws reflects a longer tradition in Irish politics of managing this ethnic minority group on their behalf and without their consent. Indeed, many leading organizations advocating for Travellers' rights are operated by settled Irish, and, despite good intentions, have been known to patronize their clients and promote ineffectual or inappropriate solutions (Lentin 2006).

Animal Nationalism

Political discourse in the early years of the Irish state animalized Travellers as an infestation given their resistance to social norms and state control, yet, as I have argued, it also leveraged their perceived cruelty to Nonhuman Animals as impetus for intervention (Helleiner 2000). That is, concern for the well-being of other animals is conditional, and the *disdain* for the well-being of other animals can easily surface via processes of race- and class-based animalization. Following the abolition of slavery in the United Kingdom and United States and the construction of an imperialist global system, for instance, citizens of African descent and colonized subjects were each stereotyped as especially cruel to other animals (J. M. Davis 2013; Deckha 2013; Lundblad 2013). Live export protest in Australia demonstrates how concern for the well-being of Nonhuman Animals may be leveraged to maintain boundaries internationally as well. The killing of Australian-born sheeps in Indonesian slaughterhouses with purportedly lower standards of treatment and dispatch for intended victims created a massive outcry in Australia, but this outcry was not against the killing per se. Instead, protests organized by settler Australians provided a coded means of demarking white Australians from "foreign" Indonesians of color. International and interracial colonizer-initiated disputes over the treatment of other animals underscore colonialism's construction of boundaries between developed and backward, and civilized and savage. Outrage over Australia's live export and Indonesia's treatment of said "goods" became a battle between Australian humanity and Indonesian animality, with actual Nonhuman Animals serving only as referents.

Dalziell and Wadiwel (2017), like Wright (2015), refer to this politicization of violence against other animals for state power as animal nationalism. More than a concern over "civil" treatment, these disputes often relate to colonialism's emphasis on land and resource ownership, given their importance to the building of nations. Subsequently, colonialism's value system assigned ethnic superiority to those who owned property, while otherizing ethnic minorities who were generally prevented from doing the same. In the case of Nonhuman Animals, they themselves become the property linked to status and power, and those owned by Western nations are typically granted greater value in trade relations. Ireland has historically been disadvantaged in this way, given its colonized status, but, as a postcolonial nation, it has aligned with the dominant Western countries and also exports much of its "stock" alive and often to Muslim countries. The export of Ireland's cows to Libya, for instance, has drawn the ire of Irish activist organizations as the violent killing of cows in Muslim Africa is thought to be less acceptable than the violent killing of cows domestically. Living, breathing nonhuman individuals with capacities for suffering and pain are thus, like Australian sheeps, granted only symbolic value as property of the state. It is Irish nationhood that is truly perceived to be slighted. Protests and letter writing campaigns have been organized to demand an end to the export of Irish cows to Muslim countries, but not the consigning of Irish cows to *Irish* abattoirs.

An element of animal nationalism is present in the tension between Travellers and settled Irish as well, not only with regard to the Travellers' treatment of other animals but also with regard to the animalization of Travellers themselves. Travellers, in other words, become the contested animals disrupting Ireland's nation-building project. Media accounts of "gypsy" life in the nineteenth century frequently portrayed them as averse to cleanliness, unable to learn civilities, and living and dying like dogs (G. Smith 1880). Because they frequently scavenged for a living, they were stereotyped as pilferers and poachers, not unlike feral dogs and foxes. Popular depictions of Travellers living out of doors and surrounded by various Nonhuman Animals underscored their animality (figure 4.1).

Figure 4.1. Travellers in 1960s Ireland. This image is reproduced courtesy of the National Library of Ireland (TIL850).

The experiences of Travellers and other animals, in fact, hold many similarities, given their shared desire for self-determination and the discrimination they face. Like many nonhuman species, Travellers resist human constructs such as property, fixed employment, institutionalized education, and permanent residence. Many live close to the elements without running water or electricity. Travellers and other animals are seen as stunted in their evolution, not quite as "developed" as privileged human groups in power (Ó hAodha 2011). For these reasons, they become an aggravation, if not a threat, to the modern establishment. Like other animals, Travellers find themselves increasingly marginalized into ever-shrinking free spaces. Photographers and journalists routinely penetrate the "wild spaces" that Travellers and other animals call home, documenting them in photo essays and educational documentaries. They are both curiosities and specimens of interest to the settled world. To be animal is to be lesser than, always exposed, and subject to exploitation by the dominant class.

The animal-based subsistence lifestyle of Travellers certainly contributes heavily to their animalization. Consider the term "knacker," a common slur levied against Travellers in reference to their occupational involvement in the purchasing of Nonhuman Animals, alive and dead, for slaughter and rendering. The transformation of the term from descriptive to pejorative demonstrates the entangled debasement of vulnerable humans and other animals. The world over, jobs that involve the slaughtering and dismembering of other animals tend to be reserved for social minorities and are low in status (Nibert 2003). For Travellers, the association with dead and dying Nonhuman Animals extends even beyond knackery, as many have also traditionally been in the business of killing farm-dwelling mice and rats deemed to be pests (Keet-Black 2013). Like rodents, Travellers, too, were treated like vermin, believed to spread disease and pilfer from farms. Vulnerable humans and nonhumans are therefore intertwined in the cultural schema, and the animality ascribed to both ensures their shared subjection to systemic violence.

The colonial categorization of human minority groups as subhuman and racially distinct demonstrates that nation-building has been critical in demarcating racial boundaries through qualifications of citizenship. Yet, Ireland's own project of nation-building in the wake of independence also engaged in identity construction, specifically in the manufacture of an imagined Celtic and Catholic homogeneity to distinguish it from British culture and justify self-government. Postcolonial Ireland marked not only Britons as "other" in this boundary-making, but also Travellers (and later immigrants from Eastern Europe), given their perceived incompatibility with new definitions of Irishness (Fanning 2002). The Travellers' commitment to bartering, subsistence living, and other alternative economies outside of capitalist channels further threatened the political-economic values of the new Irish state (Helleiner 2000). So keen was Ireland to earn the appearance of respectability in the world system, the openly visible deviance of Travellers was considered an embarrassment to national pride. Just as stray dogs and other nonhuman miscreants were rounded up and cleared away by a house-proud new nation (Wedderburn 2016), Travellers, too, faced extreme persecution and social control. Furthermore, conceptualizing them as animals provides a rationale for the extreme inequality they face. Science, which had been leveraged to naturalize the subjugation and poverty of colonized Ireland, would resurface to make sense of disadvantage in the Traveller community by redirecting attention from structural oppression to individual behaviors thought to be "genetically determined and instinctive" (Mayall 2009, 80). Because settled life in Ireland had become institutionalized and normalized, deviation is more easily comprehended as biological difference and inferiority. Given this history, the recent recognition of Travellers as an ethnic minority is not simply a recognition of their uniqueness, but a recognition of their personhood. Delinking Travellers from other animals, however, does not necessarily address the vulnerability still facing Nonhuman Animals.

Human-Nonhuman Boundaries in Long Kesh

Animality politics would also surface in civil rights tensions along the northern border, where settled Catholic minorities faced similar patterns of dehumanization, discrimination, and otherization. In fact, Nonhuman Animal imagery and bodies played an unassuming but consistent role in Ireland's Troubles of the mid to late twentieth century. Bobby Sands, a republican nationalist martyred in the Troubles in the early 1980s, actively drew on nonhuman symbolism to communicate the plight of Catholics in Northern Ireland. His writings make frequent mention of the various birds who kept him company during his long imprisonment in Long Kesh prison. In his nine years of incarceration, he found solace in watching them fly and sing outside his barred window. In the warmer months, when the human excrement and rotting food accumulating in his cell became especially pestilent, he would befriend the birds with leftovers, scraps, and handfuls of maggots. He relied on the Long Kesh avian community for inspiration, friendship, and making his abysmal living quarters tolerable. Not surprisingly, he relied on metaphors of birds to explain his condition and that of his comrades. Remembering his grandfather's story about a man who caged a lark, tortured her, and eventually killed her in his effort to force her to sing for him, he writes, "I feel something in common with that poor bird. . . . Like the lark, I too have fought for my freedom, not only in captivity, where I now languish, but also while on the outside, where my country is held captive" (Sands 1981, 34). Today, the iconic Bobby Sands memorial mural on the street-facing wall of Sinn Féin's headquarters in Belfast depicts a small bird in flight below his portrait and, above him, a phoenix rising (figure 4.2). Both birds are illustrated as breaking the colonial chains that bound him.

Birds feature most prominently in narratives of Long Kesh, but other species have also offered solidarity or symbolic value. For instance, Sands (1981) also writes of a spider with whom he shared his cell. Day after day, he watched the spider helplessly crawl about the room, a constant reminder of their joint entrapment. For Sands and the other political prisoners, birds, maggots, and other insects were a fundamental part of their social world and integral to their identity. They understood themselves to be animalized, and they looked to other animals as comrades. Prisoners also animalized their oppressors, a strategy that allowed them to rationalize the confounding violence they endured. They may have understood themselves to be like

Figure 4.2. Bobby Sands mural, Sinn Féin office, Belfast. Source: Gráinne McCormick.

birds starved of freedom, but guards were regarded as brutish and predatory. Prisoners invented the phrase, "bear on the square," for example, to alert fellow inmates to the presence of guards entering the block.

I will further argue that the prison protests that Sands and his comrades engaged in were themselves a challenge to the boundary between human and nonhuman. Prison is a dehumanizing institution that is designed to remove identity, propensity for agency, and personal determination (Guenther 2012). In effect, prisoners are no longer persons, but rather anonymous numbers subsumed within a mass of similarly clad and similarly treated inmates. In a short story titled "Imagine," Sands asks his readers to

> try and imagine just what it is like to be in this situation in surroundings that resemble a pigsty, and you are crouched naked upon the floor in a corner, freezing cold, amid the lingering stench of putrefying rubbish, with crawling, wriggling white maggots all around you, fat bloated flies pestering your naked body. (1981, 22)

Depictions of this kind leave little doubt with regard to the acute similarities between oppressed Nonhuman Animals and H Block prisoners. They also support Morin's (2018) contention that carceral logic applies to both human and nonhuman oppression in comparable ways. Due to its shocking nature, the treatment of Irish political prisoners drew international attention as a gross violation of human rights. Detained and imprisoned for their supposed association with the Irish Republican Army (IRA), their incarceration was a consequence of the British government's move in the 1970s to crack down on Irish resistance fighters, republicans, and other protestors. In labeling republicans as criminals, they immediately stripped them of their political prisoner status and took away their ability to freely associate, wear civilian clothes, and abstain from prison work. A number of inmates responded with a protest of resistance, refusing to wear prison clothes and opting to cover themselves instead with prison issue blankets. The institution retaliated with violent treatment by prison staff and a sharp reduction in inmate privileges (including their right to slop waste) with expectations of breaking the protestors resolve. Instead, they graduated the blanket protest into a "dirty protest" whereby the accumulating excrement was spread across the cell walls.

The dehumanization of Long Kesh prisoners was thus a joint effort between the prison (which aimed to bully the prisoners into submission through a regimen of degradation) and the prisoners themselves (who embraced that degradation in hopes of shocking prison officials and the public into recognizing the political injustices facing Catholics in the North of Ireland). To be clear, the routine experiences of Nonhuman Animals under anthroparchy were not at all critiqued. Instead, prison activists capitalized on the human-animal boundary to emphasize that their treatment was inappropriate as members of the "superior" human species. The protest escalation, in any case, was difficult for outsiders to comprehend, and visitors were horrified at the sight of the blanket men. Frail, disheveled, unclothed, unbathed for many months, and surrounded by urine-soaked foam mattresses and feces-smeared walls, the blanket men and women (women later joined the dirty protest in Armagh women's prison and added to the dehumanization strategy by bleeding freely during menstruation) were shockingly animalistic in appearance and behavior. That said, I would argue that their resolve in these grisly and prolonged resistance efforts was almost *super*human, or rather, *super*animal. Few animals, human or not, could persevere in the face of such extreme psychical and psychological degradation.

Sadly, it was a resolve that proved fatal. The protestors' eventual move to hunger strike would only underscore their departure from humanity. Having given up clothing, cleanliness, and regular visits from friends and family, many would also give up the most basic of necessities: food. As in earlier years, the stereotypes of Irish resisters as barbaric, wild, uncontrollable, and nonhuman persisted in media coverage of the protest. The inmates' condition drew the attention of humanitarian organizations, but the British government firmly opposed negotiation. It was not until the momentous death of the hunger striking Sands and his comrades that some prison rules were relaxed. The rejection of food tested not just the limits of human endurance, but the prisoners' very animal condition as well. Prior to 1975, British institutions often force-fed prisoners, some of whom died (such as Thomas Ashe of the Easter uprising and IRA prisoner Michael Gaughan). Women were force-fed as well, a dangerous and humiliating violation that was described as akin to rape (Miller 2016).

The Troubles may have since subsided, but the efforts of the hunger strikes remain poignant. At the time of this writing, the hunger strikers are buried in Milltown Cemetery, Belfast, across from a large Sainsbury's grocery store (figure 4.3). Having suffered for weeks under the slow agony of starvation in their fight for freedom, Sands is now laid to rest under the shadow of a looming British grocery chain store, a testament to an Ireland colonized by British industry and the ever-politicized nature of

Figure 4.3. Hunger strike memorial, Milltown Cemetery, Belfast. Source: author's collection.

food. Yet, the aforementioned comradery Sands built with his nonhuman cellmates serves as a poignant example of interspecies solidarity that could, if acknowledged, prove as a useful strategy of resistance in total institutions like Long Kesh. Prisoners centered the human experience in their perceptions of other animals who were primarily reduced to metaphors, but there is reason to believe that some, like Sands, built meaningful relationships with the Nonhuman Animals they lived with. Should prisoners (arguably among the most oppressed victims of the West's "civilizing process") acknowledge this connection in tandem with an explicit rejection of anthropocentrism, its destabilizing potential might be advanced beyond rhetorical use.

Anti-speciesist Activism in the Twenty-first Century

The twentieth century was thus a deeply transformative point in Irish history, challenging the status of Nonhuman Animals and, by association, the status of marginalized human groups. While the identity politics of earlier decades have not fully subsided, Ireland has entered a new era of multiculturalism and peacemaking that is poised to relieve much suffering. Paradoxically, this very aura of positive change and fellowship presents its own barriers. It becomes all too easy to presume that violence and inequality are relics of the past, thus undermining the impetus for further collective action. For Nonhuman Animals, this tendency is especially problematic, as speciesism remains so deeply entrenched. In spite of nearly two centuries of consistent anti-speciesist and vegetarian agitation in Ireland, the economic stranglehold that animal-based agriculture has on the Irish state continues to confound social justice efforts for other animals. Public engagement with anti-speciesist rhetoric offers insight into this phenomenon. Consider, for instance, an interview with Tom Regan (a leading figure in Nonhuman Animal rights theory whose work defined and invigorated the modern movement in the West) featured on Ireland's iconic program the *Late, Late Show* in 2001. Audience members chosen to engage in the dialogue were predominantly involved in "meat" and dairy production, and humanewashing and nationalism framed many responses. For instance, a butcher emphasized the respect he felt for the Nonhuman Animals who provide his living and "feed Ireland."

Little has changed in the time since Regan's visit. In the 2010s, the Irish nonprofit organization Go Vegan World published a full-page advert in Irish papers that captured the attention of *Newstalk Drive* and ignited a debate on air. The ad was defended by Go Vegan World director Sandra Higgins who was pitted against the dairy establishment as represented by the president of the Irish Creamery Milk Suppliers, John Comer. Higgins's advert highlighted the fallacy that cows' milk is humanely produced by emphasizing the heartbreak experienced by cows and their babies upon routine separation (figure 4.4). Although the image only depicts a cow with a matter-of-fact description of regular dairy practices, host Chris Donoghue (2017) described it to listeners as "militant" in design. Veganism's threat to the economy was palpable in the debate. Comer evaded the vegan critique

Figure 4.4. Go Vegan World anti-dairy campaign poster. Source: Go Vegan World.

with sensationalistic predictions of a dairy-free dystopia in which the populace would devolve into disease-ridden apes limping about a landscape overrun by wandering, unattended cows. Perhaps mindful of colonial simianization and the deep injustice it legitimized for at least two centuries, it is likely that many cling to the established anthroparchal order as a means of preserving their newly gained status of "human."

More recently, Higgins has been attacked by the Irish Farmers' Association (IFA) on grounds that Go Vegan World was funded by large foreign companies specializing in animal product analogs (an accusation Higgins denies; Go Vegan World is funded by individual donors and some small businesses) (Higgins 2020). In this instance, the very heart of Ireland—its farming community—was depicted as a victim of predatory and foreign plant-based food interests, a narrative that fits firmly within Wright's (2015) theory of animal nationalism. "Beef" and dairy are framed as inherently and authentically "Irish," while vegan consumption is cast as an enemy to the state. This countermovement framing is powerful. Irish advertising company Exterion, for instance, rejected several Go Vegan World bus and rail ads based on their perceived potential to provoke backlash and complaints, and, presumably, this assumption was related to pressure from agricultural interests (V. Flynn 2017). In neighboring Scotland, the National Farmers' Union reported to the *Herald* that Higgins's campaigning was akin to a hate crime, as it depicts "farmers" as abusive and cruel (Chiorando 2018).

This fearmongering suggests a strategy of misdirection made necessary by the indefensibility of the cruelty inherent in dairy production that is highlighted by Higgins's campaign. The exploitation of Nonhuman Animals in Irish agriculture, when examined, clearly runs counter to national values, such that industry leaders must reframe the practices to align with aspirations of sovereignty, autonomy, order, and development. The *Newstalk Drive* episode and others like it may present Ireland as unreceptive to anti-speciesism, but the flustered responses of Comer, the IFA, and the National Farmers' Union Scotland suggest a chink in the industry's armor. In fact, Ireland lays claim to a number of groups specifically catering to anti-speciesism and veganism that have emerged in the new millennium. As with other developed nations, this social movement space is dominated by larger, professionalized organizations attending primarily to dog and cat welfare or to issues facing popular free-living animals. Some medium-sized organizations with a lesser degree of professionalization also contribute to anti-speciesism and tend to grant more attention to the interests of food animals and free-living species. A number of less organized, unprofessionalized grassroots groups also exist, usually with a more radical, vegan-centric focus. These organizations are too many to document here, but some of the more prominent groups will be introduced.

Perhaps it is most appropriate to begin with the history of the aforementioned Irish Society of the Prevention of Cruelty to Animals (ISPCA), the largest animal welfare charity on the island. Established in 1949, it now hosts twenty affiliated member societies across various counties (Irish Society for the Prevention of Cruelty to Animals n.d.). The ISPCA and other welfare groups in Ireland enjoy state support and can receive large grants to fund operations (*Irish Times* 1998). As with large welfare organizations in the United States and the United Kingdom, the ISPCA has been unclear on its position regarding those species commonly exploited by industries and elites for food and entertainment (Kiernan 1999), fostering tension with more rights-based organizations. The Irish Wildlife Trust (IWT) (n.d.) has also been relatively inconsistent with regard to its protection of free-living animals. It denounces "hunting" and badger "culling," for instance, but condones killing as an option for the "management" of deer communities.[2] Groups such as the Irish Whale and Dolphin Group (IWDG) can be even more species-specific in their activities. The IWDG monitors regional cetacean communities and was instrumental in achieving sanctuary status for Irish waters in 1991.[3] Likewise, County Cork's Donkey Sanctuary is a popular visitor's attraction and, as of this writing, has rescued over four thousand donkeys since its founding in 1987.[4]

Not all sanctuaries in Ireland are single-issue. With a more explicitly anti-speciesist framework, Higgins's Eden Farm Sanctuary cares for a number of nonhuman refugees while also engaging in public vegan education.[5] In 2015, it launched Go Vegan Ireland, and, subsequently, Go Vegan World. It would be Ireland's first large scale public awareness campaign, consistently advocating a vegan lifestyle across buses, billboards, and other public spaces (S. O'Reilly 2015). Prior to Go Vegan World, Alliance for Animal Rights (AFAR) (founded in 1989 and still in operation) and Animal Rights Action Network (ARAN) (founded in 1994) were leading contributors to Irish anti-speciesism. There is also the Dublin-based Vegan Society of Ireland (also known as Vegan Ireland) launched in 2009. Unlike its American and British counterparts that are more health-oriented, Ireland's vegan society explicitly promotes veganism within an anti-speciesist framework.[6] Also worth mentioning is the much older Vegetarian Society of Ireland (VSI), a registered charity formed in 1978 that also heavily supports vegan aims and concerns itself with Nonhuman Animal welfare (Hillis 2012/2013). Notably, it hosts World Vegetarian Day in Dublin each September.

There is a lively grassroots presence in Ireland as well. A number of local meetup groups serve for socializing, pot lucking, or dining out, some of which are affiliated with or supported by the larger organizations. In addition to activity in Dublin, a 2013 issue of the *Irish Vegetarian* makes mention of vegetarian groups in Clare, Galway, Kerry, Kilkenny, Northern Ireland, and Sligo. Cork Vegans exists in the southern part of the country, primarily focusing on supporting other vegans in navigating restaurants and accessing specialty vegan products (Slater 2011). Active since about 2013, the Vegan Information Project (VIP) adheres to a more radical approach of abolitionist education in prioritizing anti-speciesism and anti-oppression values.[7] It can be found tabling regularly in Dublin city center. Based in County Westmeath, the Irish Council against Blood Sports (ICABS) advocates against "hunting," "coursing," "fighting," and some forms of trapping. Formed in 1966, it is one of Ireland's oldest Nonhuman Animal rights organizations, once operating support groups in major cities across the country. It relies heavily on petitioning today, but it engaged in more direct interference with these speciesist practices in the past.[8] As has been discussed, pressure against "hunting" has a long history in Ireland. Despite these prolonged efforts, the "hunting" of foxes remains legal today, while it is illegal in neighboring Britain. There has been hesitancy for the Irish state to interfere with the practice, given its connotations of traditional Irishness and its ties to the lucrative Irish horse market (BBC 1999). As ICABS' John Fitzgerald (2001) points out, a great number of powerful forces have negatively impacted Irish "hunting" over the years, including railroad interests, the Great Famine, protracted Nonhuman Animal rights activism, and the more recent outbreak of foot-and-mouth disease. None of them have been successful in putting an end to it.

I have argued that Ireland experiences a unique collection of speciesisms that can be traced to colonial interference, but this same colonial legacy has inspired fierce resistance. For that matter, Irish culture does not only inform speciesism; it has also impacted global protest culture. There are several symbolic appropriations from Irish republicanism that emerge in the tactics of the Animal Liberation Front (ALF), for instance. The ALF formed in 1970s Britain at a time when the Troubles were dominating news and politics. These self-proclaimed "freedom fighters" mimicked the style of Irish rebels by dressing in black and covering their faces with balaclavas. The ALF employed undercover operations to disrupt speciesist industries and terrorize any operators, employees, and consumers involved. This repertoire popularized in the movement and quickly made its way to the United States where American activists also took on the IRA persona. Unlike Irish rebels, British and American activists were committed to nonviolence, explicitly avoiding the possibility of physically harming speciesists (Best and Nocella 2004). The tactics of terror that the ALF favors do challenge this claim of nonviolence, particularly for the industries and politicians threatened by anti-speciesist protest, but the only recorded acts of serious injury and death related to anti-speciesist protest to date have befallen activists at the hands of counterprotestors and speciesists. Other protestor deaths have been self-inflicted. One such activist, Barry Horne, had been jailed for planning the violent disruption of speciesist industries across Britain with a series of firebombs. Bombs were not the only tactic borrowed from Irish independence fighters; he also undertook a hunger strike. Forgoing even water, he died in just two weeks. His death was considered to be the first incurred on behalf of Nonhuman Animals, as reported by the *Irish Times* (2001).

The ALF's forceful tactics and aggressive posturing restricted its ability to resonate in Britain and the United States and have been criticized by many as counterproductive to the activist agenda (Best and Nocella 2004). Its aggressive activism is thought to turn the public against Nonhuman Animal activism and create a convenient rationale for extreme state repression, but it also made fundraising difficult for an increasingly bureaucratized movement.[9] Increasingly, activists wished to be viewed as professionals, not insurgents. By the turn of the twenty-first century, American and British organizations had mostly disassociated from the direct action faction (Wrenn 2019). Meanwhile, ALF-style activism did not take root in Ireland itself until the early 2000s, coinciding with the tenuous achievement of peace in Northern Ireland. The ALF's cultural appropriation of Irish political violence probably meant that protest meaning would be misconstrued to the detriment of their cause. Certainly, the real IRA was not especially admired by the majority in the Republic (Hayes and McAllister 2007), and anti-speciesists mirroring the IRA style could have proved confusing if not outright dangerous.

In a personal correspondence, ALF founder Ronnie Lee recollected that anti-speciesism in the image of the IRA did not fail to take hold in Ireland because of any sensitivity to ongoing sectarian tensions. Instead, he suggested that the slow development of Irish Nonhuman Animal activism in general was responsible. It is true that Irish anti-speciesism was in a period of abeyance during this period. As was explored in the previous chapter, Ireland experienced vigorous mobilization in the nineteenth century, and, by the early twentieth century, it was even eliciting envy from the American movement. This activity settled down considerably in the mid-twentieth century, as was consistent with American and British activism. The International Vegetarian Union and the Vegan Society were active in the North of Ireland throughout the 1960s and 1970s, but there was much less activity in the Republic. Nonhuman Animal rights activism in the West had entered its second wave by the early 1970s (Wrenn 2019), and Ireland seems to have been slightly delayed in riding it, but not significantly so. In any case, I would argue that it is inaccurate to characterize Ireland as devoid of activism. The ALF did not take root in Ireland until the 2000s, but AFAR and ARAN had been active many years prior to that. The Vegetarian Society of Ireland was also busy in the 1970s and 1980s. The first issue of *Irish Vegetarian News* published in 1978 listed a number of meetings and public events happening during this supposed dry spell.

The aforementioned Go Vegan World may be one of the more potent organizations in recent years. Go Vegan World's uncompromising billboards, bus posters, and newspaper features have been covered extensively by the Irish and British media, while founder Sandra Higgins is regularly interviewed by numerous radio stations to the ire of Ireland's agricultural institutions. Other speciesist institutions have been ruffled by activists as well. Ireland's robust pharmaceutical industry has increased in strength and influence in recent years as the relatively vulnerable postcolonial state struggles to attract business and create jobs. This economic shift ensures that Nonhuman Animals by the hundreds of thousands will be subjected to vivisection. Despite the European Union's intention to phase out Nonhuman Animal testing, Ireland was responsible for the exploitation of about a quarter of a million animal subjects in 2014 alone (D'Arcy 2015). Scientists are not prone to openly discuss this exploitative practice, with some citing a fear that "extremists" (such as those affiliated with the ALF) will mail bombs to the premises in retaliation (King 2013). Although their efforts have pushed violent scientific research into secrecy, these "extremists" have been successful in pressuring airlines to cease their involvement in the importation of test victims to Ireland.

Anti-speciesism and the Irish State

As has been alluded to thus far, Ireland is often stereotyped as hesitant in its propensity for protest. Dismayed over rampant environmental deterioration and extinction, the Irish Wildlife Trust's Pádraic Fogarty (2017) finds Ireland's lackluster efforts exceedingly subpar compared to those in England. Vegan sociologist Roger Yates (2011) is equally negative, with his research reporting an apathetic response to systemic violence against other animals. His ethnographic work in Irish movement ranks indicates a shared activist belief that anti-speciesist mobilization is tempered by state repression. Other researchers point to research emphasizing the stagnating effect of low cultural modernization in the wake of colonialism, or the tenuous state of Irish industry, which could divert attention to survival over progress (Tovey and Share 2000).

Frustration with the sluggish pace of social change understandably encourages finger-pointing and cultural critiques, but criticism in this regard is misdirected. Using the Irish water charges movement as a case in point, sociologists (Cox 2017; Layte and Landy 2018) have observed a noticeable growth in protest related to twenty-first-century experiences with austerity. The use of Nonhuman Animals for food has been at the heart of exploitative Irish trade for centuries, and there is already reason to believe that a convergence of anti-austerity sentiment, worsening climate change, and concern over Nonhuman Animal welfare will continue to put pressure on cracks emerging in elite-centered governance, a governance under which open markets and industries are prioritized over a strong state that might otherwise prioritize welfare and social equality. For sociologist Laurence Cox (2017), Ireland lays claim to a powerful heritage of grassroots resistance. Likewise, Tovey (2007), having spent a career studying environmentalism in Ireland, may be wary of postcolonial stagnation, but she also sees the grassroots, community-based nature of Irish protest as strategic. Bureaucratic charity structures that dominate the United States and the United Kingdom have limited reach in Ireland, at least in regard to environmental protection and Nonhuman Animal welfare. This absence is a positive one. As nonprofits institutionalize, they bargain with the state and elites, cooperating for financial stability (Wrenn 2019). In effect, they become complicit in, rather than resistant to, exploitative economic relations.

Thus, it may be more accurate to describe Ireland as a *leader* in social protest rather than a late bloomer. As a postcolonial nation, Ireland is tuned into the mechanisms of oppression and has sustained many centuries of organized resistance. The water protests of the 2010s, which are, according to Cox, "among the largest protests in living memory" (2017, 174), have reawakened this spirit. The growing tension of capitalist exploitation brought to a breaking point by Ireland's colonial legacy has manifested in an explosion of street protest, so much so that Cox suggests it may indicate a crisis in the hegemony of European governance. Indeed, it has not gone unnoticed that Ireland pursued independence for so many years only to enter immediately into union with Europe and effectively acquiesce in a dilution of its sovereignty. It is a compromise that does not sit well with all. The groundswell response to landlordism, gay marriage, abortion, and water charges in addition to centuries of Irish resistance to British imperialism depicts a culture that is sensitive to injustice and prepared to correct it. Indeed, Ireland's oppression has sharpened its concern for equality and freedom (Baker 1990). Traditional culture may not always act as an impediment to social progress; it can also be employed as a powerful and resonant framework for protecting and respecting nature and its human and nonhuman inhabitants.

Although it could be argued that the Irish vegan movement does not exist on the same scale as its British and American counterparts, collective action on behalf of other animals is probably proportionate, given Ireland's limited geographic space and small population. In any case, it is enough activity for the Irish state to take some notice. Similar to collectives working in other parts of the West, direct action activists in Ireland have met with police surveillance, intimidation, and arrest (Fitzgerald 2011). Peaceful protestors, too, are experiencing similar state management and interference (Yates 2011). As is the case in the United States and many parts of Europe, anti-speciesism advocacy of any kind is increasingly considered to be terrorist behavior. Yet, Irish society seems poised for change, despite these powerful obstacles.

For social movements, acknowledgment by the state, media, and public is fickle and difficult to secure. The resonance of anti-speciesist and vegan claimsmaking, furthermore, will fluctuate based on economic conditions and sociopolitical circumstances. The Irish reliance on animal flesh in diet and export reflects its new relative wealth in the global system and a determination for self-sufficiency. It also accounts for the state's interest in repressing anti-speciesism activism. Nonetheless, Ireland's deepening relationships with other nations and cultures have popularized veganism and plant-based eating to some extent. Modern Ireland is beginning to care about the welfare of its nonhuman inhabitants. This can be reflected in politics as well. Christopher Fettes, founder of the Irish Green Party, is also the founder of the Vegetarian Society of Ireland and is the former chairman of the Irish Anti-Vivisection Society. While its influence is limited in Irish government, the Green Party does advance a strong position on Nonhuman Animal welfare. As this book was going to press, the Green Party had entered a historic coalition government with the traditional parties of Fine Gael and Fianna Fáil. Perhaps this offers hope that the Irish state will develop a critique of oppressive economic relations, encouraged by transforming cultural values, a changing geography, and the hard work of a diverse advocacy community.

Conclusion

After the dust of independence and war had settled, activism for other animals reignited in Ireland, beginning with the humble reestablishment of the Vegetarian Society and the outreach efforts of Britain's Vegan Society. The North of Ireland was a hot spot for plant-based protest and was home to many of the movement's leaders and celebrities, such as vegan athlete and activist Jack McClelland. In fact, collectives emerged and thrived throughout the island. This mobilization was sorely needed. As Ireland entered the twentieth century, Nonhuman Animal oppression grew ever more industrialized. This chapter has not attempted to survey the entirety of nonhuman oppression in Ireland, but it has highlighted some important acts of violence and protest that are integral to Irish species politics, such as sulky "racing" and live export. Activists have been faced with the difficult task of negotiating conflicting interests in an increasingly multicultural society. Too often, Nonhuman Animals are simply used as ammunition in power disputes and are overlooked as a minority group with interests of their own.

Modern Nonhuman Animal advocacy must contend with the tendency for speciesism and animalization to impede the advancement of Nonhuman Animals, but also that of marginalized human groups. The civil rights disasters facing Catholics in the North of Ireland and Travellers in the Republic that culminated in severe state repression in the mid-twentieth century indicates that speciesism—discrimination based on perceived animal difference—has ramifications for humans and nonhumans alike. Activists drew on the intersectional nature of human-nonhuman oppression to challenge inequality in the postcolonial world, but agents of the state would seek to inflame divisions between various social groups, both human and not. This strategy worked to legitimize an Irish republic that, due to its continued dependency upon Britain, was bound to mirror the system of inequality instilled there after centuries of colonialism. The design of the modern Irish state has introduced new difficulties with police surveillance, capitalist agendas, and the consolidating power of speciesist industries. Such barriers have led observers to argue that Ireland possesses a low propensity for protest, but this characterization overlooks a rich history of collective action as well as the many long-lived organizations fighting on behalf of Nonhuman Animals.

Resistance is also evident in Ireland's twenty-first-century foodscape. As the next chapter will explore, food has always been integral to the national identity, but the strain of globalization and European economic policies would paradoxically renew the commitment to speciesist production despite its documented detriment to the environment. In the era of austerity, Nonhuman Animals would once again become a point of conflict between "farmers" and vegan activists, both of whom have dramatically different understandings of sustainability and progress. Gramsci emphasized that hegemonies must continuously adapt to maintain themselves, often through the development of philosophy, science, and other ways of knowing. "Farmers" and policymakers alike would manipulate cultural understandings of nutrition, Nonhuman Animal welfare and ethics, and climate change to reinforce the anthroparchal hegemony. Yet, as one Gramscian historian explains, because hegemony is not static, but rather "a process of continuous creation" on a massive scale, it is "bound to be uneven in the degree of legitimacy it commands" (Adamson 2014, 174). As a result, hegemony inevitably allows space for "antagonistic cultural expressions to develop" (174). This trend appears to be consistent with Ireland's experience.

Chapter 5

Nonhuman Animal Welfare and Irish Food Sovereignty

Modernization has led to a number of consequences for Nonhuman Animals and humanity's relationship with them. Not all of these changes are attributable to protest activity. Nibert (2002), recall, argues that these relations more often relate to economic shifts. Because Ireland is a deeply agricultural nation, its food system is the largest contributor to nonhuman exploitation. How a society is organized will determine what (or who) is defined as food, what foods are thought appropriate and desirable, and what foods are available to consume. In Ireland's case, Gramsci might appreciate that Britain's cultural hegemony was considerably strengthened by its ability to normalize both exploiting Nonhuman Animals and eating them, facilitating a speciesist Irish culture well suited to perpetuating British interests beyond colonialism. Too frequently overlooked as a mundane facet of social life, food is actually of paramount importance to sociological analysis, since food behaviors have less to do with taste and nutrition than they do with political endeavors, economic structure, and social stratification. For a country that is, per capita, in fifth place on the list of the world's top food producing countries (Food and Agriculture Organization 2015), the political nature of food is only amplified in Ireland.

Both the production and consumption of food profoundly shape the Irish identity. Kneafsey and Cox (2002), for instance, concede that stereotypes about the consumption of potatoes have fueled anti-Irish prejudice, but also highlight the fact that food has been integral to the Irish diaspora in maintaining family networks, tradition, and a sense of home. "Politicised and racialized," they observe, "social relations of food production-consumption have played a pivotal role in Irish history" (8). As I have argued in previous chapters, it is animal-based agriculture more specifically that dominates in postcolonial spaces in nation-building projects. India, for example, intentionally framed animal products (specifically cows' milk) as essential to the independent Indian identity and the new country's ability to access political power on the global stage (Wiley 2017). Likewise, dairy production and consumption in China is increasingly associated with modernization, Westernization, and global competitiveness, processes that are especially poignant for a country that experienced considerable oppression and humiliation through colonialism and several major wars (Gambert and Linné 2018). As this chapter will explore, Ireland took a similar path. As was the case with India and China, Irish consumption of animal products had been relatively minimal prior to independence, but animal-based agriculture had been symbolically coded as a necessary component for growth and development for the nation and its people. Nonhuman Animals and their products, Wright (2015) has observed, become the building blocks of nationhood.

As was outlined in chapter 1, the Irish diet comprised a dizzying variety of fruits, nuts, grains, vegetables, herbs, and plants prior to British colonization (Lyons 2015). Forced absorption into the world system would swiftly restructure food systems and knowledges such that the average Irish diet became perilously simplistic. Modernity, with its industrialized, centralized, and rather monopolized modes of production, has offered greater choice as far as its ability to increase the accessibility of exotic, seasonal, and ready-made items, but this choice is primarily restricted within the parameters of animal products and processed foods. Thus, rationalized food production has expanded in some respects but shrunk in others (Carolan 2011). Foods available today are those that can be efficiently produced, such that species diversity is greatly reduced to increase control and predictability. The variety once familiar to precolonial consumers is now reduced to high volumes of "beef," "chicken," "pork," cows' milk, and various configurations of sugar, fat, and salt in shelf-stable offerings.

In addition to the 18,000 dairy farmers and 11,000 "seafood" workers, there are over 10,000 people working in the Irish "meat" industry (Food and Drink Industry Ireland 2015). Thus, at least 39,000 members of Ireland's population of 4.6 million are directly employed in businesses of speciesism. This does not include the thousands of others employed in processing facilities, animal feed farming, shops, and restaurants, all of which also rely on Nonhuman Animal exploitation. Although a large portion of

Irish farms are not profitable and would not exist without subsidy from the Irish state and the European Union, farming is frequently conflated with Irish national identity and fiercely protected (Armstrong 2015). The European Union, for instance, offered the Irish state €100 million in funding to support struggling "beef" production in preparation for Britain's planned departure (Power and Clarke 2019). Indeed, most "meat" and dairy farmers in Ireland do not earn a profit and rely heavily on government support (Dillon et al. 2018). The average "cattle" farm received €16,000 in subsidies in 2018, while the average sheep "farm" received €19,000 and the average dairy "farm" received €21,000.

Comparable to other Western nations, the Irish consume great quantities of "meat" and dairy. Most eat "meat" on a daily basis, primarily the flesh of pigs and chickens and to a lesser extent that of cows (Central Statistics Office 2012; Kiely 2001). Most of the population consumes about 280 grams of dairy every day. As past chapters have indicated, the standard diet represents a significant change from that of just a few generations ago. Ireland's changing global station and adoption of industrial farming techniques have allowed it to load animal products on to the market shelves of other countries with more than enough left over to fill its own. To be clear, these practices are not just a matter of good fortune or flavor preference. For instance, Ireland is now the top consumer of chickens' flesh in the European Union, a direct result of their artificially lowered prices, the pressure of the 2007 recession, and European austerity measures (Linden 2016).

The Irish adoption of decidedly nonvegan foodways is an economic strategy with a distinctly political history. This chapter will explore these influences, beginning with the rise of the new Irish state and the symbolic role that "meat" and dairy would play for its new citizens and their goal of economic independence. The production of Nonhuman Animal products and their consumption would become integral to the new Irish national identity, one that continues today in an uncertain global market that is regularly plagued by recessions, disease outbreaks, and outsourcing. Nonhuman Animals become commodities in the Irish project, characterizing vegan alternatives as nothing short of state sabotage.

Feeding Independence

Though times of mass hunger and deprivation are associated with times gone past, historians note that the poignant memory of famine and war would shape Irish culinary imagination (or lack thereof) well into the twentieth century. Directly following the Great Famine, the production of "meat" and dairy increased significantly under British market influence, and considerable land was also forfeited for the growing of Nonhuman Animal feed (Turner 1996). This British influence insured the popularity of "beef" long after colonialism had ended, and the imagination for indigenous Irish foodstuffs had been nearly eradicated (Armstrong 2015). Concern with the continued nutritional paucity of diets after the Great Famine led to a concentrated effort to convince citizens to switch from tea, bread, and potatoes to cows' milk and "meat." The state and civil groups cooperatively campaigned to restructure the Irish diet to one dependent on flesh (Miller 2015). Farmers, now responsible for nurturing and advancing a free Ireland, took on a sacred quality, and nationalists equated the well-being of farmers with that of the country itself.

By the mid-nineteenth century, farmers had moved from tillage to pasturage to accommodate this expanding animal economy. In doing so, they dramatically altered the landscape, creating the green-pastured Ireland that is romanticized today. Recall that many nationalists were keenly aware of the relationship between food production and Irish oppression. Dairy cooperatives, for instance, formed as an important collective resistance to capitalist exploitation of Irish farmers by allowing farmers to collaborate and pool resources to collect and market milk (Tovey 2000). Likewise, the land wars of the late nineteenth century (a period in which nationalists worked to redistribute land to tenants) demonstrated another instance of Irish defiance against the oppressive qualities of modern agriculture. "Beef" production, already well established in the country from colonization, was identified as the most appropriate strategy for achieving self-sufficiency. The ironies of relying on colonial foodways to resist and recover from colonial oppression was not lost on all. Some nationalists, such as James Connolly, were critical of the animal-based agricultural system, given its propensity to displace peasants for pasturage and the limited job opportunities it provided (Armstrong 2015). In any case, Nonhuman Animals became the collateral damage for achieving an independent Ireland.

It is impossible to overemphasize the role that animal-based agriculture played in Ireland's quest for freedom. With independence finally within reach, Ireland's long bondage to British markets was a major point of concern. Although this dependency would never fully be overcome, nationalists hoped to at least further their cause through alternative channels of consumption. The "Buy Irish" campaign of the early twentieth century, for instance, encouraged citizens to purchase anything and everything Irish-made to weaken Britain's hold. As the mainstay of the household, this duty oftentimes fell on women, and women's magazines (even feminist ones) featured propagandistic advertising to reinforce women's responsibility to "buy Irish" (Columbus 2009). With consumption and nationhood thus bound together, ordinary products suddenly became impregnated with political meaning. This did not bode well for Nonhuman Animals, since meals came to center kidneys, "tripe," and forequarter cuts from cows' legs. Once disvalued as cheaper "meats" suitable only for lower classes, these body parts came to symbolize sources of national pride. Eating "meat" became rebellious and socially desirable. *Báin-bhiadh* was a key feature of the campaign as well, and many "butter" labels proudly displayed the product's Irish origins.

"Meat" production and consumption in the early twentieth century was increasingly a global symbol of wealth, status, and strength, but not all nationalists supported the strategy of "meat" as resistance. Some positioned vegetarianism as a wiser path to the nation's advancement. The burgeoning scientific establishment was beginning to identify "meat" and dairy as serious conduits of contagion, particularly as inspection practices were minimal and insufficient in production facilities (Miller 2015). Nutritional science could thus be wielded in favor of vegetarianism. Consequently, while some nationalists had pushed "beef" production as a means of achieving self-sufficiency, others celebrated the promise of wheat and bread production (Armstrong 2015).

George William Russell (AE) ([1913] 1978), a practicing vegetarian himself, despaired of Ireland's poor nutrition, relying as it so heavily did on a diet of tea and white bread. While Irish vegetarian reformers of his era pointed to the robustness of the Irish people as evidence of the suitability of flesh-free diets, Russell could not overlook the paucity of forced vegetarianism among the very poor. A diet of white bread, tea, canned products, and adulterated foods was nutritionally devoid and aggravated the oppressed condition of Irish slum dwellers, millworkers, and peasantry. As he understood it, this was "dead food for half dead bodies" ([1913] 1978, 375). He harkened back to an earlier time when Ireland's people consumed porridge, brown bread, and cows' milk, emphasizing the healthful potential of vegetarianism. The new diet of refined products was more expensive in terms of both finances and health cost. An anti-vivisectionist as well, AE also blamed the "dictates of the black magicians of science" for inoculating the Irish people with "horrible animal matter" (vaccinations) (376) instead of encouraging preventative wellness. That said, Russell's concern for the plight of the rural poor led him to advance a strategy of cooperative farming as a means of self-sufficiency. Though he was himself a vegetarian, he did envision "meat," dairy, and egg production as cooperatively operated in the service of a more socialist, independent Ireland (Russell 1916).

Famed author James Joyce also entertained vegetarianism in his writings on nationalism. Notably, he included trends in dietary reform and critical analyses of "meat" and food production in his celebrated work *Ulysses*. Joyce, too, positioned vegetarianism as an embodiment of modernity. To him, it nurtured a capacity for critical thought and enlightenment, whereas the flesh diet inhibited productivity and elicited aggression (Plock 2007; Regan 2009). Grisly depictions of slaughter and rotting flesh abound in *Ulysses*, as does the allegorical association between the state of society and its consumptive practices. "Hot fresh blood they prescribe for decline," his protagonist, Leopold Bloom, observes. "Blood always needed" (Joyce 1922, 163). Indeed, a shift from the consumption of "offal" to vegetable foods is used to illustrate Bloom's character development. Nonhuman Animals also feature as agential characters throughout the story (Norris 2017).

Although Joyce was himself critical of vegetarianism, his writing picked up on the idealistic vegetarianism that had been adopted by the Celtic-revivalists of the late nineteenth and early twentieth century (Adkins 2017). He found irony in the movement's romanticization of Ireland's agrarian past, bound as it was to the crude exploitation of other animals. Written two centuries previously, Swift's ([1726] 1900) *Gulliver's Travels* also employed themes of vegetarianism and flesh-eating to illustrate the savagery of the British "civilization" project in its penchant for cruelty and war-mongering. The humanoid Yahoos that Gulliver encounters are depicted as depraved scavengers who tear into raw flesh and terrorize cats, donkeys, and other animals. Their civilized equine overlords, by contrast, dine on cooked oats and milk (Hinnant 1987). For Swift and other political theorists, diet was a barometer of cultural constitution, maturity, and capacity for sovereignty.

Meanwhile, Shaw, who might similarly be expected to align with this vegetarian nationalism, was more skeptical. Born of a Protestant family, Shaw was less than enthusiastic about Ireland's chances of achieving full independence, advocating that Ireland become a member of the Commonwealth instead. He was critical of militant nationalism, and, like Wilde, believed vegetarianism to be a diet conducive to aggression. Irish protest that mobilized in Trafalgar Square in November of 1887 served as an example of the relationship between food, patriotism, and violence:

> The recent spread of fire-eating fiction and Jingo war worship—a sort of thing that only interests the pusillanimous—is due to the spread of meat-eating. Compare the Tipperary peasant of the potatoes-and-buttermilk days with the modern gentleman [sic] who gorges himself [sic] with murdered cow. The Tipperary man [sic] never read bloody-minded novels or cheered patriotic music-hall tableaux; but he [sic] fought recklessly and wantonly. (Shaw [1898] 1990, 401)

For Shaw, a flesh diet made cowards and weaklings out of its consumers, but vegetarianism was a combative diet. "Ninety-nine per cent of the world's fighting has been done on farinaceous food" he claimed. This logic emerged from his understanding that critical thinking and vegetarianism were tightly correlated. Nonvegetarians did not only consume the status quo in diet, but the status quo in social values as well. This consumption suited them to acquiescence over rebelliousness. His solution to structural inequality and social conflict was not diet, but breeding. Quite controversially, Shaw was an advocate of eugenics, not out of a desire for racial purity, but rather a yearning for moral and social progress. To the dismay of his humanitarian colleague Henry Salt, he extended this logic to the practice of "hunting," finding little fault in the practice given its role in the evolutionary process (Griffith 2002). This is not to suggest that Shaw's vegetarianism lacked a humanitarian component. He did advocate vegetarianism as a means of coping with poverty, and espoused the economic virtues of a plant-based diet (Holroyd 1997).

If vegetarian nationalists were hoping to free Ireland through dietary reform, they were fighting an uphill battle. The plant-based quality of Irish consumption was already becoming a relic of the past. Reports from the 1916 uprising, for instance, provide insight into new eating habits. Food shortages created by Ireland's ongoing struggle for independence were only amplified by the tumultuousness of World War I and caused considerable frustration to soldiers and civilians alike. Detainees in the Frongoch internment camp complained of frozen "meat" from New Zealand and tinned cows' milk that were certifiably unfit for human consumption. They also described soapy potatoes, improperly cured herring bodies, and unpalatable margarine that poorly substituted for the dairy "butter" they were accustomed to (Irish Prisoners 1916a). Preserved vegetables were provided instead of fresh, causing skin diseases to break out in the camp. Worse, the provisional "meat" had a noticeable stench, and prisoners were directed to wash the flesh in vinegar to improve its palatability (Irish Prisoners 1916b). Even these meager offerings needed close guarding, as the soldiers' rodent cohabitators devoured these foods without complaint.

Clearly, by the early twentieth century, animal products had come to be expected in the Irish diet, especially in the diet of the soldier. As was typical elsewhere in Europe during wartime, "meat" production, a costly and complex endeavor, was frequently disrupted, and what little was available was funneled into the war effort. The redirecting of animal flesh to soldiers was consistent with the patriarchal belief that fighting men must have access to "meat" for strength, vigor, and battlefield prowess (Adams 2000). The citizenry, however, found the disruption of regular flesh supplies a great burden. Several letters from the era complain of having to make do without animal products or their tinned variants (Martin 1916). The diary of one County Wicklow woman reports the family having gone nearly vegetarian out of necessity, relying instead on potato cakes, seaweeds, rice, and the occasional loaf of brown bread bulked up with ground byproducts from chicken corpses (Gittins 2015).

As animal products are essentially luxury items and can be omitted from the diet without negative health consequences, they become especially precious during wartime, given the high cost of their production. By 1916, the Irish army seemed to have already forgotten the palatability of the vegetarian eating that had characterized the island for so many years. Records illustrate a number of risky and outlandish efforts made to obtain "meat" and other animal products. On one occasion, some republican soldiers raided a British storehouse and absconded with two lorry loads of "meat." They were ambushed at their drop-off point, however, and were sentenced to twenty years in Arbour Hill Prison (Mullen 1913–21).[1] Irish butchers who sent "meat" to English markets rather than reserving it for the war effort were bullied by nationalists. One such purveyor who failed to comply found his stores dumped in the River Lee (Spillane and O'Sullivan 1913–21).

Elsewhere, soldiers compensated for the scarcity by stalking free-living deer communities. The grisly and drawn out killing of one such victim is recorded in the report of IRA member Michael O'Donoghue, who jovially spent the better part of a morning with his compatriots shooting and pursuing a wounded deer to death (O'Donoghue 1913–21). While "hunting" may have offered soldiers a distraction, "venison" tasted foreign and disagreeable to the soldiers. Members of Cumann na mBan, the women's auxiliary, were enlisted to improve its palatability with little success. As soldiers scavenged for sustenance, domesticated Nonhuman Animals along their path were also shot and consumed (Dalton 1913–21; Kettrick 1913–21).

This intersection of patriarchal violence against Nonhuman Animals and the violence of combat was not lost on all. In fact, there was a vocal minority who found war and Ireland's participation in it unconscionable. Many feminist and pacifist activists of the era positioned vegetarianism as a counter to violence (Adams 2000). However, Ireland had been feminized through hundreds of years of colonialism, and this complicated the resonance of such a framework. Ireland was struggling to assert itself with masculine power for recognition in the patriarchal world system, and "meat" was essential to this project.[2]

Radical author and activist Francis Sheehy-Skeffington was at least one exception to this relationship between male dominance and violence to other animals in the making of a free Ireland. Although not involved in the fighting, his radical politics made him a target. A feminist, pacifist, and vegetarian, he found himself in want of food while imprisoned for his involvement in the rising (it would be almost a century later until Britain recognized prisoners' right to vegetarian food). The issue of animality shaped his politics and imprisonment, but also his death. Observers recollect that he had been "shot like a dog" upon his execution (Mulhall 2016). Both he and AE, incidentally, appear in Joyce's *Ulysses*, suggesting that, while in the minority, their pacifist vegetarian positions were influential on the political discourse.

Ireland Enters the World System

Following independence, "meat" and dairy had become staples of the Irish diet, but food production would become relatively stagnant as the state strove for stability and recognition. It has not been until relatively recently that Ireland's foodscape would begin to witness any significant change with the coming of economic security and prosperity. A food consumption survey completed in the year 2000 suggests that "increasing affluence and changing lifestyles" had resulted in a dramatic change in Irish dietary habits (Kiely 2001). Certainly, the industrialization of Nonhuman Animal agriculture was partly responsible, with Ireland seeing a 74 percent increase in general "meat" consumption and a tripling of fish consumption since the 1930s (Friel and Nolan 1996). It was not unheard of for poorer families in the mid-twentieth century to have only one "meat"-based meal per week. The

Food and Agriculture Organization of the United Nations records a modest consumption of 19 grams of animal protein per person each day in Ireland in 1961 (Food and Agriculture Organization n.d.). This level would only increase across the decades, peaking in the years of the Celtic Tiger with 37 grams per person each day. Today, foodstuffs marketed to lower income families are highly processed, calorie dense, and, if not based in "meat" or dairy, then otherwise laden with animal derivatives. The Irish food industry has industrialized such that animal products are now superabundant and new uses for byproducts are regularly invented and imposed upon consumers to absorb this heavy production and keep the industry viable. Millions of Nonhuman Animals lose their lives and liberty as a result. As recently as 2003, Ireland ranked tenth in global consumption of "meat" and quite high in its consumption of dairy (Speedy 2003). Consumption of "meat" dipped during the recession to about 27 grams per person each day, but, by 2013, this had increased to prerecession levels. Although the Central Statistics Office no longer measures "meat" consumption, the *Irish Times* has estimated that the average Irish citizen was consuming about 90 kilograms of flesh in 2016, a rise from 77.5 kilograms in 2011 that is explained by the increasing popularity of chicken bodies in the diet (Cleary 2017).

Such trends in "meat" consumption reflect larger market forces. At the turn of the twentieth century, agricultural production remained the primary Irish industry. Relationships between tenants and landowners had improved, but international competition was straining Irish farmers and impoverishing rural dwellers. The farm cooperatives movement that resulted, along with the Irish Agricultural Organization Society formed to coordinate it, would create a much-desired sense of self-reliance. These measures may have offered Ireland some leverage in the market, but they also increased dairy production considerably (King and Kennedy 1994). "Farmer" protections thus came at the cost of nonhuman labor. Cooperatives would only grow more precious to farmers as the agricultural landscape continued to shift under globalization. The Irish food industry experienced significant restructuring in the mid-1980s, and animal-based agriculture would see even greater growth thanks in part to rationalization, concentration, and product diversification (Harte 1997).

Although entry into the European Union expanded Ireland's economy, which had hitherto been dominated by agriculture (such as technology services and pharmaceuticals), "meat" and dairy remain high priority business (Friel and Nolan 1996; McDonagh and Commins 1999; Tovey 1991), accounting for 69 percent of food and drink exports. In 2014, the country traded in approximately 6.6 billion euros worth of living and nonliving Nonhuman Animals and their excrements (Bord Bia 2015). The agrifood sector has become the island's leading indigenous industry, with dairy and "seafood" demonstrating the strongest growth. While only responsible for 1 percent of the global dairy supply, there are about a million dairy cows "farmed" in Ireland and the industry is projected to grow. Between 2012 and 2016, for example, cows' numbers increased by 22 percent (K. O'Sullivan 2017). Irish dairy imports have also recently risen by as much as 30 percent in some recipient countries (particularly in Asia) where dairy was not traditionally consumed (Bord Bia 2015). Like Ireland, Asia's entry into the world system has brought with it Western consumption norms, providing a fertile new market.

With 7,500 kilometers of coastline, Ireland's sizable "seafood" sector is also strong. The value of aquatic exports has risen by 70 percent since 2009 (Bord Bia 2015). This is in spite of European Union restrictions which prevent "fishing" for several months out of the year and allow Irish seafarers exclusive access only within six miles beyond the shore (Marine Institute 2009). These regulations, incidentally, are generally interpreted as a raw deal for Ireland, as other EU members have much larger oceanic jurisdiction. The relative disparity in Ireland's allocation compared to other EU member states results in part from division in the "fishing" community, which made powerful representation in EU negotiations difficult. "Farmers," by contrast, were much more successful, although their practices are often blatantly contrary to sustainable methods. In truth, the EU's policy impacts on Ireland have been inconsistent with regard to their benefit to both Irish agricultural *and* sustainability goals (B. Flynn 2009). Subsidies in the 1980s and 1990s that rewarded "farmers" for the number of Nonhuman Animals they maintained created an increase of half a million sheeps, putting a tremendous strain on the environment. Fishes in Irish waters, at least, have benefited from the regulation, limited though this may be given the current collapsing of ocean ecosystems. The industrialization of "fishing," particularly the advent of bottom trawling, has decimated sea-dwelling communities and the ocean landscape they once occupied (Fogarty 2017). Indiscriminate netting multiplies the number of dead, as the bodies of unwanted "trash" fishes and the occasional seal become trapped alongside intended victims.

Tovey (1993) expands on this tension in what she observes as two competing Irish environmentalisms: one taking a conservationist perspective and the other prioritizing sustainable "farming" practices. Although both approaches seek to address the impact of modern development on the environment, the two are often at odds. Aggravating this tension is the tendency for conservationist environmentalism to be located in urban centers and led by educated, middle-class professionals, while agricultural environmentalism more often relies on rural communities and informal knowledges. Official, professionalized environmentalism too frequently disregards rural environmentalism, and these structural differences disrupt potential for alliance and successful policy implementation.

An additional variable to consider is international governance and the many frustrations it brings. As was just mentioned, EU membership tests Ireland's sovereignty as the country struggles to grow its speciesist industries under environmental regulations (B. Flynn 2009). What regulations have been implemented tend to be desperately underfunded and poorly enforced. Many "farmers" simply disregard what they feel to be the overstretched reach of faraway bureaucrats. Sheeps and other animals have grazed much of the countryside to the point of desertification, precipitating considerable soil erosion and decimating ecosystems. Illegal fires are regularly burned in an effort to encourage grass growth for sheeps and cows. Meanwhile, turf-cutting in Ireland's shrinking bogs continues unabated to such an extreme that less than 1 percent of natural raised bogs remain intact and untouched. Even national parks, which exist as some of the few remaining refuges for free-living animals, are heavily degraded in the name of economic progress (Fogarty 2017).

Loving Ireland, Buying Local

The enormous pressure to bolster Irish food production must be understood in relation to Ireland's global station. As was previously explained, food was central to colonization, and thus became central to independence and postcolonial state-building. In no way is the present Irish diet a reflection of some authentic Irish heritage. Instead, what Ireland eats is directly related to Ireland's relationship to the world economy. The encroachment of Western foodways represents more than a colonized diet; it also colonizes culture. As a semi-periphery nation shaped by British commerce, Ireland remains heavily agricultural and reliant on tourism, with high unemployment and high emigration. Economic policies in Ireland of the early twentieth century were heavily protectionist to discourage foreign competition (Baker 1990; Tovey and Share 2000). Unfortunately for Ireland, this strategy quickly proved unrealistic, given the already international and interdependent nature of the nation-state system it was now a part of. Today's Ireland repackages this independence-era sentiment and celebrates and supports Irish farmers while *also* capitalizing on global markets. The response has been a more or less positive and profitable one, but the growing role that transnational corporations play in the Irish economy is cause for concern, given that the benefits of growth are unevenly distributed. Nonhuman Animal production is supported by a system of extreme inequality that impacts humans and nonhumans alike. It is also a leading contributor to climate change (Steinfeld et al. 2006). While some do profit from this openness, fewer regulations mean that Ireland's most vulnerable inhabitants will be exploited to support this growth.

Some level of regulation has been necessary, however, to preserve this unstable system. To what extent these regulations protect the interests of capitalists and to what extent they protect the vulnerable is unclear. Marx, for instance, described the free trade system as "destructive." By cultivating less powerful nations to the "command of the world market," he observed, "one nation can grow rich at the expense of another. . . . It breaks up old nationalities and pushes the antagonism of the proletariat and the bourgeoise to the extreme point" ([1848] 2000, 295–96). Unrestrained global capitalism, he posited, had revolutionary potential given its propensity for fostering extreme inequality, but Ireland's entry into the world system would not provoke an anti-capitalist revolution. Instead, the strength of British hegemony would maintain Irish dependence.

Marx was correct, however, in predicting the expansion of exploitation without protectionist measures. Ireland's admission into the European Union in 1973 majorly revised and developed the country's animal-based economy. EU membership allowed animal-based agriculture to expand, while it also, paradoxically, promoted more sustainable practices (Tovey 2006). Ireland's 1994 Rural Environmental Protection Scheme and the EU's Common Agricultural Policy (CAP) were two of the more influential measures in this regard, but a number of additional events and arrangements have encouraged the resurgence in local sustainability-oriented production and consumption, including the collapse of the Celtic Tiger and Ireland's subsequently reduced global competitiveness. Several devastating outbreaks of disease arising from animal-based agriculture certainly did much to disrupt faith in industrialized production as well. The discovery of equine DNA in imported flesh intended for human consumption was, in particular, a leading cause of distrust among Irish consumers (Bord Bia 2013). Outbreaks of foot-and-mouth disease, bovine spongiform encephalopathy ("mad cow" disease), and dioxin contamination associated with the 2008 Irish "pork" crisis (which resulted in a massive international recall) (Bánáti 2011) were also devastating to consumer trust. That said, cultural changes have piqued Irish interest in sustainable agriculture as well. Rising incomes, increased vacationing, greater media attention to gastronomic cultures (McDonagh and Commins 1999), and the efforts of Irish celebrity chefs like Myrtle and Darina Allen (Sage 2003) have raised the profile of locally produced foodstuffs.

Buying Irish has once again become an important political action that resists the colonization of Irish economies by international corporations and imported goods and energy. The buy local campaign's strength lies in its strategy of reskilling Irish farmers and supporting rural communities (Tovey 1997). In addition to ensuring food security within its borders, this food initiative also provides Ireland with an international presence and allows for greater political and economic cooperation. Subsequently, Tovey and Share (2000) insist that Ireland's vigorous commitment to agriculture represents not its late modernization or "backwardness," but rather its forward thinking. No indication of slow development, agrarianization is instead a marker of achievement. One outgrowth of the Irish agricultural campaign, however, is a persistent distrust of outside intervention. EU regulations are too often regarded with suspicion and resentment, particularly so as decisions about Ireland's economic future are made in mainland Europe and are rigidly bureaucratic without sufficient incorporation of local knowledges (O'Mahony 2009).

Beyond self-sufficiency, these new food systems are a means of instilling a sense of trust and confidence in a time of much economic insecurity. The recession may not have caused suffering on the level of the nineteenth-century famines, but it was disastrous in its own right, throwing many into poverty and unemployment. Once again, the basic ability for Irish families to put food on the table became a serious worry. The rather serious problem of corruption in the food industry has only complicated this vulnerability. Fattened by government subsidies, the industry steadily concentrated its power and overreached its authority. The great importance placed on the "beef" industry granted it considerable political and cultural leverage. The temptation to exploit this power and legitimacy proved too great. Systematic irregularities in government oversight, subsidies, and labeling schemes were uncovered in the 1990s, including the upgrading of lower grade "meats" and the obfuscation of slaughtering methods (L. Hamilton 1994). The distinction between government and industry thus blurred, there could be no clearer indication as to the political potency of Ireland's "meat" export trade.

The weakened post-recession economy thus fell on the heels of several decades of serious corruption in the food sector, creating a genuine interest in wholesome, transparent production. Food producers seized on this marketing opportunity and obliged consumer desires for fairer, more trustworthy food. Products increasingly touted their cleaner ingredients, healthier recipes, and, perhaps most importantly, their Irish origins. These new products claimed to be homegrown with integrity. They touched something in the consumer imagination, and people were prepared to pay. Like the earlier cooperative measures, these made-in-Ireland products were poised to keep production local and thus protect Irish jobs and culture. Regional imagery is now a commonly applied marketing technique that is used to denote quality of product and stimulate underdeveloped areas in Ireland (Henchion and McIntyre 2000). Alternative food systems resonate because they highlight the social embeddedness of the economy, facilitating an element of moral awareness, community, personal relationships, and reciprocal exchange in the market (Sage 2003).

This social embeddedness is an added value that can be commodified. For an Ireland made anxious by an economic downturn and eager to take pride in Irish heritage and community, food has taken on a new level of political relevance. The Irish Food Board's "Origin Green" initiative has capitalized on this relationship to benefit the Irish economy, but several privately owned grocers and food brands are adopting the approach as well. German-owned Irish discount grocer Aldi launched a "Love Ireland" campaign in 2012. In doing so, it hoped to lend itself a sense of authenticity and quality by encouraging customers to buy locally and support Irish farmers and businesses (Barrington 2012). EUROSPAR's "Yes to Irish!" campaign attempts the same (*Retail News* 2011). Likewise, dozens of Irish brands entered into a cooperative arrangement in 2009 to form the "Love Irish Food" association, specifically to promote Irish products and protect Irish jobs (Cullen 2010; Love Irish Food 2014). All of these efforts rely heavily on promoting images of family, nationalism, nostalgia, and a romanticized Irish countryside. And they are effective. The campaigns increased sales dramatically by tapping into the population's desire to support the local economy, but also by exploiting the perception that local Irish products are superior in quality (*Irish Independent* 2013). Indeed, research conducted by Love Irish Food finds that over three quarters of Irish customers seek out Irish-made products when shopping. After so many decades of insecurity and disruption, there is a real hunger for local and sustainably grown food. Given the environmental consequences of traditional, industrialized methods, the support for alternatives is promising.

Greenwashing Speciesism

ANIMAL AGRICULTURE AND SUSTAINABILITY POLITICS

Agricultural growth in Ireland has brought wealth and independence to "farmers," but these benefits have been unevenly experienced. Indeed, some researchers point to reforms such as the aforementioned Common Agricultural Policy (an EU program that regulates and subsidizes farming) as exploitative and stratifying (Crowley 2006). Corporatized and productivity-oriented, the modern Irish agrifood sector has had unfortunate consequences for Nonhuman Animals living in Ireland, too, as agriculture moved from a model of subsistence to surplus. It would likely surprise most consumers that the "Love Ireland" campaigns have done little to advance Nonhuman Animals' interests. In addition to reinvigorating domestic consumption, evocations of Irish regionalism and imagery of happy, healthy, and consenting Nonhuman Animals have been successfully promoted to the effect of significantly increasing the international market's interest in Irish animal products (Henchion and McIntyre 2000) and thereby the number of Nonhuman Animals who will be exploited.

A major consequence of this growth is that smaller farms are less able to compete as larger, intensive operations flourish under new agricultural policies (Crowley 2006). While nonhuman domesticates experience unimaginable violence on "farms" of *all* types, intensive larger "farms" equate to more intensive oppression and more victims. That said, even smaller operations harbor similar dangers, including outbreaks of zoonotic diseases. The 2020 COVID-19 outbreak has clearly demonstrated that slaughterhouses, too, are hazardous in this regard, and the Nonhuman Animals who are killed there come from "farms" both big and small. Smaller operations, furthermore, cannot avoid the stressors of confinement and exploitation, as Nonhuman Animals continue to fall ill. In response to outbreaks of avian flu, for example, the Department of Agriculture began requiring the confinement of layer hens, and, consequently, the relinquishment of "free range" labeling. Ireland's agricultural interest, in abandoning battery cage systems, has yet to account for routine practices of painful beak mangling without anesthesia, extreme crowding, and skeletal damage to birds caused by genetic manipulation and environmental stressors (Hackett 2017). Facilities that exploit and kill Nonhuman Animals for food are regulated by the Department of Agriculture, according to the Animal Health and Welfare Act of 2013, but, although Nonhuman Animal welfare organizations such as the ISPCA are responsible for enforcing this act in tandem with the department, prosecutions are extremely low, as enforcement is lacking. Just twenty-two prosecutions were initiated by the ISPCA in 2018, for instance, only eighteen of which were finalized and almost all related to Nonhuman Animals categorized as "pets" (Dowling 2018). Another complication is the distribution of responsibility for welfare measures across different governmental departments, an arrangement that creates unnecessary confusion in relation to jurisdiction and added bureaucratic hindrances.

Sadly, for Nonhuman Animals, local and humane labels are frequently misleading, and the customers' imagination rarely matches with reality. The persistence of disease indicates the shortcomings of alternative production strategies and the unnaturalness of domestication. Indeed, it symbolizes the exploitative character of animal agriculture as an institution. Tovey (2002) has pointed to zoonotic disease outbreaks as opportunities for identifying state and industry collusion in exerting control over both nonhuman bodies and humanity's empathetic response (or lack thereof). The mass slaughter of curable cows, pigs, and other animals during a foot-and-mouth outbreak was an exercise in risk management that made painfully clear that smooth industrial function and profit were to be prioritized over saving lives. This can only be the case, as the danger to humans was minimal and nonhumans could have been vaccinated or nursed back to health. The speciesist devaluation of their lives did not warrant this investment, such that any notions that the food industry harbored concern for "welfare" cannot be seriously entertained. Conversely, food scandals like the spread of foot-and-mouth so disrupt consumer trust that they can sometimes work in favor of consumers and other animals alike. The Vegetarian Society of Ireland, for instance, experienced a marked increase in membership and donations following the horse "meat" breach in which large amounts of horse DNA were discovered in Irish "beef" products (O'Sullivan 2013). Likewise, both the Vegan Society and the Vegetarian Society of the UK reported a surge of interest following the "mad" cow disease crisis of the 1990s (Vegan Society 1996).

As modern Irish agricultural policy exacerbates human inequality by widening the gap between the haves and have-nots among farmers, so too is inequality worsened for Nonhuman Animals, who must produce, reproduce, and die at ever higher numbers. Large-scale farming brought growth not only in Nonhuman Animal production but also in environmental degradations inherent in the practice. Ireland's export-focused agrarianization is increasingly industrialized and its ownership concentrated despite the popularity of alternative, more sustainable practices. In 2014, the overall value of "meat" and "livestock" export rose by 3 percent, and violence against cows, in particular, undergirds a large part of this growth. Irish cow's flesh is available in more countries than any other nation's "beef" (Bord Bia 2015). Just prior to the Great Famine, the Irish cow population was 1.8 million (Clarkson and Crawford 2001). Today that population has increased by three and a half times to 6.3 million (Central Statistics Office 2015). Despite the remarkable growth the food sector has already experienced, the Irish state at the time of this writing hopes to increase exports *even further* to the tune of 19 billion euros by 2025 under its "Food Wise" ten-year initiative.

Drafted by the food industry, the primary focus of Food Wise 2025 is "meat," dairy, and "seafood" (Department of Agriculture, Food and the Marine 2015), but it is debatable how "wise" this proposal actually is. Because expected growth in export will necessitate even greater growth in the Irish Nonhuman Animal population, the environmental impacts of increased flesh and dairy production are likely to be significant. Not surprisingly, some have criticized this strategy as dangerous with regard to the climate change crisis (Burke-Kennedy 2015; Crowley 2006). In light of the fact that Ireland is, per capita, the highest emitter of greenhouse gases in the European Union (Kijewska and Bluszcz 2016) and has already demonstrated an inability to meet reduction requirements, the *Guardian* has referred to Ireland's plans to increase "meat" and dairy production as "breathtaking hypocrisy" (Gibbons 2017). Even the most "humane" and "sustainable" of production entails the emission of massive amounts of waste into the countryside, and the United Nations lists Ireland as one of the leading consumers of fertilizer. Although fertilizers like nitrogen help food intended for cows and other animals to grow, they leach into surrounding land and water and become poisonous to ecosystems (Food and Agriculture Organization 2015). At the time of this writing, the EPA has recorded that nearly half of Irish lakes and rivers do not meet satisfactory ecological standards (*Thejournal.ie* 2019a). Irish animal-based agriculture also destroys hedgerows—vital respite spaces for free-living species—in a bid to increase field sizes to accommodate Nonhuman Animals and the production of their feed (Fogarty 2017).

The Department of Agriculture, Food and the Marine downplays the risks entailed in its plans for expansion, projecting that much of the growth will be attributed to technological advancements and not from an increase to the number of domesticated Nonhuman Animals. Indeed, "sustainability" rhetoric saturates Irish policymaking despite clear conflicts between growth and what is truly required to leave a lighter footprint. As with many postcolonial countries, the desire to play catch up following so many years of suppression and the financial dependency wrought by colonial exploitation makes strategies for truly sustainable industrialization less appealing or practical (McLaren 2003).

The department's plan to rely on technology to reach quotas without increasing the number of farmed nonhumans, if achievable, *may* stave off additional environmental consequences, but it will nonetheless ensure greater strain on Nonhuman Animals, who will be forced (and genetically manipulated) to produce to greater capacities. The recent growth in Irish dairy has created a "calf tsunami" resulting in hundreds of thousands of additional male calves who are exceeding current capacities. Many farmers kill the calves a few days after birth to avoid the costly veterinarian bills necessary to allow them to live long enough for live export and slaughter for food (Kevany and Busby 2020). Furthermore, despite the Irish focus on "environmentally friendly" practices, "overfishing," overgrazing, pollution, and the heavy use of water, grain, and energy are inherent in speciesist industries and will continue to threaten Irish ecosystems even if the number of Nonhuman Animals exploited on "farms" does not increase (Hogan 2012). There is reason to believe the situation is even more dire than is officially acknowledged. Records of Ireland's emissions, already far too high, are not inclusive of other major sources of greenhouse gases, such as the mass respiration of millions of cows, chickens, pigs, and others (O'Donovan 2014). Greater international interaction resulting from increased trade has also opened up the island to "invasive" species that further threaten natural systems (Montgomery, Lundy, and Reid 2012).

While the plight of cows, pigs, sheeps, and chickens dominate environmental concerns, fish species are also experiencing considerable oppression under the food industry's expansion efforts. Fish, shark, and shellfish communities living in Irish seas have been slaughtered to unrecoverable levels, with some species disappearing from the area altogether. Inland, lake-dwelling crayfish communities are subjected to plagues, population crashes, and extinction due to "overfishing" and agricultural runoff (Reynolds 1988). As "fishing" techniques become more and more specialized, water dwellers have little opportunity to escape. Today's kill rate is just a fraction of that reported in the nineteenth century, not because the "fishing" industry has relaxed, but because it has obliterated the ocean's ecosystem (Fogarty 2017). Just as the domestication and exploitation of "livestock" has physically altered the Irish landscape, "fishing" has altered the seascape. Regular dredging has transformed a clear, complex ecosystem into a murky dead zone with flattened ocean floors. Many Irish shorelines are regularly littered with the dead and dying bodies of nontargeted species who wash ashore.

Indeed, fishes are thoroughly integrated into the agricultural system. Their bodies are of course marketed as food to directly feed humans, but still more are killed and processed to provide food and fertilizer in support of Ireland's "meat" and dairy production. The state of the oceans surrounding Ireland have reached crisis levels, yet the government continues to subsidize "fishing" in an attempt to sustain an unsustainable industry. Any killing is an injustice to sentient inhabitants of the ocean, but, as previously alluded to, "fishing" restrictions could provide at least some relief. Alarmingly, the "fishing" allocations permitted by Irish law are as much as 20 percent higher than levels advised by scientists to prevent full-out collapse of aquatic life. In 2017, Ireland reached a compromise with the EU that allowed for massive quota increases for a litany of marine species (Siggins 2017a). While neighboring oceanic countries such as Norway have actively sought sustainable strategies, Ireland has resisted, insisting instead on persisting in its "quest to catch the last fish" (Fogarty 2017, 36).

The plan to both sustain and increase Ireland's animal-based agriculture is also a death sentence for free-living nonhuman land dwellers. It is not just the species exploited for consumption that are at risk, but also those thought to interfere with food production. Bears, wolves, and golden eagles, for instance, have been exterminated from Ireland, while badgers may well be in the future. Red grouses, corncrakes, and grey partridges have all but disappeared (Fogarty 2017), while magpies are also persecuted for daring to interfere with animal-based agriculture despite old Celtic fables that identified them as sacred (Locke 2017). Speciesist agriculture also threatens otters, horseshoe bats, bottle-nosed dolphins, and natterjack toads (Crowley 2006). Carnivorous birds, such as peregrines, hen harriers, kites, ospreys, and eagles have been disparaged as vermin and subsequently executed by farmers with guns, poison, nest-robbing, noose traps, net traps, and slow-killing pole traps (which clamp down on the legs of any bird misfortunate enough to choose the pole as a perch) (G. D'Arcy 1999). Countless other birds quietly died out as woodlands were cleared and wetlands drained.

The industrial exploitation of "wild" species was easily accomplished, since, prior to the nineteenth century, the only protection afforded to free-living animals could be found in aristocratic decrees that reserved their killing for nobility. The efforts of the Royal Society for the Protection of Birds in the late nineteenth and early twentieth centuries helped raise awareness about decimated avian communities (the Irish chapter formed in 1904), while the Bird Protection Act of 1931 offered respite to songbirds and outlawed the use of pole traps for the killing of carnivorous birds. It also introduced seasons to restrict the killing, as birds had been killed indiscriminately, offering little chance for population relief and recovery. While these protections were certainly helpful, agricultural practices in the twentieth and twenty-first centuries continued to involve the massacre of undomesticated animals. It would not be until 1976 that Ireland's Wildlife Act attempted to seriously deal with nonhuman endangerment, although many loopholes remained for "farmers" wishing to kill nonhumans who were deemed pests. According to Fogarty (2017), illegal killing still takes place as well. The gruesome shooting, clubbing, and decapitating of seals believed to compete with the "fishing" industry is a regular occurrence. Pressure to begin the "culling" of seagulls for similar reasons has dominated news media. Even the reintroduction of eagles has been rocky going as "farmers" continue to shoot them. EU regulations that supplement the Wildlife Act are similarly limited in reach. The Green Party's Pippa Hackett (2017) points to these "ambiguities and contradictions" as a "sad mockery" of conservation efforts, while lack of enforcement remains as an ongoing problem.

Species labeled "invasive" are especially subject to various injustices. Grey squirrels, for instance, have been competing with native red squirrels such that the population of reds has plummeted. Lethal attempts to control their spread have entailed great suffering for grey squirrels, but they have been largely unsuccessful. Greys have proven resilient, forcing the consideration of far less violent birth control methods (Fogarty 2017). More fundamentally, this assault on "vermin," "pests," and "invasive" species demonstrates the political nature of species construction. Classifications of "naturalness" for free-living animals have consequences for the fate of nonhumans, just as do classifications regarding their economic value or their potential to threaten agriculture (as is true with eagles). Vegan socialism emphasizes that these classifications are predicated on the utility that Nonhuman Animals serve for human interests (Cole and Stewart 2014). Nonhumans who interfere with human interests (in this case capitalist profit and reparations for a destroyed environment) are vulnerable to categorization as "pest" or "vermin." Van Dooren (2011) has argued that the default, lethal response to managing "invasives" relies on "exclusionary logics and vilifying discourses" that simplify complex, multispecies ecosystems that cannot, regardless of intervention, realistically return to precolonial conditions (294). The dualistic antagonism constructed between "good," "native" species and "bad," "invasive" species is itself an epistemology of colonialism. For these reasons, Irish strategies are often confused and contradicting. The interest in reintroducing boars has met with government resistance, for instance, as pigs are deemed non-native, having been introduced in the Neolithic era. But, as Fogarty (2017) points out, deers, too, were introduced by Neolithic persons but nonetheless warrant protection. Cows, sheeps, and chickens, of course, are also not native to Ireland, and they do great damage to the environment, yet their presence is welcomed and accommodated. Species identity and symbolic value are thus highly politicized, and economic arguments invariably triumph. The divisive and antagonizing categories of social distinction that once allowed for the prolonged colonialization of Ireland retain their utility to a "free" Ireland still locked into Britain's logic of oppression. In an effort to define and protect "native" Ireland, Irish conservationists and policymakers unwittingly entrench colonialism's legacy.

Native or not, free-living species are under continual threat so long as animal-based agriculture persists. By way of additional examples, lynxes and beavers are being considered for introduction into Ireland to help restore ecosystems destroyed by animal-based agriculture. If this were to occur, however, their continued existence in Ireland would depend on their not disrupting "livestock" (Viney 2015). Consider also the plight of Ireland's rabbits. In the 1950s, farmers intentionally introduced a deadly virus into the population (Mac Coitir 2010). All but 1 percent of the rabbit population died a painful, drawn-out death during which they experienced fever, tumors, and blindness over the course of two weeks. Rats and mouses, at least, have been more fortunate, developing resistances to poisons set by "farmers." In any case, Nibert's (2013) assertion that an economy based on the exploitation of domesticated Nonhuman Animals is one that is extremely inhospitable to free-living nonhumans seems to hold weight given the conflict over space and other resources. The full impact is only now becoming clear. A global analysis of megafauna conservation efforts found Ireland to rank among the world's worst performers (Lindsey et al. 2017). In Fogarty's words, Ireland is "not as green as we'd like to think" (2017, 1).

Without further environmental protection commitments, Ireland's "green" branding could be jeopardized. Research warns that the pressure for sustainable operations to compete, turn a profit, and find new markets can threaten the integrity of smaller industries and their ability to maintain control along supply channels (McDonagh and Commins 1999). Increasing privatization of agricultural production has even been undermining Ireland's long history of cooperative farming (Breathnach 2000; Harte 1997). Fogarty (2017) suggests that better government regulation, a stronger environmental protection sector, and even more "sustainable" "farming" practices could move Ireland toward a better balance. Yet, the notion that animal-based agriculture and environmental sustainability are somehow congruent under proper management remains magical thinking. While pasture-based, locally produced "meat" and dairy systems are generally believed to be in the interest of both vulnerable humans and Nonhuman Animals (at least before they are inevitably killed), it remains the case that corrupting market forces, in tandem with the unavoidable health and environmental burdens associated with animal-based agriculture, challenge the integrity of this "sustainable" system (Wrenn 2013). Adding to this, the numerous health risks associated with animal production and consumption (an issue that might otherwise discourage consumption) have been masked by Ireland's strategic emphasis on local, value-added production (Mahon and Cowan 2004; O'Donovan and McCarthy 2002).

POST-SPECIESISM

Sustainability rhetoric has had serious consequences for Nonhuman Animals embedded in the food system. Irish food sovereignty and its reliance on the bodies of Nonhuman Animals facilitates a *post-speciesist* ideology, or what I would describe as a system-wide, false assumption that humanity's injustice to other animals is waning or has otherwise ceased altogether. Ideologies are relevant to sociological analysis, as their function is often to impede the legitimacy of alternative social arrangements. Marx ([1846] 2000), for instance, identified elite-produced ideologies as absolutely vital to the maintenance of extreme social inequality under capitalism in the industrial revolution of Great Britain. So powerful are these mechanisms that socialist or communist alternatives remain heavily stigmatized or dismissed as utopian (Marx himself lived much of his life in exile due to the provocativeness of his ideas) (Craib 1997). Likewise, post-speciesist ideology has been levied by industry elites and the state to render invisible alternative economic measures that would not center the exploitation of Nonhuman Animals. When this posturing is also couched in nationalism, as Wright (2015) observes, it can be an especially potent barrier. Although hemp, nuts, and other vegetable sources can provide both protein and profit, post-speciesist ideology protects an inherently unsustainable and unethical animal-based social structure in presenting it as normal, natural, and most appropriate. The strength of Britain's cultural hegemony with regard to foodways, deemed legitimate in its former colonies, only complicates the development of alternatives.

Post-speciesist ideology is a modern adaptation of a much older system of animal inequality. The institutional discrimination against Nonhuman Animals based on their species, or *speciesism*, is a coordinated, systematic, and state-sanctioned act of structural violence against Nonhuman Animals that is perpetuated by humans for human benefit. Nibert (2002) understands speciesism to be both ideological and structural in that it emerges from economic conflict over limited resources, unequal power or abuse of power (particularly that power that is wielded by the state), and socialization (which provides legitimation for this conflict and inequality). Culturally, speciesism relies on the shared understanding that there is an "us" and a "them," with humans positioned as the dominant class and other animals subjugated. I introduce the concept of *post-speciesism* as an ideological variant of speciesism that misleadingly suggests that species as a symbolic category is no longer especially relevant. That is, speciesism is, in general, conceptualized mainly as a relic of the past such that any lingering speciesism is believed inconsequential and not likely to persist.

Post-speciesism, most critically, works to ideologically obscure the continued and robust existence of speciesism. The illusion of realized social change and social justice attached to the concept of post-speciesism becomes a powerful means of securing and normalizing oppression. Minor adjustments to the material conditions of other animals used by humans (such as stunning before slaughter or allowing animals outdoor access) supports this process. Scholars have observed the same phenomenon manifesting in modern racial politics as well (Bonilla-Silva 2006). Most whites today find racism morally repugnant, yet clear structural racisms remain. Post-racial ideology, like post-speciesist ideology, manifests an attitude of inclusiveness that renders difficult any potential for critical attention to persistent structural violence. Thus, post-speciesism acts as an ideological countermovement to the traditional analysis of speciesism like that advanced by Nibert and other Critical Animal Studies scholars. Sociologist Bonilla-Silva (2006) notes how "post-racial" white supremacy curiously manifests as "racism without racists"; Ireland's "humane" "farming" likewise preserves speciesism for "animal lovers."

Nonhuman Animals are obviously used and killed to create human foodstuffs, and this implicit awareness necessitates some level of consumer reckoning with this suffering. Post-speciesism ideology addresses this disquieting reality by promulgating the notion that species as an identity category is irrelevant, and that animals, both human and nonhuman, are "one." The concept of a "circle of life" in which all animals inhabit their rightful place in the evolutionary community is another potent variant that resists the speciesist critique. If the power differentials between humans and other animals are erased, it is difficult to recognize and critique speciesist exploitation. "Farmers" frequently erode the human-nonhuman boundary even further by referring to their nonhuman victims as children, family, or friends (Cole and Morgan 2011a). Violence against other animals that is inherent in agricultural practices, of course, continues to the benefit of humans, but dismissing the differences between humans and other animals in a supposedly post-speciesist society ideologically negates Nonhuman Animal oppression. Clear and significant differences in life opportunity that are based on species identification are erased from the narrative. This erasure is essential to upholding oppression in a society where social justice ideology has been gaining momentum, particularly so in the Republic of Ireland where values of freedom and liberty hold such poignancy after centuries of colonial rule.

Again, Marx identifies the economy as the originator of prevailing ideologies, and post-speciesism is certainly evidence of this. Ireland's commitment to a "green" economy commodifies humanity's concern with speciesism, rebrands speciesist institutions, and markets what are essentially similar products for a much higher price. Here, post-speciesism confers added value. "Humane" labeling, for instance, denotes quality and relies on consumer trust to extort higher prices (Swanson 2013). Post-speciesist ideology facilitates this trust by obscuring systems of oppression and relationships of domination; it allows human supremacy to fade into the background. In traditional speciesist frameworks, violence was out, open, and celebrated. In the post-speciesist world, however, hurting other animals is considered antiquated. Nonhumans killed or exploited for "meat," dairy, "wool," and labor are "happy" and "respectfully" treated. This post-speciesist rebranding allows speciesist industries to stand out in a heavily competitive marketplace. As with all capitalist endeavors, ideologies are necessary to obscure exploitation, to make consumption pleasurable, and to encourage the fetishization of the product.

The aforementioned "Produced in Ireland" labeling scheme exemplifies this process. It is designed to challenge globalized food production, an environmentally taxing process that outsources agricultural work, threatens the state in creating a dependency on outsiders, and strains the local economy with job loss and import costs. As I have argued, localizing food is an important form of resistance, but, paradoxically, local production can sometimes be prohibitively expensive in a global society in which cheaper competitors are readily available from developing regions where human rights, Nonhuman Animal rights, and environmental regulations are lax. Advertising campaigns seek to reframe local food as patriotic, moral, and familial to counter this.

By way of an example, Aldi's "Love Ireland" campaign produces television spots and in-store full color booklets that pull on Irish nationalism and nostalgia to push product. Green pastures, families, and happy Nonhuman Animals are themes that repeat to frame the purchase of "Love Ireland" products as an ethical choice and a political action. Nonhuman Animal welfare is consequently commodified. Consider an in-store booklet distributed in the summer of 2015. A dairy cow featured on the cover is identified as "Daisy," although it is clear from her ear tags that her real identification is 0722 (figure 5.1). Fabricating her name for the brochure

Figure 5.1. Aldi Love Ireland store flyer. Source: Aldi.

creates the perception that she is individualized and treated as a person with interests. The reality of dairy production in Ireland is far less pleasant. Even cows raised on "happy" farms are separated from their mother at a young age (often just a day or so after birth) (Kelleher 2019). While male calves are funneled directly into "meat" production or killed soon after birth, female calves will follow the paths of their mothers, facing repeated forced impregnations and separations from her own calves (although many females are also deemed surplus and killed in infancy). She, like her brothers and sons, will enter the slaughterhouse before reaching adulthood, her body spent from the laboriousness of repeated pregnancy and tremendous levels of milk production made possible by genetic alteration. Indeed, "Daisy" was probably long dead before her image graced the catalogs stocking Aldi stores.

To be clear, local food production is, at its heart, a capitalist enterprise. Happiness and humaneness are often touted in tandem with the celebratory economic support of Irish farmers and their families. Producers featured in this Aldi catalog, for instance, assure the customer that their purchases allow them to "reach a much bigger market," and that "Aldi's support has contributed to our ability to maintain our long tradition." Callan Bacon Ltd., a family company applying "traditional" curing methods on its "humble premises," reports that Aldi's "Love Ireland" program has enabled it to increase its staff to almost 200. The town of Monaghan's "small indigenous fresh dairy produce manufacturer" claims to depend heavily on the support of retailers to reach customers. Aldi's support has helped it to establish a presence in the marketplace. ABP "beef suppliers" have also reported remarkable growth since working with Aldi. ABP now works with a network of over 35,000 farmers, spending over €450 million each year in the "acquisition of cattle" and staff employment. Post-speciesist ideology does not simply obscure systemic violence, it *increases* it. Vasile Stănescu (2010) furthers this point by highlighting that the nationalistic undertones to locavorism not only misrepresent the experiences of Nonhuman Animals, but, in romanticizing and glorifying the importance of "the soil and the local" (19), also fan repressive ideologies with regard to women, immigrants, people of color, homosexuals, non-Christians, and other minorities whose citizenship status is partially defined by their relationship to food production, preparation, and consumption.

"Sustainability" programs ultimately do little if anything to challenge the property status of Nonhuman Animals, who remain as machinery and products to be used, bought, sold, consumed, and discarded as it suits the dominant class: humans. Sustainability narratives only undergird the false belief that Nonhuman Animals, although firmly beneath humans in status and life opportunity, can enjoy human care and respect. Speciesism can be said to exist when, in a conflict of interest between humans and nonhumans, the interests of humans take automatic or assumed precedence. Post-speciesism, however, masks this conflict by describing the interests of Nonhuman Animals as *congruent* with that of humans. It should take no stretch of the imagination to concede that Nonhuman Animals—as sentient, emotionally complex individuals—desire to live and to do so free from systematic suffering. Animal-based agriculture can never fulfill such interests.

In 2009, the Lisbon Treaty, a constitutional document of the EU, officially recognized the sentience of other animals. Sentience is a characteristic that science had known to be present in other animals for at least a century, but it apparently still needed official recognition in order to motivate regulatory bodies. Following the treaty, the EU moved to require certain welfare standards for those exploited and killed for food. However, farmers, who still view Nonhuman Animals as commodities, products, and machines, necessarily have limited compassion for their suffering and accept welfare measures only in so far as they will draw a financial return (Miele and Lever 2013). Because "farmed" animals have been genetically manipulated through domestication, or what Nibert (2013) refers to as *domesecration*, they are fully controlled by humans, sexually manipulated by humans, and eventually killed by humans, simply to fulfil the elite-constructed penchant for animal products in society. Such an irrational system could not genuinely be described as humane, just, or consensual, but *greenwashing* and *humanewashing* have effectively maintained these myths for considerable economic benefit (Stănescu 2010).

Emerging Vegetarianism and Veganism in Modern Ireland

For much of the developed world, the dangers of animal products have been gradually registering with medical practitioners and policymakers, but this has happened to a much lesser degree in Ireland. Although dietetic associations in neighboring countries now lend evidence-based support for plant-based diets, the Irish Nutrition and Dietetic Institute has been slow to condone veganism. In a 2015 interview with the *Irish Examiner*, for instance, it explicitly warns that veganism is not healthy (Ní Chonchúir 2015). The institute does produce fact sheets offering advice for achieving a vegan diet, but only with clear reservations about the healthfulness of doing so (N. Donnelly 2016; Irish Nutrition and Dietetic Institute 2004). Nibert (2002) asserts that the capitalist state works in the service of speciesist enterprise by wielding its authority in such a way as to elevate the importance of animal products. It achieves this through legal protections and subsidies for animal-based agriculture, but also through ideological dissemination via various government offices and entities. Undoubtedly, the economic importance of animal agriculture to Ireland is influencing the ability of state institutions to promote alternative diets. Without these official recommendations to offer it legitimacy, veganism is in danger of remaining a foreign concept and a practice at odds with the Irish national agenda. It has been argued in previous chapters that Irish history supports a much richer history of anti-speciesism and plant-based living than is presently acknowledged, but the state's failure to recognize veganism as critical to Nonhuman Animal welfare, human health, and environmental protection has ensured that modern Ireland remain compliant with colonial foodways.

Statistics on veganism are lacking, but between 5 and 10 percent of Ireland's population identifies as vegetarian (Irish Nutrition and Dietetic Institute 2004; Leahy, Lyons, and Tol 2010; Pichler and Blackwell 2007). Bord Bia (2018) estimates as much as 4 percent may be vegan. These estimates are comparable to the United States, Great Britain, and other parts of Europe, and it is no more difficult to be vegan in Ireland than other Western countries. In fact, Bord Bia (2018) research indicates that about one in five Irish persons are either vegan, vegetarian, or flexitarian, while nearly 60 percent of the population is reportedly open to considering a vegan diet in the future.

In a story covering the growing vegan scene in Ireland, the *Dublin Inquirer* declares, "The vegans are coming" (D. Murphy 2015). Vegan restaurants are still few in number, but demand for vegan options in restaurants is building. Vegetarian restaurants are not difficult to find in larger cities like Belfast, Dublin, Cork, Galway, and Limerick. Cornucopia, Dublin's most prominent vegetarian restaurant, in successful operation since 1986, is now almost exclusively vegan in an effort to meet demand. Even Cork's historic English Market, a leading representative of Ireland's local and sustainable branding initiative that is renowned for its selection of regionally produced animal flesh, now includes vegan and natural foods vendors. Many of its restaurants also offer explicitly vegetarian menu items. In fact, all major grocery chains in Ireland now sell specialty vegan options, including soy milk and veggie patties. As one Irish vegetarian cookbook author explains it, "Ireland is in the middle of a culinary revolution" (Cotter 1996, 5). Even the *Irish Catholic* reports that "vegetarianism seems to be everywhere these days," providing readers with an overview of vegetarian and vegan ethics and offering advice on how to best transition to the diet (Keery 2014).

Another milestone in Ireland's vegan metamorphosis is evidenced in the 2015 arrival of Dublin Vegfest. Held on World Vegan Day (November 1), the festival celebrates vegan food, culture, and anti-speciesism ethics. As one participant reminisced, "One of the things I remember most of the day is the number of Irish activists who came up saying words to the effect: 'where have all these vegans come from?' They were remarking on the huge numbers of people who no-one active in the Irish movement had seen before" (Yates 2015). In the North of Ireland, Farplace Animal Rescue began hosting the similarly structured annual Irish Vegan Festival. The 2015 year truly was a turning point in Irish veganism. Sealing its success was Guinness's announcement that the legendary brew and popular symbol of Irish cuisine would no longer be made with nonvegan ingredients extracted from the bodies of fishes. This change in recipe, the company insists, comes from its desire to market the beer as suitable for vegans and vegetarians (Stack 2015). A year later, Bailey's Irish Cream joined suit, releasing a vegan, almond-based version of its liqueur.

To be clear, vegetarianism and veganism are not simply emerging, but *resurging* in popularity. As chapter 3 explored, plant-based politics infused a modernizing, independence-minded Ireland. Dublin laid claim to the Sunshine Vegetarian Dining Rooms, operated by the Dublin Vegetarian Society on Grafton Street in 1891. There was also the College Vegetarian Restaurant, which opened at about the same time, touting the digestible, economical, and scientifically proven superiority of its "pure diet of Fruit and Vegetables" (figure 5.2). Advertisements in the *Irish Times* also lauded the diet's ability to ease and restore influenza victims, a claim that probably resonated well in disease-prone nineteenth-century Ireland. Remarkably, this institution operated for over twenty years. The College was part of Leonard McCaughey's vegetarian chain, which also included an outlet in Belfast. McCaughey hailed from the North of Ireland. Active with the Irish Vegetarian Union, he was a food reformer and vegetarian restaurateur into his seventies (Gregory 2007).

McCaughey's Dublin location included a vegetarian hotel, and the restaurant attracted Irish nationalists, suffragettes, and other liberals who met there regularly. The College Restaurant even makes an appearance in James Joyce's *Ulysses* (Plock 2007). Indeed, vegetarian restaurants across the United Kingdom were frequent hotbeds for activists and revolutionaries

> Those Visiting Horse Show this Summer will be pleased and benefited by Dining at
>
> # THE COLLEGE
> # Vegetarian Restaurant
>
> ### 3 & 4, COLLEGE STREET, DUBLIN,
>
> Where the Science of Cooking is Adopted.
>
> This Rational System of Food is HIGHLY DIGESTIBLE and STRICTLY ECONOMICAL. Beautifully Light, yet Richly Nourishing. A pure diet of Fruit and Vegetables—Nature's own production—therefore best.
>
> ## OUR SIXPENNY TEAS
>
> In all our Establishments stand unrivalled.
>
> A NEAT HOTEL is attached to our Dublin Restaurant, which is a great favourite for Comfort and Cleanliness.
>
> ### THE McCAUGHEY RESTAURANTS, Ltd.

Figure 5.2. The College Vegetarian Restaurant advertisement. Source: *Irish Times*, September 11, 1900.

who understood the political nature of food production and its relationship to other social justice causes (Leneman 1997). As such, this restaurant surfaces in the Bureau of Military History database more than once, as it was a meeting place for nationalists and loyalists alike. In one instance, a waiter overheard diners from Trinity College planning to attack the Sinn Féin headquarters on Harcourt Street. He duly reported the plans to rebel leader Seán MacMahon, and nationalists were able to prepare for the mob attack (Lynch 1913–21). Hindu vegetarians also congregated at these restaurants, imparting an early Indian influence that would continue into modern times. Former Indian president V. V. Giri, for example, was a regular guest at the Irish Farm Produce Café on Henry Street, Dublin. Operated by member of the Dublin Women's Suffrage Association and first president of the Cumann na mBan, Jennie Wyse Power (Central Statistics Office, n.d.) (figure 5.3), this vegetarian café was connected with the newly formed and radically left-wing Sinn Féin party and advocated home-grown food and consumption as a means of colonial resistance. Regular police surveillance at the café indicates how important this vegetarian space was to the Irish resistance. Indeed, Ireland's 1916 Proclamation was signed on its premises in April of that year (McNally 2019).

The Irish Farm Produce Café became a casualty of the Irish Civil War on account of Wyse attracting the ire of anti-treaty activists. As for the College Restaurant, it had become part of a larger enterprise. Records suggest that the McCaughey family also operated the Ivanhoe Hotel and Vegetarian Restaurant and the Princess Restaurant (both in Dublin) (Mac

Figure 5.3. Jennie Wyse Power. Source: Wikimedia Commons.

Con Iomaire 2008), but the chain was not to last. This first wave of vegetarian restaurants petered out by the era of Irish independence. The only mid-century holdout was McCaughey's Belfast location, known as the X.L., which remained open until 1950. The aforementioned Eastern influence was resurrected in the first restaurant of Dublin's second wave of vegetarian gastronomic culture, Good Karma. This facility operated for a short time in the 1970s, apparently offering a trendy hippie vibe. A number of health food shops catering to vegetarian and vegan diets also appeared in Dublin in the 1970s. Journals produced by the Vegan Society advertised vegetarian bed and breakfasts in Ireland as early as 1948, but more regularly beginning in the 1980s. Several vegetarian restaurants also opened in the 1980s, and, from thereon, vegans and vegetarians could easily enough find restaurants to cater to them.

Of course, food tourism, grocery shopping, and fine dining represent only the surface level of a complex food system. With food comprising such a large part of the economy, substantial replacements to "meat" and dairy will be necessary to achieve a viable vegan system. Fortunately, vegan alternatives have shown promise in the agricultural sector. Ireland's mushroom sector has expanded significantly and is considered one of the most successful in the world (Teagasc Mushroom Stakeholder Consultative Group 2013). Thanks to subsidies and advertising programs, the industry now provides over 3,000 Irish jobs and is worth well over a hundred million euros (McCall 2015). It constitutes one of the largest horticultural exports and demonstrates that nonanimal proteins can flourish with the state support that is most often reserved for speciesist industry. The Mushroom Bureau (n.d.) promotes fungi as a healthy alternative to animal protein and deliberately situates it within Ireland's growing interest with vegetarian eating, even suggesting mushroom-based meals for "meat free Mondays."

Unfortunately, the mushroom sector's success also lies in its ability to make profitable the burdensome waste products from animal-based agriculture like chicken litter and cow's manure. This could mean that even vegetable alternatives to Ireland's animal-based economy will have difficulty disentangling from speciesist institutions. Mushrooms are a standard element in the vegan diet, but their source leaves activists ambivalent. As the Vegan Society summarizes it, "Button mushrooms are cheap and the main reason for this is intensive animal farming" (Prowse 2004). Recognizing that the glut of cheap manure and the pressure of cheap imports discourages ethical production, the society advocates less popular varieties such as oyster mushrooms, shitake, and enoki, which are grown in cellulose. Just how feasible large-scale production of these varieties could be remains unknown in Ireland, and will not likely be explored so long as the agricultural structure is centered on Nonhuman Animal production and muddies any imagination for alternatives. Recent interest in veganism in the United Kingdom has been credited for a massive growth in demand for these exotic mushrooms, however, indicating that it could prove a fruitful venture for Irish farmers (Smithers 2020).

It is also important to note that, like Nonhuman Animal production, nonanimal protein production can also cause harm to vulnerable human groups if the capitalist framework in which that production is supported is not itself challenged. The Irish mushroom industry has become infamous for its systemic labor violations. Women, mostly from Eastern Europe and Asia, work for well below minimum wage, as they are paid by the weight of the mushrooms picked. According to Migrant Rights Centre Ireland, the industry's structure creates a dangerous race to the bottom, as it is, "virtually impossible to achieve the minimum rate of pay per hour even when the mushroom harvests are at their best and picked by the most experienced pickers. The result is that workers are being pushed to work faster and faster" (Sheen 2006, 11). Neither are employees entitled to overtime pay or holidays. They work dangerously long hours and are exposed to toxic, lung-damaging chemicals used in the production process. Adding to this precariousness is the fact that the work is largely part-time for women (men are generally placed in operative positions, which are more stable). This arrangement used to be suitable employment for Irish housewives in an era when women's employment was severely restricted. Today, however, immigrant women have largely replaced native-born Irish women, and they have the same need for a full day's pay as any man. This exploitation is not unacknowledged by the workers, but their often weak English skills and geographic isolation in a country that is foreign to them impedes their ability to fight for fairer treatment. Black vegan feminists have observed this conundrum in the production of other vegan foods deemed "cruelty-free" (Harper 2010), such as avocados, bananas, berries, cashews, and chocolate. In the bid to promote alternative Nonhuman Animal products, the suffering of marginalized *human* animals can easily be overlooked in the absence of careful attention to the intersecting nature of oppression in capitalist systems.

This is not to exonerate "meat" and dairy production, as it is the leading industry in human abuse. In fact, the mushroom sector relies so heavily on Nonhuman Animal products to feed its mushrooms that it might be accurate to categorize it as a subset of animal-based agriculture. Nonhuman Animal industries of all varieties have been identified as major sources of human trafficking. Again, it is disproportionately vulnerable individuals from Eastern Europe and Asia who are targeted. The "fishing" and fish "processing" industries stand out as especially abusive, with workers enduring hazardous conditions, forced sleep deprivation, erratic payment, and crowded living conditions (Allamby et al. 2011). These abusive practices are only aggravated by a changing political climate that threatens Ireland's special relationship with Britain, increasing the pressure to produce and remain profitable. The Brexit vote of 2016 has rocked the mushroom industry. In fact, it was one of the hardest hit, with several farms closing as the price of sterling plummeted and Irish mushroom growers bargained for new contracts in competition with other European countries (Cadogan 2016).

Perhaps kelp will prove more promising. Already a thriving business in Asia, the industrial production of seaweed is growing in Ireland. Seaweed was a major export in the nineteenth century until the introduction of railroad infrastructure undermined ecosystems and access to seaweed. The Irish Free State, eager to move away from industries painted as backward and associated with poverty, took little interest in revitalizing the industry (Dowd-Smith 2020). Farmers today, however, are revisiting the practice (Ceurstemont 2014), and it is positioned as a means of protecting Irish industry and Gaelic culture in remote coastlands where it is harvested. In addition to its suitability for cooking, it is also useful for biofuel, toiletries, and food additives. Notably, it has been applied as a fertilizer for centuries (Friel and Nolan 1996), and this could serve as an ethical and sustainable replacement for Nonhuman Animal manure. It is also used as a cheap "livestock" feed, however, suggesting that the industrialization of kelp will more likely be employed in the streamlining of speciesism instead of reducing its reach.

That kelp is being marketed to "farmers" as a "green" alternative that reduces methane gas released by cows' digestion, improves cows' health, and increases their reproductivity (O'Brien 2017a) only underscores this potential. Worried by growing calls for a reduction in "meat" consumption to lower the number of cows living in the country, the Irish Farmers' Association has eagerly welcomed this new development. Seaweed extracts are also used as antibiotics for cows, artificially sustaining herds weakened by the stress of agricultural exploitation. Likewise, seaweed is often grown alongside salmon "farms" as fish waste works as a potent fertilizer. It is also utilized to support free-living fish populations who rely on it for shelter and are, in turn, relied upon by the Irish "fishermen" who exploit them. Like mushrooms, seaweed may be too bound to speciesist industries to become a viable vegan alternative on a large scale. There are also fears that kelp aquaculture could disrupt natural ecosystems, as modified plant species may escape and interbreed with wild growing varieties. Consequently, capitalist industrialization must itself be examined in any plan to develop sustainable food production, as it has the potential to turn even the most innocuous of products into ethical and environmental threats. The seaweed boom has already invited appropriation by absentee corporations, and, as a result, hand harvesting is vulnerable to mechanization. These processes damage the sensitive marine environment and erode the industry's potential to protect traditional cultures (Siggins 2017b). If industrialized kelp should continue down this path, it is unlikely to offer much relief to the problems caused by intensive food production.

Hope is not lost. Ireland's ancient cereal, oat, is now experiencing a resurgence. Oat milk sales have exceeded production capacities, signaling to the Irish food board that vegan alternatives are here to stay and worth investing in. Farmers are now encouraged to develop vegan-friendly formulas in environmentally sustainable packaging to take advantage of this "key innovation trend in dairy" (McKeown 2019). Wheat and pea protein might also be mass-produced in Ireland to meet domestic and global protein requirements. Citing rising consumer concerns with climate change, political unrest, culinary adventurousness, and veganism, Bord Bia (2018) (which has been historically committed to protecting and expanding animal agriculture) is evidently concerned by the threat to Irish "meat" production. It now advises all manner of rebranding initiatives for "livestock" farmers to get "in tune with emerging needs and new meat expectations" and resist the growing tide.

Conclusion

Food is central to the construction of Ireland as a country and a culture, and it has always been political. Boycotts in the land wars squeezed landlords, dairy cooperatives resisted capitalist exploitation, and early twentieth century "Buy Irish" campaigns revitalized consumer trust with nationalist sentiment. Anthropologist Sidney Mintz (1996) has observed that agency over foodways, no matter how limited, can become a vital act of resistance to deeply oppressive economic systems. "The tasting of freedom," he writes, "was linked to the tasting of food" (37). Certainly, in Ireland's case, the character and success of the new republic was nurtured through the practices of growing, cooking, and eating, or even just the *ideas* of how these practices might unfold. Just how Ireland would make and use food was fiercely debated in the trenches of war, on the floors of parliament, and over the dining tables of vegetarian cafés. The political practice of animal nationalism, as history would unveil it, has come to have a significant influence over the fledgling nation-state. The hegemonic belief (cultivated by centuries of colonialism) that animal-based agriculture demonstrated a country's power and wealth would take precedence. Conversely, vegetarianism—a foodway far more familiar to pre-independence Ireland and championed by some as a fairer and healthier system—would fade from the political discourse. In Gramscian terms, vegetarian and vegan campaigning contributes to an important counterculture or even proto-alternative hegemony. The entrenchment of colonial values is firm.

Vegan feminism might explain this marginalization as a result of its association with the radical, feminist left. This was a connection that challenged the anthroparchal, patriarchal order. Ireland had something to prove: it was as robust as Britain and could hold its own in the world system, but, at the same time, it was *not* British. For this reason, in its early years of independence, Ireland adhered more strongly than ever to its conservative Catholic culture with the assumption that doing so would delineate cultural differences between Britain and Ireland and provide a measure of resilience. As this chapter has outlined, this strategy had limited economic and political success, but, more importantly, it had lasting negative consequences for feminized members of free Ireland, especially Nonhuman Animals. Following independence, Ireland adopted an extreme isolationist policy that led it into a state of stagnation before it was finally conceded in the 1950s and 1960s that protectionism was futile. Following the end of this policy, Ireland experienced a marked increase in agricultural concentration and an industrialization of "meat" and dairy production, causing concern for the livelihood of small-scale farmers and the well-being of the nonhumans oppressed in the food system.

Resistance to this rationalization process, however, comes with its own set of problems. Rather than motivate a move to plant-based alternative production practices, greenwashing and humanewashing have created a veneer of sustainability that is more useful for branding purposes than it is for mitigating the problems inherent in animal-based agriculture. Indeed, speciesist food production remains afloat only with the help of intense government subsidies that keep the industry financially viable and allow it to artificially increase consumption rates. Old productivist economic values are today protected by new values of pseudo-sustainability. Increased production continues to be advocated by state and industry, while sustainability rhetoric works to deflect criticism and interference. As became clear following the "beef" tribunal of the 1990s, the unchecked power of the industry creates a situation in which products may be packaged to meet regulations and consumer desires, but this packaging can easily mask production practices that are adverse to public health and Nonhuman Animal welfare. With little government oversight and lured by the temptations of subsidies, producers are free to alter labeling and advertising without having to significantly alter the product itself. Labels touting "fresh," "happy," and "humane" animal products shield customers from immeasurable violence inherent in Nonhuman Animal "farming."

The harm to Nonhuman Animals thus remains relatively undiminished, but environmental degradation also continues unabated. Zoonotic diseases continue to emerge even from "sustainable" operations and threaten all life, human and nonhuman alike. Plans to increase Nonhuman Animal production could bring Ireland to the point of crisis. In the meantime, the wrangling over food sovereignty gives insight into the difficulties faced by a postcolonial state in a globalizing market and governance scheme. Ireland's green agriculture as it currently exists only applies a veneer of Irishness to an old colonialist arrangement. The Gaelic Irish diet, composed of hazelnuts, sorrel, dock, knotgrass, goosefoot, clover, celery, parsley, cress, cabbage, wild radish, bracken, mosses, nettle, chickweed, corn cockle, buttercup, cherries, plums, apples, raspberries, rowan, strawberries, bilberries, blackberries, peas, legumes, oats, barley, bread, and flax has long been lost to the modern consumer. The archaeological and historical research surveyed in chapter 1 demonstrates that nothing could be more Irish than a rich and varied diet of fruits, nuts, vegetables, legumes, and grains. Yet, veganism is characterized as threatening, while animal-based agriculture is slated for continued growth in the face of worsening climate change and diet-related health crises.

Nibert (2002), Torres (2007), myself (Wrenn 2016), and other Marxist sociologists have highlighted the economy as the basis for structuring social roles, values, norms, and relations with regard to humans and other animals. Therefore, an economy bound to speciesism would be predictably resistant to veganism. With so much riding on animal-based agriculture, veganism becomes a dangerous threat to the social structure, primarily in its potential to disrupt the inequalities that make a speciesist economy possible. Nevertheless, a vegan scene is burgeoning across the island, as is evidenced by numerous restaurants, grocery store offerings, and festivals sprouting up in the past few decades. There is reason to believe that Ireland is on the edge of a plant-based renaissance, one that could alleviate human illness, nonhuman suffering, and environmental devastation. In the remaining pages, these strategies for change are explored as they speak to an Ireland in the twenty-first century. With globalization and corrosive neoliberal policies only growing more relevant to state decision-making, the relationship between humans and other animals is as strained as ever. Social movement scholars and community changemakers, however, have identified a potential crisis in hegemonic governance, suggesting that vegan ethics may have means to permeate and facilitate a more equitable social arrangement.

Conclusion

Human-Nonhuman Relationships in the Global Era

Nonhuman Animals play a vital, yet underappreciated role in Ireland. To its discredit, the field of Critical Animal Studies has almost exclusively focused its attention on Britain and the United States, forgetting the little nation in the middle. To address this shortcoming, I have presented three general theses in support of Irish Nonhuman Animal studies. First, it was argued from a vegan Marxist perspective that Nonhuman Animals are materially and ideologically key to the functioning and development of Irish society. Second, I also advanced a vegan feminist perspective to argue that the experiences of Nonhuman Animals are entangled with that of Irish persons living both at home and abroad. Third, the vibrancy of Irish vegan protest has been documented as deeply influential to the advancement of Nonhuman Animal rights on the world stage, and, furthermore, Ireland's story might be conceived as a dual narrative of both oppression *and* resistance. In this conclusion, I briefly revisit these themes, but I also consider how they may inform contemporary and future human-nonhuman relations as Ireland contends with political and economic challenges in the twenty-first century.

Animality in Irish Society

One would be hard pressed to identify any human society that has freed itself from anthropocentrism, but ancient cultures were certainly far closer to species egalitarianism than those of today (Mason 1993). In the premodern era, Nonhuman Animals positively saturated human societies. They constituted the basis of the economy, legitimated politics and kingships, permeated knowledge systems and mythology, shaped the physical landscape, lived as housemates, and served as food, clothes, and entertainment. As society modernized, animality was symbolically and materially constructed to delineate humanity as superior. This hierarchical thinking would extend to order and oppress marginalized human groups as well. Explains Ko, "*Animal* is part of the vocabulary of white supremacist violence; it signifies the rhetorical and social branding of certain bodies, which white supremacy wants to consume, exploit, and eliminate without question" (2019, 99). Modern society has cemented the species hierarchy and fully normalized the exploitation of Nonhuman Animals, and animality continues to play an important role in shaping boundaries and defining values. Recall that nationalistic Celticism proved highly detrimental for Travellers and other nonconforming groups in the years following independence.

As societies undergo great change and transition, their established social orders can destabilize and subsequently stoke anxieties over identity difference. What it meant to be "animal" truly became a point of contestation as Ireland modernized. The Irish at home and abroad were likened to Nonhuman Animals (a practice legitimized by the pseudoscience of biological racism), while the rise of anti-cruelty advocacy forced the populace to consider who was animal and who was not. Recall the case of blood "sportsman" Kit Burns, who roundly denied that chickens and rats were animal in his attempt to protect his fighting industry from activist intervention. Concurrently, as an Irish immigrant, he himself was constructed as a nonhuman as the modernizing American nation grappled with rapidly fluctuating demographics and economies. Most damningly, farmers were able to categorize cows, pigs, chickens, and other animals exploited and killed for food, clothing, and scientific research as something more object-like than animal so as to facilitate their industrial practices. Obviously, these species are superficially acknowledged to be sentient, but not sentient enough to be spared the suffering and death inherent to agriculture and scientific experimentation. Unfortunately, the experience with animalization shared between Irish humans and nonhumans has not encouraged human solidarity with other animals. As the Irish have assimilated and aligned with whiteness and humanity, they have leveraged this privilege to the increased otherization of Nonhuman Animals.

Many persistent Irish traditions that involve the use of Nonhuman Animals relate back to the oppressive days of colonialism and are relatively removed from Ireland's animist history, despite their cultural branding as quintessentially Irish institutions. The oppression of other animals for entertainment was obviously not unknown to Ireland before British rule, but it significantly expanded and institutionalized after the 1600s. The ritualistic exploitation of other animals in "zoos," "racing," plowing, fairs, "hunting," "breeding," vivisection, and food systems served to instill ideologies of oppression and normalize extreme social stratification. In adopting these British customs, Ireland has become complicit in this project of inequality. Perhaps the cultural attachment to these speciesist practices indicates an attachment to romanticized colonialist pasts. More likely, it illustrates Ireland's effort to assimilate into the modern world system as fully developed, civilized, and *human* equals.

Sociologist Anthony Giddens (2004) has argued that modernity has great potential to lift a society by fostering improvements in knowledge, technology, sanitation, and access to resources, but he also warns that these benefits come at a cost. The growth they facilitate, for instance, is most often achieved by the extreme exploitation of society's most vulnerable, while the benefits are unevenly distributed. Personal autonomy and environmental integrity are also undermined as economic processes rationalize and expand to the effect of prioritizing business over individual and environmental health. This struggle with modernity is familiar to many nations and cultures, but it has special potency in regions like Ireland where colonial exploitation shaped their progress. Consequently, Ireland and other postcolonial nations characteristically seek to maintain or resurrect traditions damaged or destroyed by colonialism, with colonialism and modernity often symbolically linked as problematic (Skonieczny 2010). There is, to be sure, a paradox to this response. On one hand, Ireland, like other postcolonial countries, is eager for success and acceptance in the world system. On the other hand, it is wary of the cultural, political, and economic costs of assimilation in a system that was built on the oppression of former colonies like itself. In any case, traditions may take on a magical quality as emblems of some glorious, purer past that can render them dangerously impervious to critique.

Giddens, to be clear, did not mean to suggest that modernity is an entirely detrimental process. Many attitudes and behaviors associated with the premodern era were quite harmful to marginalized groups such as women, poor persons, ethnic minorities, and Nonhuman Animals. Rationalization and modernization may have created considerable social change and disruption (including unimaginable nonhuman suffering in the production of science and food), but they have in other ways offered a chance for a better life for the very marginalized. All modern societies today rely on the economic exploitation of other animals and have thus constructed ideological barriers to recognizing species-based injustice. Ireland's traumatic history with colonialism, however, presents unique difficulties for any positions or policies that could potentially interfere with its aim for economic and cultural independence. Its slowness to modernize has created a burning desire to adopt the markers of modernization, but also anxiety over rapidly eroding traditionalisms. In its bid to mimic the status and mores of the dominant nation-states, Ireland has unfortunately institutionalized inequality for Nonhuman Animals and other minority groups such as the Travelling community.

Entangled Oppressions

What it means to be Irish has thus depended upon the social configuration of animality, but antagonistic boundary-maintenance overlooks the fact that the humans and other animals of Ireland have many intersecting interests. Marx observed that capitalist exploitation was facilitated by separating "nature" from humans and also by alienating individuals from one another ([1844] 2000). In Ireland's case, this was accomplished by privatization of property (solidified by mass displacement of the peasantry and the installation of a tenant system) and the creation or aggravation of boundaries based on species, class, ethnicity, race, and gender. Failure to acknowledge the shared circumstances of humans and nonhumans, I have argued, inhibits Ireland's ability to identify and address systems of inequality. The persistence of speciesism, in other words, threatens social progress. Vegan feminist theory points to the symbolic role of animality in upholding other systems of oppression: so long as Nonhuman Animals are treated like "animals" and like "meat," this framework remains accessible for the similar treatment of women and other minorities (Adams 2000; Ko and Ko 2017). This line of argument is only strengthened by the work of Nibert (2003), Torres (2007), and other vegan socialists (Wrenn 2016) that highlights the role of economic arrangements in fueling the objectification, commodification, and intensified oppression of these groups.

In an opinion piece for the *Irish Times*, political commentator Fintan O'Toole observed that Irish culture remains inhibited by the effects of what he has termed the "moral-industrial complex," a nexus of colonialism, nationalism, and Catholicism that manifested within industrial schools, mother and baby homes, and mental asylums (O'Toole 2017). Decades of socialization under these institutions, he explains, have predisposed the populace to ignoring injustice and avoiding demands for accountability.

Charity has become the institutionalized response to inequality such that it has replaced civil rights initiatives. Ireland ranks as the fifth most giving country according to the World Giving Index (Charities Aid Foundation 2018), but charity can obscure structural inequalities. Indeed, sociologist Marcel Mauss (2002) recognizes gift-giving as a means of maintaining the inferior status of those on the receiving end. Reliance on charity over rights preserves a hierarchy of worth in relegating those in need to the whims of those with the power to relieve suffering. Charity also maintains structural violence because it so commonly allows for the stigmatizing of victims, such as destitute and homeless persons, "wayward" women, and disabled persons. If O'Toole is right, could this socialized complacency with human injustice in Ireland also support a complacency with regard to the wrongs imposed on Nonhuman Animals?

Ireland's strained history has undoubtedly influenced its present values and norms with some degree of conservatism, but it would be wrong to presume it to be uniquely uncaring to nonhuman suffering. Sociologists have suggested that denial is a normal process of social conditioning (Cohen 2001); it takes considerably more mental effort to deviate from speciesist paths of least resistance created by social institutions (Morgan and Cole 2011). It also entails risk of ostracization (Cole 2011). The inconsistent Irish response to inequality, then, is less a marker of deviance, and more a predictable communal complacency with social arrangements that have been successfully normalized by the state and industry. O'Toole's concern over the debilitating legacy of shame resulting from institutional oppression in Ireland, however, does point to the reality of shared trauma and the propensity for victims to deflect that trauma further down the hierarchy of societal membership. Frustratingly, as Marx feared, deflection is more likely to manifest than solidarity (LeDuff 2000).

Throughout this book, I have emphasized the economic influence over human relations with other animals as consistent with the vegan socialist theories of Nibert (2003) and Torres (2007). Ireland's current malaise, linked as it is to earlier colonialist insults and the speciesism Britain would institutionalize there, supports this assertion. The diet of Ireland's populace from prehistory until modernization in the twentieth century was largely plant-based. This vegetarianism increased under colonialism as animal products were shipped to England and became much too expensive for Ireland's poor. Recall that the versatility of the potato would be responsible for an incredible increase in the Irish population in the eighteenth and nineteenth centuries, but this reliance also created extreme vulnerability in the context of colonialism and environmental unpredictability. As one historian describes it, "The collapse of Ireland's population along with the potato crops only emphasizes how important a lacto-vegetarian diet was to most Irish people" (Cotter 1996). Given this history, it is strange that Ireland's dietary heritage is today eclipsed by stereotypes of flesh eating, as the relationship between plant-based consumption and Ireland's political and economic trajectory is so strong.

The encroachment of famine in the nineteenth century led to the animalization of poor persons who were reduced to scavenging and were often scavenged by other animals themselves. British elites, whose market policies had created the economic devastation, looked at the collapse of Ireland's peasantry as a matter of evolution (Clarkson and Crawford 2001). The Irish species had simply overpopulated and strained its ecosystem, leading to a very natural crash. The extreme poverty of this era also saw a swelling in Irish insane asylums (Finnane 1981). Hundreds of destitute and desperate individuals and families abused the system by forcing inmate admittance on the pretext that an individual was "dangerous." This only aggravated the tendency to animalize persons with mental disabilities. In America, medical institutions also targeted the Irish, primarily in vivisecting and dissecting their bodies for research purposes. Britain, meanwhile, shipped Irish subjects to the colonies by the thousands as chattel to breed and build the Empire (O'Callaghan 2000). Only through animalization could the mass incarceration of Irish women and men in asylums be justified. Only through animalization could Irish immigrants in Britain and America be denied political access and funneled into backbreaking, underpaid, and often coerced employment. Only through animalization could the coerced emigration to Australia and Barbados be rationalized.

This process extends beyond the horrors of colonization. Patriarchy also deploys speciesism in animalizing women and girls to justify their unequal status. Irish women and girls were systematically underfed and overburdened with heavy farm labor that dramatically reduced their lifespans. Unwed women fared even worse. Thousands upon thousands of "sinful," "lustful," and "unruly" mothers who had failed to follow civilized conventions of sex and marriage were institutionalized and forced to perform years of unpaid labor for the Catholic Church (a practice that persisted well into the 1990s). An untold number of women, girls, toddlers, and infants died as a result of the brutal conditions; many were buried in unmarked mass graves. Some, like those perishing in the Tuam home, were interred in a septic tank as literal waste. Likewise, the ideological categorization of racial and ethnic minorities as apes, monkeys, dogs, pigs, and vermin was a powerful psychological mechanism for subverting trans-species fellowship within a conflict-based hierarchical system. Animalization is a timeworn technique for the maintenance of structural violence in a colonial or postcolonial space in which the subjugated population is limited in its ability to access basic needs for a healthful and equitable life. Less frequently acknowledged is the experience of Nonhuman Animals, whose oppression serves only as a referent. So long as the cultural supports that normalize discrimination against Nonhuman Animals remain intact, these supports will be available for malevolent application to other vulnerable groups (Adams 2000; Ko and Ko 2017). The solution to human suffering, therefore, is not to emphasize the humanity of Irish persons who have been animalized over the centuries, but to instead emphasize their *personhood* and shared oppression. When humans abandon their animality, this ensures its continued stigmatization. It also maintains a hierarchy of worth by allowing humans to rise in status by demeaning or domineering others.

Indeed, entangled experiences are not simply an ideological or symbolic matter, but manifest readily in the material world as well. The modernization of Ireland and the changing role of agrarianism has posed a challenge to humans and nonhumans alike. As discussed in chapter 5, farming is increasingly centralized and industrialized. As a result, free-living nonhumans have suffered numerous population crashes, particularly ocean dwellers, and this devastation has all but destroyed "fishing" communities. Another consequence is the disappearance of Nonhuman Animals, like certain hounds or horses, who were once purpose bred for managing farms and are no longer deemed valuable. Free-living species who are accused of interfering with agricultural production, too, are rapidly eradicated by increasingly effective technology.

These intersecting oppressions are only poised to increase in severity and impact, as globalization has introduced new ideas, technologies, and dangers. Most notably, it has concentrated power and production to the effect of rendering community governance and sustainable practices impotent. Furthermore, the spread of capitalist ideology through the world system has encouraged the elimination of trade restrictions and subsequently locked former colonies in a dependence on global markets that disproportionately benefit former colonizing nations (Hoogvelt 2001). The consequences are countless. Intensified global relationships have allowed for the introduction of new parasites that are killing native Nonhuman Animals such as bees, while zoonotic diseases seep across borders and "invasive" species introduced by increased contact with faraway places displace squirrels, fishes, shellfishes, and other animals (Fogarty 2017). Agricultural workers, meanwhile, are subject to worsening labor conditions as the pressure to cut costs increases their work hours, decreases their pay, and undermines their dignity. Of concern to consumers, the quality and content of animal products have become questionable. Stretched and deepened by globalization, modern food chains are increasingly complex and difficult to monitor for consistent and ethical production (Carolan 2011). The COVID-19 outbreak brought into stark relief how truly vulnerable animal-based food systems are, with Nonhuman Animals and "meat"-packing employees (most of whom are marginalized immigrants) especially hard hit (Hilliard 2020). The status of Nonhuman Animals thus holds considerable relevance throughout all levels of Irish society. Because speciesism serves as a lynchpin in Ireland's material conditions, efforts to eradicate speciesism can only stir waves of positive change for humans and nonhumans alike.

Irish Vegan Ethics

Recall Wright's (2015) observation that a nation's identity is shaped by its relationship to animal food. This has only been heightened in an era dominated by intensified global connectivity and the moral panic of terrorism. Veganism, in particular, is frequently scorned as an act of domestic terrorism. Wright further notes that the foods associated with veganism, such as falafel, soy, tofu, or tempeh, threaten this national identity as they evoke non-Western spaces occupied by "others." Britain's exit from the European Union testifies to growing uneasiness with globalization. Many traditionally homogenous societies like Britain fear infiltration by "others," and predictably so, as racism and ethnocentrism contribute to a false consciousness as to the true root of inequality (a capitalist system) and are thus strategically employed by state and industry as diversionary measures. Veganism is easily swept into this nationalistic discourse, becoming code for nonwhite, non-Western foreignness. Because Ireland's identity has been bound for so long to its exportation of "beef," dairy, and other animal products, anything that threatens this practice is liable to be viewed as inherently anti-Irish.

While Ireland currently has no intention of leaving the EU, being as it is well over 90 percent white and heavily committed to animal-based agriculture, Wright's work suggests that veganism in Ireland may be interpreted as a threat to national security. Sometimes this association is explicit. In an 98FM Dublin radio interview with Go Vegan World founder Sandra

Higgins, for instance, a sheep "farmer" called in to accuse her of trying to "shut down the whole country" and suggested that she was in alliance with ISIS (Dublin's 98FM 2015). Callers on other radio interviews have emphasized the anti-Irishness of veganism by evoking the importance of animal-based agriculture to Irish culture, landscape, and heritage (Higgins 2017). When Taoiseach Leo Varadkar announced a personal interest in reducing his animal product consumption for reasons of sustainability, he was met with shrill protest by farmers accusing him of being vegan and acting against the interests of Ireland (*Thejournal.ie* 2019b). Again, this Irish speciesism is more constructed than indigenous. Modern Ireland's carnivorous identity is a result of government and industry campaigning to normalize and encourage speciesist consumption in response to Britain's influence. As Nibert (2003) emphasizes, the state is heavily vested in speciesism and may reconstruct or obscure any history adverse to its economic interests. Vegans are the butter witches of the modern day, an untrusted feminine force interfering with the livelihood of "farmers."

Yet, while Ireland may be an island, it does not exist in a vacuum. More than homegrown, Ireland's culture is also *globally* grown. Its intermingling with various invaders, traders, and immigrants has created a culture more diverse in values than is commonly acknowledged. Globalization's transferal of culture and capital has entrenched speciesism, but it has also created awareness to alternatives. Observes the *Irish Times*:

> Being vegan in Ireland where beef and dairy are our largest industries has long been dismissed as a crank sport, a barely noticeable blip on the chart. But we've come a long way in a short time. You no longer have to go into a health food shop smelling of patchouli oil to find oat and almond milk. (Cleary 2017)

Ireland has absorbed concerns about the healthfulness and environmental impact of animal-based consumption, while it has, in turn, played an important role in the formation of the Western Nonhuman Animal rights movement. Indeed, it continues to participate with its own indigenous contributions to vegan and anti-speciesist activism today. As this book has emphasized, Ireland exhibits a greater anti-speciesism consciousness than it is generally given credit for. The popularly held notions that Ireland is comparatively backward in its treatment of other animals or that Irish culture is somehow antithetical to veganism rely on centuries-old classist and ethnic stereotypes that were successfully employed in the suppression of Irish civil rights.

There are pockets of anti-speciesist activism that bring renewed attention to nonviolent, plant-based eating and alternative economies. Comparatively few Irish families remain in the Nonhuman Animal "farming" business, and, of those that do, even fewer can rely on the exploitation of Nonhuman Animals as a primary source of income (Tovey 2000). The status and power once associated with "farming" other animals is being eroded in the wake of urbanization. As animal-based agriculture becomes increasingly concentrated under the jurisdiction of large corporations, Irish "farmers" must look elsewhere for survival. Ireland's quickly expanding mushroom and kelp sectors have been identified as potentially relevant to increasing interest in vegetarianism, while vegan alternatives are becoming more and more familiar to Irish grocery stores and restaurants. Sales of avocado (a popular alternative source of fat that could be grown indoors in Ireland) increased by nearly 100 percent between 2013 and 2018. Likewise, plant milk sales increased by 66 percent (over fourteen million packs of the product sold in 2017) (Cleary 2017). Quinoa, which can be grown in Ireland, has also been recommended, given its popularity and nutritional completeness (Armstrong 2015). Irish farmers would be wise to invest. It is predicted that plant-based proteins will claim a third of the market by 2054 as the world's protein needs and environmental pressures only continue to increase (Lux Research 2015). Even without the benefit of state subsidies, a move from animal-based agriculture would be strategic.

The rich variety of Nonhuman Animal welfare and rights organizations that work across the country likewise speak to another side of Irish identity, one that is less about "meat and potatoes" and more in line with contemporary social justice efforts. Growing political and cultural interest in multiculturalism is poised to advance the cause. That is, vegans are increasingly recognized as a minority group with unique and valid interests that should be recognized by the state. The Vegetarian Society of Ireland has begun inquiry into extending the interpretation of anti-discrimination laws in the Irish Constitution and the European Convention on Human Rights to include vegans (M. O'Sullivan 2014). Meanwhile, the media campaigns of the radical grassroots group Go Vegan World have become so attention-grabbing and resonant that British and American charities have begun to emulate their claimsmaking.[1] Irish animal agriculturalists have also voiced their fears that vegan campaigning has been disrupting youth recruitment (Fox 2019). There are reasons to be hopeful for Nonhuman Animals and their human allies in Ireland.

Advances in reducing dog and cat homelessness offer another significant example of positive change. While Ireland is currently the center of "puppy milling" in Europe, it also has a remarkably low kill rate for homeless dogs. According to the Department of Housing, Planning and Local Government (2016), only 1,500 dogs were killed for want of rehoming in 2016, just 12 percent of the total individuals impounded (Hackett 2017). This is still an extremely low number compared to previous years. A decade ago, the overwhelming majority of dogs entering "shelters" (approximately 25,000–30,000 individuals) were killed. This relief has been made possible by neutering and educational campaigns. There is reason to expect that Ireland will become completely "no kill" in the future.

The continued existence of "breeding" for racing purposes, however, impedes this goal. The Irish state encourages the increased "breeding" of greyhounds by subsidizing the "racing" industry, and rescue shelters report that they are receiving greyhound surrenders at numbers disproportionate to other breeds. In their short lives, they are subject to horrific institutional violence, such as doping and beatings, not unlike that which was experienced by dogs in the nineteenth-century "fighting" industry (Hackett 2017). According to RTÉ, 16,000 greyhounds are "bred" in Ireland each year, about 6,000 of whom are "culled" due to slowness (*Thejournal.ie* 2019c). The country's love of "racing" has prevented the campaign to end canine homelessness from reaching its full potential, but there are signs that the "racing" industry is coming to an end. Despite large government subsidies to support the "sport," lack of attendance is threatening the closure of some facilities (Cosgrove 2017). Likewise, Ireland has also joined in the global push to ban Nonhuman Animal use in circuses. Hurting Nonhuman Animals is no longer the entertainment it once was.

Despite these victories, using Nonhuman Animals for food remains a formidable barrier to achieving a vegan society. Despite calls for Ireland to reduce its greenhouse gas emissions, these emissions continue to rise due to its heavy reliance on animal-based agriculture. Recall that the Department of Agriculture's (2018) Food Wise program hopes to increase food exports (primarily "meat" and dairy) by €19 billion before 2025, but the state is already on track to receive an EU fine for its high emissions in 2020 (K. O'Sullivan 2017). Reeling from the economic crash and the pinch of austerity, the state may, nevertheless, be willing to take the hit and absorb EU fines as a cost of business.

The problem is that, after several thousand years of dairying and "meat" production, the Irish economy has become path dependent on the exploitation of Nonhuman Animals, and the ability to introduce truly sustainable and nonviolent agricultural practices is greatly limited (Tovey 2000, 2007). Varadkar's support for lowered "meat" consumption drew strong condemnation from Dáil members, particularly those hailing from rural regions who cited the importance of animal-based agriculture to farming communities and the wellbeing of the nation (O'Halloran 2019). The DAFM (2018), furthermore, is deeply committed to supporting and expanding "meat" and dairy production.

Even potential governmental challengers to this speciesist economy are reluctant to take on animal-based agriculture. In a personal correspondence, the Green Party spokesperson for Agriculture and for Animal Welfare, Pippa Hackett, communicated that "animal welfare" only refers to the "humane" treatment of Nonhuman Animals on route to slaughter. The Green Party indicates an interest in plant-based eating, but only for matters of environmentalism, explicitly avoiding veganism as a matter of ethics. Other European countries have already begun experimentation with nonanimal forms of protein and textile production, and there is no reason that Ireland might not investigate the same. Over 90 percent of Ireland's arable land is currently used for animal-based agriculture (O'Mara 2008), suggesting that the elimination of even a small portion would provide ample space to support the production of plant-based alternatives. If the Green Party, however, cannot even commit to the promotion of veganism and allies itself with animal-based agriculture, it is unlikely that the systemic change necessary to curtail violence against the environment and nonhuman communities, both domesticated and free-living, will be achieved anytime soon, at least through institutional channels.

Ireland's agricultural decisions are not independently made, however. They are instead shaped heavily by EU regulations. While the EU has pressured Ireland to reduce its emissions, it also paradoxically subsidizes animal-based agriculture, thereby artificially increasing the production and consumption of animal products. A Greenpeace (2019) report, for example, finds that approximately one fifth of the EU's total budget is injected into animal-based agriculture. The end of 2019, meanwhile, witnessed an eruption in violent "farmer" protests regarding mass layoffs in the Irish "meat" industry and plummeting prices for animal products. Rather than address the fundamental unsustainability of animal production, protestors targeted giant European retailers such as Aldi and Tesco with repeated blockades, eventually prompting the government to form a "beef taskforce" to appease them (Bowers 2019).

Even if these barriers were to be overcome, there remains a danger in placing too much stock in plant-based alternatives to exploitative animal-based production. Chapter 5 considered that a move to vegan agriculture would not ensure equality so long as capitalist structures remained intact. For instance, the mushroom sector, one of the largest horticultural industries in Ireland, is perhaps well positioned to provide a healthy source of protein and nutrients to replace "meat." Yet, while the mushroom industry may spare vulnerable Nonhuman Animals, it horribly exploits vulnerable immigrant women, many of whom are from racial or ethnic minorities. In response to these issues, many vegan scholars advocate the consolidation of Nonhuman Animal ethics with anthropocentric food justice efforts (Harper 2010; Wrenn 2016). Irish food producers would thus need to take into consideration these deeper connections should plant-based eating continue to grow in popularity. No food product, be it "meat" or mushroom, can be said to be cruelty-free so long as its production relies on exploitation and coercion.

Looking Forward

Respecting differences and achieving liberation is, of course, easier said than done. So deeply embedded is speciesism in the fabric of Irish culture and its landscape, it will be difficult to dislodge. EU regulations may represent progress in terms of sustainability and Nonhuman Animal welfare, but enforcement will remain insufficient so long as it retains the weak confederal approach that relegates policy implementation to the local (B. Flynn 2009). Irish agriculturalists require and receive considerable state subsidies before considering any sort of compliance, but funding is in general inconsistent. As Ireland presses forward into modernity with ever-increasing demands on production, consumption, and resource extraction, the capitalist agendas of the elite are sure to conflict with the necessities for nonhuman survival and well-being. Nibert (2003) and Torres (2007), recall, are highly skeptical that a capitalist world system can respect the dignity and autonomy of Nonhuman Animals given their vulnerability to exploitation and the profitability to be derived from their bodies and labor. Rather than address systemic inequalities, environmental and economic policies alike ensure that Nonhuman Animals will absorb the brunt of capitalist pressure. Efforts to deal with concerns over climate change are invariably undermined by the state's insistence on protecting animal-based agriculture. "Meat," milk, eggs, and other animal products are not necessary for human consumption; they are only *desired* for human consumption. Climate change is teetering on a point of no return with loss of biodiversity, changes to the ocean chemistry, extreme temperatures, and increasingly frequent "natural" disasters, while Ireland, like other countries, is paradoxically investing its energies in *increasing* animal-based agriculture, one of the largest and most expendable contributors to climate change. This is not a sustainable path.

The sector's growth seemingly recognizes no limits. Having saturated domestic markets, Ireland and other Western countries with animal-based economies now reach out to Asia. China has subsequently become a major consumer of Irish dairy even though Asian populations are predominantly lactose intolerant and soy milk has been traditionally consumed in preference to animal milk. The introduction of Western diets is already wreaking havoc on human health in these countries (Campbell and Campbell 2006). The live export of cows and other animals to Middle Eastern countries and Turkey also helps to buoy industry growth. The few EU welfare standards that are in place to regulate the "meat" trade, furthermore, are systematically breached (O'Brien 2017c). Some have called for these victims to be killed in Ireland to ensure better standards, but "farmers" rely on export so as to avoid domestic processing plants, which offer low returns. Unfortunately for nonhuman "commodities," even fewer policymakers advocate for a switch to a truly humane, plant-based production system.

Potential is found in the EU's increasing attention to welfare regulations in response to public criticism and zoonotic outbreaks. The European Food Safety Authority launched in 2002 in an attempt to trace food supply chains and provide transparency. Its Welfare Quality project aims to monitor the well-being of Nonhuman Animals and validate often misleading industry rhetoric (Miele and Lever 2013). Welfare regulations are inevitably leveraged to legitimize exploitative operations that, regardless of standards, necessitate the separation of mothers from babies, genetic modification, restricted movement, and eventual slaughter. Despite the project's commendable goals, welfare alterations are ultimately limited in their ability to relieve the suffering of Nonhuman Animals, designed as they are to maintain and protect the food industry from consumer pressure and public scrutiny. Indeed, sociologist Matthew Cole (2011) applies Foucauldian theory to suggest that the seemingly animal-centered rise in welfare standards for food animals is an exercise in "pastoral" state and industry power that manipulates public knowledge and guides the population to align with the speciesist interests of animal-based agriculture. Stănescu (2010) furthers this point in his observation that sustainability rhetoric also works to protect animal-based agricultural interests by masking the heavy environmental and ethical costs inherent in "raising," using, and killing other animals.

Relationships with free-living animals further expose these inconsistencies. Consider the reintroduction of species that were wiped out of Ireland to protect agricultural interests. Their right to life depends entirely on their profitability. Efforts to reintroduce golden eagles, for instance, rely heavily on claims related to their ability to attract tourism (Golden Eagle Trust n.d.). Given that capitalist exploitation has been at the root of environmental destruction and violence against other animals, it remains questionable how well a framework based on financial profitability will facilitate restoration efforts. For that matter, "wildlife" agencies have suggested killing foxes to make room for eagles (Woodworth 2016a), signifying that anthroparchy remains the baseline for environmental decision-making.

Consider also gull populations, which have dropped by 90 percent due to habitat destruction and collapsing populations of fishes (D. Griffin 2017). Despite such devastatingly lowered numbers, they are labeled as disease-spreading nuisances as they encroach into human spaces scavenging for survival. In a pattern that has been familiar in human society, gulls are perceived to breach the superficial boundary between humans and other animals by brazenly encroaching into human habitats, thus necessitating measures of human control to preserve the hierarchy (Carr and Reyes-Galindo 2017). Reframing them as pests has justified the disruption of seagull nests and persistent calls for "culling." Consequently, the "green Ireland" motif that launched Irish agriculture into the global market appears to be complacent with global trends in environmental destruction. What (or, in this case, *who*) exactly is determined to be worth "sustaining" and "conserving" is ultimately based on human economic wants. Although there has been great progress in Irish environmental ethics, the general response to handling conflicting human and nonhuman interests is to eradicate or contain nonhumans.

Badgers, too, have come under fire due to similar accusations of endangering humans and industry. Specifically, they are targeted for spreading tuberculosis to cows. Although the Irish Wildlife Trust has contested the targeting of badgers as vectors of the disease and tuberculosis continues unabated in spite of the cull, the killing of badgers has persisted since the 1980s. Indeed, the killing increased dramatically after official sanctioning in 2001, despite life-saving badger vaccinations, which are now available (Woodworth 2016b). These vaccinations have been shown to be more effective and are more popular with the public (McCulloch and Reiss 2017), yet, in support of animal-based agriculture, the state pours several millions of euros into the mass killing each year. It is unclear if badger populations will survive the onslaught. The same "cull" has been underway in Britain as well, but the number of British badgers impacted is significantly lower, given the groundswell of activist protest. In Ireland, there appears to be some reluctance to interfere with the state's agricultural agenda. As explored in chapter 4, it is difficult to attribute this to a cultural aversion to protest, particularly as Ireland is a leader in anti-globalization resistance. Indeed, it would presumably be of interest to those protesting against austerity that the Irish state invests so heavily in the morally and scientifically reprehensible persecution of badgers while Ireland's economic turmoil has been used as justification for severe cuts to social services.

IRELAND INTERNATIONAL

The ramifications of Britain's 2016 vote to exit from the European Union could complicate these agricultural strains on the environment, Nonhuman Animals, and vulnerable human communities. Government officials fear that Brexit's influence on the Irish food industry is a threat comparable to that experienced during the isolationist turmoil of the post-independence era in the 1930s (O'Brien 2017b). Following the vote, a major UK supermarket chain, the Co-operative, launched a "British Only" "beef" campaign to capitalize on Britain's cultural discomfort with multiculturalism and desire for independence from its European neighbors (Moran 2017). This isolationist move is predicted to be replicated by other grocers. Here, animal nationalism surfaces again as cows become politicized objects. The Co-op specifically cites the "soaring" influx of foreign flesh from European countries and the desire to support British farmers as motivation for its bid to supply "British Only." The Irish Farmer's Association has reason to worry, as €1.65 billion in cows' flesh is shipped from Ireland to the United Kingdom each year. It is *possible* that this could reduce the number of cows born into oppression and relieve the enormous environmental strain caused by this practice. More likely, the suffering of Irish cows bound for British markets will only be replaced by British cows. For other supermarkets seeking cheaper deals, victims' bodies could be shipped in from Brazil. All animals entering the UK as food are liable to especially horrific deaths since the Tory government negotiating Britain's exit voted down EU slaughter regulations, which were based on a recognition of nonhuman sentience. The future of welfare regulation there is unclear (Gove 2017).

"Pet" and entertainment industries have globalized as well. Irish greyhounds have become increasingly popular exports to Asian countries, where they will be "raced." Unlike in Ireland, where racing castoffs are at least given a chance at adoption before meeting with "euthanasia" (McMahon 2017), China processes them in slaughterhouses for "meat." For a country that loves its dogs, this practice has mobilized substantial protest, putting pressure on the Department of Agriculture to cease export to Asia (Pollak 2017). Campaigns of this nature highlight the increasing complexity of combatting speciesism in a globalized market, but they also denote the potential for anti-cruelty efforts to bolster racist ideologies in a white-dominant society made anxious by new connections to new cultures.

Not unrelated, Ireland harbors a massive puppy mill industry, producing thirty to forty thousand dogs every year, mostly for export under cruel conditions (Lillington 2016; O'Halloran 2017). As with any variant of intensive animal-based agriculture, puppy mills are extremely oppressive and have been under severe scrutiny elsewhere in the West. Irish legislation was in enacted in 2012 to ban these mills, but laws remain unenforced. Furthermore, "hunters" who desire the availability of "hunting" breeds to fuel their industry continue to lobby against any interference with their canine "breeding" operations (P. Donnelly 2016). "Farmers," too, rely on puppy "milling" for supplementary income, making anti-"breeding" efforts politically dangerous for lawmakers. The ISPCA, AFAR, and other activists thus face an uphill battle in promoting a culture of adoption over the more established logic of growth.

Recall that thousands of horses are born, raised, and trained for racing in Ireland as well. Castoffs of the racing industry strain equine welfare organizations and populate slaughterhouses (Collins et al. 2008). In a recurring theme, the romanticization of Ireland's past preserves exploitative practices while masking the violence against Nonhuman Animals that is inherent in the system. As with greyhounds, thousands of horses are shipped to China, where they fuel the Asian "racing" industry (*Irish Times* 2017a). Horses also fuel the global food system. The complexities of food production and distribution in such a system make it very difficult to monitor and control the food chain, given that consumer items are increasingly pieced together from a variety of sources across a variety of countries. To the dismay of Irish consumers who primarily relate to horses as "pets" and laborers who are not to be eaten, in 2013, tests found that Irish "beef" products could contain as much as 29 percent horses' flesh (mostly horses from Spain and Portugal) (*Irish Times* 2017b). The scandal led to the arrest of dozens of people, and yet the killing of Irish horses for human consumption in other countries remains standard practice. Indeed, it is made necessary by incessant "breeding," which produces more horses than can be cared for and rampant abandonment of those who are no longer fit to "race," pull, or plow. More than a thousand years after the cultural negotiations between Christians and pagans over the status of horses, hippophagy continues to create unease by disturbing carefully constructed boundaries and hierarchies between and amongst human and nonhuman groups.

Welfare initiatives are seriously challenged in their ability to curtail this mass oppression. In addition to the profits garnered from sponsorships, betting, and licensing, the "racing" of horses and greyhounds receives millions of euros in state funding in hopes of attracting tourists and further domestic engagement. State support and superficial welfare reforms are critical in their ability to legitimize and perpetuate these speciesist practices. Although the 2016 budget increased funding for Nonhuman Animal welfare organizations by 27 percent, to €2.7 million, it allocated €74 million for horse and greyhound "racing" (Gleeson 2015), thus ensuring the continued treadmill of dog and horse production from racetrack to slaughterhouse. While the rest of the Western world is gradually moving away from entertainment industries that exploit Nonhuman Animals, Ireland (although it has turned away from circuses) is determined to increase its reliance on "racetracks." Furthermore, while other countries have introduced bans on the killing of foxes, deers, and other animals, Ireland remains open for business, attracting foreign tourists who find sport in killing. Deers and hares are protected species, and yet they remain as legal targets. Colonialism's legacy of dependency and economic insecurity undoubtedly accounts for this persistent but profitable speciesism.

The temptation to provide an outpost catering to vice banned elsewhere is too great, given the potential profits to be realized. Other countries have resisted welfare trends in order to attract tourists as well, such as Cuba and its steadfast protection of "cockfighting," and Spain with its notorious "bullfighting." Unfortunately, as tourism increases in economic importance, traditional Irish culture has been commodified such that stereotypes about "old Ireland" are reified and the very self-image of Irish citizens begins to bend to these romanticized and otherized constructions (Kneafsey 1998). Tourism provides an important source of resilience and independence in a globalizing market, but the continuity in culture it necessitates is poised to protect speciesist practices that have become emblematic of Ireland in the global imagination. That said, ritualized violence against Nonhuman Animals is notoriously conflated with national identity in Spain, and, yet, "bullfighting" has been gradually losing favor with the Spanish, particularly among women, younger persons, and urbanites (María et al. 2017). There is no reason to believe that Ireland cannot also be influenced by strengthening anti-speciesist values and move away from "hunting," "racing," and other problematic traditions.

For the time being, Nonhuman Animals remain objectified in the process of Ireland's entry into the industrializing global market. This objectification frequently relates to the symbolic role that Nonhuman Animals serve in Irish culture and, predictably, leads to widespread suffering. By way of another example, Ireland has been slow to monitor the trade in exotic species. Following the economic collapse that began in 2008, snakes (purchased as status symbols on an island where snakes are not native) were abandoned in large numbers (Chozick 2013). The plight of horses, however, is especially puzzling, given that horses have become a mascot of Irishness. If national identity is so bound to them, how is it that horses continue to be exploited and killed at such alarming rates? Culturally, there is some awareness of this contradiction. Several films produced during the economic boom, for instance, used horses to metaphorically represent marginalized groups who were made vulnerable and dislocated by modernity and industrialization. The real-life abandonment and slaughter of horses provided rich allegory. As media studies scholar Maria Pramaggiore (2015) observes, it was not coincidental that the use of horses in cinematic storytelling coincided with the horse "meat" scandal of the era. The adulteration of food chains not only disturbed the fragile species barrier that humans had created to legitimize their dominant position; it also drew attention to the social precariousness facilitated by rapidly changing global relations.

Pigs, too, have become metaphors for Ireland's struggling transition into the modern global system. Recall that Irish people were frequently depicted as pigs in the nineteenth and early twentieth centuries, given their agricultural lifestyle and purported love of pigs' flesh. These depictions resonated with stereotypes of Irish persons as dirty, ignorant, and in need of tending. Pigs were a class marker of subsistence living. Because the Irish immigrants were seen to be stressing their host countries with demands for rights and resources, portraying them as pigs was all too easy, for, like pigs are also stereotyped, they were perceived as greedy. With the EU's post-recession bailout, this trope would be revisited. Consider, for instance, the acronym "PIIGS," which was designated by market analysts as shorthand for the countries receiving this assistance (Portugal, Ireland, Italy, Greece, and Spain). Like the porcine Irish of a century earlier, indebted Ireland is once again portrayed as wanton, uncontrolled, and overconsuming (Townsend

2015). In late 2017, a document leak confirmed the existence of offshore tax havens that redirected wealth for Irish elites. This roused even greater criticism from some EU leaders who were already resentful of Ireland's heavy use of handouts. In the eyes of its old colonizers, Ireland was still a bit of a pigsty.

New Movements

European governance and Asian markets increasingly dictate the nature of Ireland's economy, but social movements, too, can be inspired by global connection. Sociologists have identified "new" movements as a phenomenon of postindustrial societies in which citizenship is more or less established. New social movements are increasingly transnational, democratic in governance, and interested in the politics of identity and daily life (Johnston 1994). For the Irish, now independent from Britain and relatively secure in their citizenship, broad-reaching agendas related to culture and lifestyle can be entertained. Ireland's environmentalism and Nonhuman Animal rights efforts have been fueled and supported by other organizations and activists in Europe and America, for instance, and, like other new movements, they are characterized by a grassroots, community focus. This type of resistance avoids the bureaucratic entanglements of professionalized charities and the frustrating compromises associated with slow moving governmental agencies and policies (Wrenn 2019).

Yet, there are costs and risks to this informal style. The near collapse of the Animal Rights Action Network in 2015, following the retirement of its leader, made clear the tenuousness of mobilization outside of institutionalized channels. Likewise, grassroots efforts that focus mainly on educating the public often do little to effect policy. The Vegan Information Project, for instance, which tables outside of Trinity College and Temple Bar almost every weekend, come rain or shine, brings an explicitly vegan message to thousands of passersby, but has otherwise failed to operationalize this agenda through legislation or policy. This disconnection may not be for want of trying. Grassroots activists find themselves regularly excluded from professional social change entities (Wrenn 2019). For instance, activists working to advance protection for free-living Nonhuman Animals and the wild spaces in which they live have been encumbered by a classist devaluing of their expertise and knowledge (Tovey 2007). Their failure to incorporate into the now standard professionalized structure becomes a liability. The modern social change arena has absorbed capitalism's logic of rationalization and expansion, corporatizing activism and thus rendering invisible any and all activists who lack capital and clout. To maintain visibility, charities are under extreme pressure to prioritize economic growth, and this is only made possible by a dilution of goals to appeal to the widest possible funding audience. Grassroots activism, while delegitimized by the social movement sector, becomes an important holdout of radical values.

Grassroots activism also melds well with an Irish culture that values community and is rightly wary of large state institutions. Local collaboration within communities has been extremely successful for collective action on behalf of free-living species such as seals, dolphins, and whales, for instance (Tovey 2007). The sense of "doing one's bit" and having a direct involvement with social justice efforts is motivating and rewarding. Unfortunately, grassroots collectives are also highly vulnerable to co-optation by professionalized organizations (Wrenn 2019). For instance, the Vegan Society in Britain has repeatedly capitalized on the hype created by Ireland's Go Vegan World campaigning to forward its own agenda, thus starving Go Vegan World of much needed media attention and resources. According to Go Vegan World's founder, other foreign organizations have usurped its imagery and frames for their own use as well.

Inequities may exist in media representation of vegan campaigns, yet the representation is in and of itself notable. *Newstalk*, one of Ireland's more influential radio stations, consistently airs interviews with vegans and other anti-speciesist activists, ensuring that the interests of Nonhuman Animals receive a good deal more coverage and attention than would be expected in a country so dependent upon animal agriculture. This media coverage is vital for movement success. Most social movements find themselves completely ignored or badly misrepresented in media spaces (Gamson 1995), but, if granted fair coverage, this exposure can be a great boon given the potential to challenge public opinion and attract resources. The twentieth-century Irish feminist movement, for example, small though it was in its founding years, strategically exploited media connections to bring the feminist agenda to the Irish consciousness (Stopper 2006). A handful of women, some of whom were journalists themselves, were able to bring great change in a deeply conservative culture through consistent, attention-grabbing newspaper and television spots. The Irish gay rights movement also credits these sympathetic media connections for its ability to advance its aims (P. Ryan 2004). There is reason to predict that the vegan movement's consistent media representation will help turn the tide for nonhumans in Ireland. Not all are convinced, of course. Vegan journalist Frank Armstrong (2017) points to the "livestock"-industrial complex as a major barrier to fair coverage of speciesism, given agricultural influence over media, politics, scientific research, and nutritional advice. He also notes that the more graphic injustices enacted on food animals are almost completely unreported in Irish journalism (2016). Industry countermovement activity has also pushed (unsuccessfully) to revoke vegan campaigning based on a claim of false advertising (Bird 2017).

Grassroots activism is locally oriented, but it is not isolationist. Increasingly, local communities have also become global communities. Like agriculturalists, activists are also influenced by transnational links (J. Smith 2004). After all, not all of Ireland's problems are unique to it. Many are instead linked to wider global processes. A recognition of shared oppression and global solidarity is a consciousness that will be necessary to finally shift structures of inequality. Indeed, Cox (2006) has emphasized that the groundswell in Irish protest has resulted from a crisis in capitalist hegemony and the government's difficulty in garnering consent and legitimacy from the citizenry. Grassroots collectives, he insists, have real potential to restructure society to a more equitable form.

Final Thoughts

A postcolonial nation, Ireland has witnessed many centuries of oppression. As this book has outlined, this inequality has been exacerbated by speciesism. With animal agriculture introduced and protected as the primary industry under colonialist and postcolonialist capitalist economies, the suffering of Nonhuman Animals increased alongside that of the Irish peasantry. The plant-based lifestyles and knowledges that were once familiar to Gaelic Ireland gave way to modern systems of oppression that normalized violence against the poor, women, ethnic minorities, immigrants, persons with disabilities, and other vulnerable human groups via the more fundamental domination of Nonhuman Animals. Animalization was an important mechanism in creating the boundaries that separated the privileged from the oppressed and normalized inequality, not just in Ireland, but also the Irish living abroad in England, America, and Australia. In fact, animalization has been observed as a foundational theme to systems of inequality across the globe. In highlighting the physical, cognitive, moral, and spiritual differences between humans and other animals, privileged groups are able to normalize hierarchies of worth and disparities in resource allocation. Given how closely associated Nonhuman Animals are with ideas of evolutionary creation and biological difference, human-nonhuman boundaries help to naturalize inequality based on these variables. Once inequality is rendered "natural," furthermore, it is highly resistant to criticism.

These old animal-based mechanisms of difference and oppression have not devalued over time but have only persisted as a highly resonant means of structural maintenance in a modern world in which civil rights are both expected *and* challenged by processes of globalization. The manifesting crisis of climate change and concerns with Nonhuman Animal welfare have spawned considerable social movement protest that is now reaching the broader public and policymakers alike. For the most part, however, the Irish economy has only responded by reframing inherently detrimental and violent agricultural practices as "sustainable," patriotic, and "humane." Modern Ireland now finds itself in the difficult position of continued dependence on foreign markets at a time in which animal-based agriculture is evidenced to be exceedingly risky.

Not far in the background, however, Irish resistance continues to gather strength, emboldened by an anti-speciesist ethic as old as the Celts but intensified by the provocations of colonial oppression and postcolonial dependencies. Nineteenth-century activists understood that the injustice imposed on Nonhuman Animals resulted from larger systems of oppression that subjugated marginalized humans and that speciesism actually worsened the condition of these humans. The Irish vegan movement developing today builds on the legacy of these early connections by challenging the entrenchment of speciesism within the context of modern postcolonialism, austerity, and globalization. Uprooting several centuries of human and nonhuman oppression will be no easy task, but the robust spirit of Irish protest gives reason to hope that change will be forthcoming. Aph Ko reminds that, freedom means "drowning out the internal voice of our oppressor and reclaiming the elements of our natural selves that once were (and unfortunately still are) seen as the colonizer's property" (2019, 111). What might a postcolonial Ireland look like if it were truly independent of Britain?

Like Gulliver, it behooves us to be a bit adventurous and imagine alternative relations with other animals. In doing so, we might also take a cue from Marx. Marx argued that social change was achieved through conflict over the mode of production (Marx and Engels [1848] 1962). If his theory holds weight, to make real social change for Nonhuman Animals and other marginalized groups, the speciesist capitalist economy must be upturned in favor of a more equitable, power-sharing, and humane society. In its commitment to social justice and potential to inform an entirely new economic mode of production, veganism offers a means to such an end. In a vegan world, we can fulfill Marx's dream of reconnecting with our species-being, that which makes us human. I argue that what it means to be human is not to dominate other animals, but rather to live alongside them cooperatively. This cooperative living might take place within an egalitarian society in which other animals are *also* free to return to their own species-being.

Notes

Chapter 1

1. Some species once extinct in Ireland, such as red squirrels, have been repopulated. Not all the species listed here went extinct in ancient Ireland; some survived into the industrial age. Red deers are not native to Ireland and were introduced with the original settlers from Brittany (Byrne 2020).

2. Ireland's famous giant elk appears to have gone extinct due to climactic changes before the arrival of humans approximately 9,000 years ago and was not a victim of human oppression (Barnosky 1986).

3. The cathedral's war memorial also features a stained-glass image of a white heron nesting in a treetop to symbolize peace and rebirth.

Chapter 2

1. This practice dates back at least to the Middle Ages (Cowan and Sexton 1997; Sexton 1995).

2. Inmates in Irish prisons who were fed cheaply on modest vegetarian foods also provided a convenient sample for vegetarian reformers eager to demonstrate that "meat" was not required to maintain health (W. Harvey 1866).

3. The Great Famine decimated the poorer classes, who were more likely to marry young and to have large families.

4. In her 1835 publication, *Nature's Own Book*, Nicholson lists rules for her temperance boardinghouse: "No animal food of any kind (including fowl and fish—salt and fresh) should be brought upon the breakfast table; nor should any such food be eaten by any of the boarders for their breakfast" (15). However, the establishment does not appear to be strictly vegetarian. Simplicity of diet was advocated to reduce the contraction of disease, discourage vice, and increase godliness among adherents.

5. A popular practice in England as well, this "sport" involved throwing clubs or sticks at a tethered chicken until the bird expired.

6. Independence-era sports were heavily politicized with the self-improvement imported from Victorian culture mixed with nationalistic hypermasculinity (Ward 2017). As a new nation-state, Ireland used sports to demonstrate the power and vigor of its people.

Chapter 3

1. As an example, see the Clements family papers of Ashfield, County Cavan, held in the manuscripts of the Library of Trinity College Dublin (TCD MSS 7258-7360).

2. See Shelley's letter to Elizabeth Hitchener, dated March 14, 1812, in Ingpen's *Complete Works of Percy Bysshe Shelley* (1965, 294–97).

3. The digitized copy of Drummond's 1838 *The Rights of Animals* is available in the Hathi Trust Digital Library is labeled as a donation from James Walker, late president of the university. See https://babel.hathitrust.org/cgi/pt?id=hvd.32044010401362.

4. Not all products of Brown's Soapworks were plant-based. Soapworks were very much a speciesist enterprise relying on animal fats in other operations.

5. The *Zoophilist and Animals' Defender* (1904) comes to this conclusion following a report in a November 9, 1904, issue of the *Irish Times* in which the president of the Dublin College of Physicians petitions for a school of research and laboratory.

6. Tufnell was English-born but took up permanent residence in Ireland after marrying an Irishwoman there.

7. This same conflation surfaced in abolitionist literature as it pertained to enslaved African Americans (Keralis 2012).

Chapter 4

1. See page 35 of the classified announcements in the winter 1973 issue of the *Vegan*.

2. "The IWT believes that a management plan for deer is required to minimise their environmental impacts. Culling may be a part of this but should only be a part of a long term management plan and should not proceed until accurate data are available on the size and location of deer in Ireland" (Irish Wildlife Trust n.d.).

3. IWDG can be found online at http://www.iwdg.ie.

4. The Donkey Sanctuary can be found online at http://www.thedonkeysanctuary.ie/.

5. Eden Farm Sanctuary can be found online at http://www.edenfarmanimalsanctuary.com/.

6. The American and British vegan societies relegate anti-speciesism to one of several aspects of veganism, spotlighting human health and environmental sustainability as equally important. Vegan Ireland can be found online at http://www.vegan.ie/about-us/.

7. VIP can be found online at http://veganinformationproject.cf/.

8. ICABS and its archive of newsletters can be found online at http://www.banbloodsports.com/.

9. The movement debate over the role of IRA-inspired direct action is explored in *Terrorists or Freedom Fighters?* (Best and Nocella 2004).

Chapter 5

1. The prisoners were released in 1922.

2. The term "meat" surfaces 116 times in the Bureau of Military History database.

Conclusion

1. This pattern was identified by founder Sandra Higgins in a personal correspondence.

Works Cited

Adams, C. J. 2000. *The Sexual Politics of Meat*. London: Continuum.
Adamson, W. L. 2014. *Hegemony and Revolution*. Brattleboro, VT: Echo Point.
Adkins, P. 2017. "The Eyes of That Cow: Eating Animals and Theorizing Vegetarianism in James Joyce's *Ulysses*." *Humanities* 6 (3): 1–15.
Ahlstrom, D. 2011. "Solving a 2,000-year-old Death." *Irish Times*, September 8. http://www.irishtimes.com/news/science/solving-a-2-000-year-old-death-1.593646.
Alkon, A. H. 2007. "Growing Resistance: Food, Culture and the Mo' Better Foods Farmers' Market." *Gastronomica* 7 (3): 93–99.
Allamby, L., J. Bell, J. Hamilton, U. Hansson, N. Jarman, M. Potter, and S. Toma. 2011. *Forced Labour in Northern Ireland*. York, UK: Joseph Rowntree Foundation.
Altheide, D. L. 1987. "Format and Symbols in TV Coverage of Terrorism in the United States and Great Britain." *International Studies Quarterly* 31 (2): 161–76.
American Humane Association. 1902. "Queenstown, Ireland." In *Annual Review*, 45.
American Sunday School Union. 1845. *Kindness to Animals, or, the Sin of Cruelty Exposed and Rebuked*. Philadelphia, PA: American Sunday School Union.
American Vegan Society. 2013. "Obituary: Brian Gunn-King, 1933–2013." *American Vegan* 13 (1): 11.
Arluke, A. 2002. "A Sociology of Sociological Animal Studies." *Society and Animals* 10 (4): 369–74.
Armstrong, F. 2015. "Beef with Potatoes: Food, Agriculture and Sustainability in Modern Ireland." In *Food and Drink in Ireland*, edited by E. FitzPatrick and J. Kelly, 405–30. Dublin: Royal Irish Academy.
———. 2016. "Take Stock! Ireland Remains Blind to Abuse of Animals, Humans and the Environment, in Abattoirs." *Village Magazine*, June 15. https://villagemagazine.ie/take-stock/.
———. 2017. "Ireland's 'Livestock-Industrial-Complex' Influences Nutritional Advice and Environmental Reporting." Agricultural and Rural Convention, December 6. https://www.arc2020.eu/irelands-livestock-industrial-complex/.

Baker, S. 1990. "The Evolution of the Irish Ecology Movement." In *Green Politics*, edited by W. Rüdig, 47–81. Edinburgh: Edinburgh University Press.
Ballymena Guardian. 1974. "VIP Visitor Calls with Broughshane Family." *Ballymena Guardian*, July 11. https://ivu.org/congress/wvc75/satguru.html.
Ballymena Times. 2013. "Gracehill Eco Warriors Keep Up Royal Connection." *Ballymena Times*, October 23. http://www.ballymenatimes.com/news/environment/gracehill-eco-warriors-keep-up-royal-connection-1-5615219.
Bánáti, D. 2011. "Consumer Response to Food Scandals and Scares." *Trends in Food Science and Technology* 22 (2–3): 56–60.
Barnosky, A. D. 1986. "'Big Game' Extinction Caused by Late Pleistocene Climactic Change." *Quaternary Research* 25 (1): 128–35.
Barrington, B. 2012. "Aldi Launches Advertising Campaign Focused on Buying Irish." *Business and Leadership*, December 9.
Batt, E. 1965. "Letter to the Editor, Herald of Health, U.S.A." *Vegan*, Winter, 40–41.
———. 1969. "My Column." *Vegan* 16 (3): 30–32.
BBC. 1999. "Push to Run Irish Hunters to Earth." *BBC News*, September 16. http://news.bbc.co.uk/1/hi/special_report/1999/08/99/fox_hunting/434711.stm.
BBC Alba. 2016. *Banished Women*. http://www.bbc.co.uk/programmes/b07b367s.
Beale, J. 1987. *Women in Ireland*. Bloomington: Indiana University Press.
Beckles, H. McD. 1990. "A 'Riotous and Unruly Lot': Irish Indentured Servants and Freemen in the English West Indies, 1644–1713." *William and Mary Quarterly* 47 (4): 503–22.
Beirne, P. 2009. *Confronting Animal Abuse*. New York: Rowman and Littlefield.
Beglane, F. 2015. *Anglo-Norman Parks in Medieval Ireland*. Dublin: Four Courts.
———. 2016. "The Social Significance of Game in the Diet of Later Medieval Ireland." In *Food and Drink in Ireland*, edited by E. FitzPatrick and J. Kelly, 167–96. Dublin: Royal Irish Academy.
Bell, J., and M. Watson. 2014. *Irish Farming Life*. Portland, OR: Four Courts.
Besant, A. 1908. "Vegetarianism in the Light of Theosophy." *Vegetarian Magazine* 11 (9): 4–14.
Best, S., and A. J. Nocella, eds. 2004. *Terrorists or Freedom Fighters? Reflections on the Liberation of Animals*. New York: Lantern.
Bird, S. 2017. "'Humane Milk is a Myth' Ad Relaunched after ASA Rejects Farmers' Complaints." *Telegraph*, July 26. http://www.telegraph.co.uk/news/2017/07/25/humane-milk-myth-ad-relaunched-asa-rejects-farmers-complaints/.
Bitel, L. 2004. "'Hail Brigit!': Gender, Authority and Worship in Early Ireland." In *Irish Women's History*, edited by A. Hayes and D. Urquhart, 1–14. Portland, OR: Irish Academic Press.
Bonilla-Silva, E. 2006. *Racism without the Racists*. Lanham, MD: Rowman and Littlefield.
Boom, K., D. Ben-Ami, D. B. Croft, N. Cushing, D. Ramp, and L. Boronyak. 2012. "'Pest' and Resource: A Legal History of Australia's Kangaroos." *Animal Studies Journal* 1 (1): 17–40.

Bord Bia. 2013. *Retaining Loyalty to Irish Brands*. Dublin: Irish Food Board.
———. 2015. *Export Performance & Prospects 2014–2015*. Dublin: Irish Food Board.
———. 2018. *Dietary Lifestyles Report*. Dublin: Irish Food Board. https://www.bordbia.ie/globalassets/bordbia.ie/industry/marketing-reports/consumer-reports/dietary-lifestyles-report-november2018.pdf.
Bourdieu, P. (1984) 2010. *Distinction*. New York: Routledge.
Bowers, S. 2019. "Beef Taskforce Meeting Is Adjourned as Farmers Protest." *Irish Times*, October 14. //www.irishtimes.com/news/ireland/irish-news/beef-taskforce-meeting-is-adjourned-as-farmers-protest-1.4049778.
Breathnach, P. 2000. "The Evolution of the Spatial Structure of the Irish Dairy Processing Industry." *Irish Geography* 33 (2): 166–84.
British Medical Journal. 1874. "Prosecution at Norwich: Experiments on Animals." *British Medical Journal* 2 (728): 751–54.
British Vegetarian. 1968a. "Notes and News." *British Vegetarian* 10 (6): 526–27.
———. 1968b. "Marriages." *British Vegetarian*, November/December.
Burke-Kennedy, E. 2015. "Analysis: Agri-food Roadmap Fails to Assess Environmental Impact. *Irish Times*, July 3. http://www.irishtimes.com/business/agri business-and-food/analysis-agri-food-roadmap-fails-to-assess-environmental-impact-1.2271717.
Byrne, M. 2020. "Astronomical Observations at Stone Age Sites." *Trasna na Tire*, lecture 19. Posted May 7. YouTube video, 1:05:28. https://www.youtube.com/watch?v=BGKHLLcnqmM.
Cadogan, S. 2016. "300 Jobs Could Be Lost in Mushroom Sector." *Irish Examiner*, October 6. http://www.irishexaminer.com/farming/news/300-jobs-could-be-lost-in-mushroom-sector-424335.html.
Cahill, T. 1995. *How the Irish Saved Civilization*. New York: Anchor.
Calvert, S. 2014. *Ripened by Human Determination: 70 Years of the Vegan Society*. Birmingham, UK: Vegan Society.
Campbell, T. C., and T. M. Campbell. 2006. *The China Study*. Dallas: BenBella.
Carolan, M. 2011. *The Real Cost of Cheap Food*. New York: Earthscan.
Carpenter, A. 2013. "The Birds and the Bees: Ecopoetry in Swift's Irish Circle." In *Reading Swift*, edited by H. J. Real, K. Juhas, and S. Simon, 351–64. Leiden: Brill.
Carr, L., and L. Reyes-Galindo. 2017. "'The Year of the Gull': Demonisation of Wildlife, Pestilence and Science in the British Press." In *Intercultural Communication and Science and Technology Studies*, edited by L. Reyes-Galindo and T. R. Duarte, 147–74. London: Palgrave.
Carroll, C. 2003. "Barbarous Slaves and Civil Cannibals." In *Ireland and Postcolonial Theory*, edited by C. Carroll and P. King, 63–80. Cork: Cork University Press.
Caulfield, S. 2013. "Ceide Fields: Europe's Oldest Surviving Dairy Fields?" In *Secrets of the Irish Landscape*, edited by M. Jebb and C. Crowley, 95–100. Cork: Atrium.
Central Statistics Office. 2012. *Meat Supply Balance 2011*. Dublin: Central Statistics Office.

———. 2015. *Livestock Survey December*. http://cso.ie/en/releasesandpublications/er/lsd/livestocksurveydecember2014.

———. n.d. "Jennie Wyse Power." *Life in 1916 Ireland: Stories from Statistics*. https://www.cso.ie/en/releasesandpublications/ep/p-1916/1916irl/cpr/cwr/jwp/.

Ceurstemont, S. 2014. "Kelp Wanted!" *New Scientist* 223 (2978): 44–47.

Chaomhánach, E. 2002. *The Lore of the Bee, Its Keeper and Produce in Irish and Other Folk Traditions*. Dublin: University College Dublin.

Charities Aid Foundation. 2018. *World Giving Index 2018*. https://www.cafonline.org/docs/default-source/about-us-publications/caf_wgi2018_report_web nopw_2379a_261018.pdf.

Chiorando, M. 2018. "Milk Boss Brands Anti Dairy Ads 'a Hate Crime.'" *Plant Based News*, January 15. https://plantbasednews.org/culture/milk-boss-anti-dairy-ads-hate-crime.

Chozick, A. 2013. "Boom Over, St. Patrick's Isle is Slithering Again." *New York Times*, March 15. http://www.nytimes.com/2013/03/16/world/europe/boom-over-st-patricks-isle-is-slithering-again.html?_r=0.

Clark, J. 1862. "The Fourteenth Annual Meeting of the Vegetarian Society." *Dietetic Reformer and Vegetarian Messenger*, no. 5, 1–15.

Clarke, L. 1998. "Mental Illness and Irish People." *Journal of Psychiatric and Mental Health Nursing* 5 (6): 555–62.

Clarke, T., S. Mac Diarmada, P. Pearse, J. Connolly, T. MacDonagh, E. Ceannt, and J. Plunkett. 1916. *Proclamation of the Republic*.

Clarkson, L. A., and E. M. Crawford. 2001. *Feast and Famine*. Oxford: Oxford University Press.

Cleary, C. 2017. "The Rise of Veganism." *Irish Times*, November 18. https://www.irishtimes.com/life-and-style/food-and-drink/the-rise-of-veganism-we-are-what-we-don-t-eat-1.3287187.

Cohen, S. 1972. *Folk Devils and Moral Panics*. New York: Routledge.

———. 2001. *States of Denial*. Cambridge: Polity.

Cole, M. 2011. "From 'Animal Machines' to 'Happy Meat'? Focault's Ideas of Disciplinary and Pastoral Power Applied to 'Animal-Centred' Welfare Discourse." *Animals* 1 (1) 83–101.

Cole, M., and K. Morgan. 2011a. "Veganism contra Speciesism: Beyond Debate." *Brock Review* 12 (1): 144–63.

———. 2011b. "Veganphobia: Derogatory Discourses of Veganism and the Reproduction of Speciesism in UK National Newspapers." *British Journal of Sociology* 62 (1): 134–53.

Cole, M., and K. Stewart. 2014. *Our Children and Other Animals*. London: Ashgate.

Collins, J., A. Hanlon., S. More., and V. Duggan. 2008. "The Structure and Regulation of the Irish Equine Industries: Links to Considerations of Equine Welfare." *Irish Veterinary Journal* 61:746.

Collins, L. 2015. "'Our Sep'rate Natures Are the Same': Reading Blood Sports in Irish Poetry of the Long Eighteenth Century." In *Animals in Irish Literature and Culture*, edited by K. Kirkpatrick and B. Faragó, 1–12. London: Palgrave Macmillan.
Collins, P. H. 1990. *Black Feminist Thought*. Boston: Unwin Hyman.
Columbus, B. 2009. "Bean na h-Éireann: Feminism and Nationalism in an Irish Journal, 1908–1911." *Voices Novae* 1 (1): 3–30.
Connolly, L. 2019. "Sexual Violence a Dark Secret of War of Independence and Civil War." *Irish Times*, January 10. https://www.irishtimes.com/opinion/sexual-violence-a-dark-secret-of-war-of-independence-and-civil-war-1.3752556.
Connolly, M. 2011. *The Story of Ireland: The Age of Conquest*. Television broadcast, November 11. London: British Broadcasting Corporation. bbc.co.uk/programmes/b00z2m1g.
Coogan, T. P. 2013. *The Famine Plot*. London: Palgrave Macmillan.
Cosgrove, L. 2017. "Doubts Hang Over Future of Longford Greyhound Track." *Longford Leader*, July 20. http://www.longfordleader.ie/news/longford-town/260842/doubts-hang-over-future-of-longford-greyhound-track.html.
Cotter, P. 1996. *Irish Vegetarian Cookery*. Cork: Killeen.
Cowan, C., and R. Sexton. 1997. *Ireland's Traditional Foods*. Dublin: Teagasc, National Food Centre.
Cowie, H. 2014. *Exhibiting Animals in Nineteenth-Century Britain*. London: Palgrave Macmillan.
Cox, L. 2006. "News from Nowhere: The Movement of Movements in Ireland." In *Social Movements and Ireland*, edited by L. Connolly and N. Hourigan, 210–29. Manchester: Manchester University Press.
———. 2017. "The Irish Water Charges Movement." *Interface* 9 (1): 161–203.
Craib, I. 1997. *Classical Social Theory*. Oxford: Oxford University Press.
Crenshaw, K. 1991. "Mapping the Margins: Intersectionality, Identity Politics, and Violence against Women of Color." *Stanford Law Review* 43 (6): 1241–99.
Crónín, D. 1995. *Early Medieval Ireland, 400–1200*. New York: Routledge.
Crowley, E. 2006. *Land Matters: Power Struggles in Rural Ireland*. Dublin: Lilliput.
Cudworth, E. 2011. *Social Lives with Other Animals*. New York: Palgrave Macmillan.
Cullen, P. 2010. "Love Irish Food Campaign Hailed." *Irish Times*, September 28. http://www.irishtimes.com/news/love-irish-food-campaign-hailed-1.864728.
Cunningham, P. 2015. "The Evolution of Cattle and Cattle Farming Systems." In *Agriculture and Settlement in Ireland*, edited by M. Murphy and M. Stout, 1–13. Dublin: Four Courts.
Curtis, L. P. 1968. *Anglo-Saxons and the Celts*. Bridgeport, CT: University of Bridgeport.
———. 1971. *Apes and Angels: The Irishman in Victorian Caricature*. Washington, DC: Smithsonian Institution Press.

Cusack, J. 2014. "ISPCA Calls for 'Sulky Racing' Ban after Latest Injury." *Independent*, June 8. http://www.independent.ie/irish-news/news/ispca-calls-for-sulky-racing-ban-after-latest-injury-30337300.html.

D'Arcy, C. 2015. "Nearly 225,000 Animals Used for Scientific Tests in 2014." *Irish Times*, July 20. http://www.irishtimes.com/news/science/nearly-225-000-animals-used-for-scientific-tests-in-2014-1.2290257.

D'Arcy, G. 1999. *Ireland's Lost Birds*. Dublin: Four Courts.

Dalton, M. 1913–21. "Statement by Witness Document No. W.S. 1116." *Bureau of Military History, 1913–21*. https://www.militaryarchives.ie/collections/online-collections/bureau-of-military-history-1913-1921/reels/bmh/BMH.WS1116.pdf.

Daly, D. 1904. "The Legend of St. Brendan." *Celtic Review* 1 (2): 135–47.

Dalziell, J., and D. J. Wadiwel. 2017. "Live Exports, Animal Advocacy, Race and 'Animal Nationalism.'" In *Meat Culture*, edited by A. Potts, 73–89. Leiden: Brill.

Davies, W. 2010. "Economic Change in Early Medieval Ireland." *Settimane* 57:111–33.

Davis, J. M. 2013. "Cockfight Nationalism: Blood Sport and the Moral Politics of American Empire and Nation Building." *American Quarterly* 65 (3): 549–74.

———. 2016. *The Gospel of Kindness*. New York: Oxford University Press.

Davis, J. 2012. *World Veganism—Past, Present, and Future*. International Vegetarian Union. https://ivu.org/history/Vegan_History.pdf.

———. n.d. "History of Irish Vegetarian Societies." International Vegetarian Union. https://ivu.org/history/societies/ireland.html.

Deckha, M. 2013. "Welfarist *and* Imperial: The Contributions of Anticruelty Laws to Civilizational Discourse." *American Quarterly* 65 (3): 515–48.

De Courcy, C. 2009. *Dublin Zoo*. Wilton, IE: Collins.

Delany, R. 2007. "James Haughton." *Oscailt Magazine* 3 (11).

Department of Agriculture, Food and the Marine. 2015. *Local Roots, Global Reach: Food Wise 2025—a 10-year Vision for the Irish Agri-food Industry*. https://www.gov.ie/en/publication/a6b0d-food-wise-2025/.

———. 2018. *Annual Review and Outlook for Agriculture, Food and the Marine*. https://www.agriculture.gov.ie/media/migration/publications/2018/AnnualReviewandOutlook2018310818.pdf.

Department of Housing, Planning and Local Government. 2016. *Dog Control Statistics 2016*.

Dewhurst, K., ed. 1983. *Richard Lower's Vindicatio: A Defence of the Experiential Method*. Oxford: Sanford.

Dillon, E., B. Moran, J. Lennon, and T. Donnellan. 2018. *Teagasc National Farm Survey*. https://www.teagasc.ie/media/website/publications/2019/NFS-2018_final_web.pdf.

Douglas, R., L. Harte, and J. O'Hara. 1998. *Drawing Conclusions: A Cartoon History of Anglo-Irish Relations, 1798–1998*. Belfast: Blackstaff.

Donnelly, J. S. 1971. "Cork Market: Its Role in the Nineteenth Century Irish Butter Trade." *Studia Hibernica* 11:130–63.

Donnelly, N. 2016. "Eating Well on a Vegetarian Diet." Irish Nutrition and Dietetic Institute.

Donnelly, P. 2016. "The Law on Breeding Puppies." *Irish Times*, August 11. https://www.irishtimes.com/opinion/letters/the-law-on-breeding-puppies-1.2751779.

Donoghue, C. 2017. *Newstalk Drive*, July 26. http://www.newstalk.com/listen_back/81889/37788/26th_July_2017_-_Newstalk_Drive_Part_1/.

Dowd-Smith, C. 2020. "Seaweed and Its Wars—Ireland's Contested Resource." *Trasna na Tire*, lecture 17. Posted May 5. YouTube video, 57:19. https://www.youtube.com/watch?v=Xx9VlXWSFCQ.

Dowling, C. 2018. Foreword. *ISPCA Inspectorate Report 2018*. https://www.ispca.ie/uploads/Inspectorate_Report_2018_final.pdf.

Drummond, W. H. 1838. *The Rights of Animals, and Man's Obligation to Treat Them with Humanity*. London: J. Mardon.

Dublin's 98FM. 2015. Sandra Higgins interview. November. Available on Go Vegan World's website: http://edenfarmedanimalsanctuary.com/wp-content/uploads/2015/01/98fm.mp3.

Duffy, P. J. 1982/1983. "The Nature of the Medieval Frontier in Ireland." *Studia Hibernica*, no. 22/23, 21–38.

Dunayer, J. 2004. *Animal Equality: Language and Liberation*. Ann Arbor: University of Michigan Press.

Earwood, C. 1997. "Bog Butter: A Two Thousand Year History." *Journal of Irish Archaeology* 8:25–42.

Egan, M. 2005. "Organizing Protest in the Changing City: Swill Milk and Social Activism in New York City, 1842–1864." *New York History* 86 (3): 205–25.

Elias, N. (1939) 2000. *The Civilizing Process*. Oxford: Blackwell.

English, E. 2017. "Plan for Cork's First Traveller Horse Grazing Site Backed." *Irish Examiner*, February 18. http://www.irishexaminer.com/ireland/plan-for-corks-first-traveller-horse-grazing-site-backed-443203.html.

English, T. J. 2006. *Paddy Whacked: The Untold Story of the Irish American Gangster*. New York: Harper.

European Pet Food Industry. 2018. *European Facts and Figures*. http://www.fediaf.org/images/FEDIAF_Facts__and_Figures_2018_ONLINE_final.pdf.

Fallon, D., S. McGrath, and C. Murray. 2012. *Come Here to Me! Dublin's Other History*. Dublin: New Island.

Fanning, B. 2002. *Racism and Social Change in the Republic of Ireland*. New York: Manchester University Press.

Farm Animal Rights Movement. 2016. "40 Years of Compassion." Posted October 19. YouTube video, 6:58. https://www.youtube.com/watch?v=ngEJKkzEAU8.

Fiala, I. 2013. "Dog Breeds: The Canine Version of a Socially Constructed Race." *Humanities and Social Sciences Review* 2 (4): 137–44.

Finnane, M. 1981. *Insanity and the Insane in Post-famine Ireland*. Totowa, NJ: Barnes and Noble Books.

Fitzgerald, J. 2001. "Dear Editor." *Vegan*, Autumn, 23.

———. 2011. *Bad Hare Days: One Man's Fight Against a Cruel Blood Sport.* Kilkenny: Callan Press.
Flynn, B. 2009. "Environmental Lessons for Rural Ireland from the European Union." In *A Living Countryside? The Politics of Sustainable Development in Rural Ireland*, edited by J. McDonagh, T. Varley, and S. Shortall, 53–67. Burlington, VT: Ashgate.
Flynn, V. 2017. "Pro-Vegan Ads Rejected for Bus and Rail Poster Spots." *Irish Times*, December 31, 4.
Fogarty, P. 2017. *Whittled Away: Ireland's Vanishing Nature.* Cork: Collins.
Food and Agriculture Organization. 2015. *FAO Statistical Pocketbook: World Food and Agriculture.* Rome: United Nations.
———. n.d. *Food and Agriculture Data.* http://www.fao.org/faostat.
Food and Drink Industry Ireland. 2015. *Meat Industry Overview.* Accessed 2015. http://www.fdii.ie/meat.
Foster, J. B., and B. Clark. 2018. "Marx and Alienated Speciesism." *Monthly Review* 70 (7): 1–21.
Fox, C. 2019. "UCD Professor Reports Students 'Mortified' by Farm Visits." *Farming Independent*, May 1. https://www.independent.ie/business/farming/agri-business/agri-food/ucd-professor-reports-students-mortified-by-farm-visits-38066599.html.
Fox, J. A. 1887. *Why Ireland Wants Home Rule.* Vol. 4. London: National Press Agency.
Freedman, P. H. 2002. "The Representation of Medieval Peasants as Bestial and as Human." In *The Animal-Human Boundary*, edited by A. N. H. Creager and W. C. Jordan, 29–49. Rochester, NY: University of Rochester Press.
Freeman, P. 2001. *Ireland and the Classical World.* Austin: University of Texas Press.
Friel, S., and G. Nolan. 1996. *Changes in the Food Chain since the Time of the Great Irish Famine.* Galway: National Nutrition Surveillance Centre.
Fuller, E. 1950. *George Bernard Shaw.* New York: Scribner's.
Gaard, G. 1993. *Ecofeminism.* Philadelphia: Temple University Press.
———. 2013. "Toward a Feminist Postcolonial Milk Studies." *American Quarterly* 65 (3): 596–618.
Galtung, J. 1969. "Violence, Peace, and Peace Research." *Journal of Peace Research* 6 (3): 167–91.
Gambert, I., and T. Linné. 2018. "From Rice Eaters to Soy Boys: Race, Gender, and Tropes of 'Plant Food Masculinity.'" *Animal Studies Journal* 7 (2): 129–79.
Gamson, W. A. 1995. "Constructing Social Protest." In *Social Movements and Culture*, edited by H. Johnston and B. Klandermans, 85–106. Minneapolis, MN: University of Minnesota Press.
Gibbons, J. 2017. "Ireland's Staggering Hypocrisy on Climate Change." *Guardian*, July 26. https://www.theguardian.com/environment/2017/jul/26/irelands-staggering-hypocrisy-on-climate-change.

Gibbs, A. M. 1990. *Shaw: Interviews and Recollections.* Iowa City: University of Iowa Press.
Giddens, A. 2004. *The Consequences of Modernity.* Cambridge: Polity.
Gittins, E. 2015. "The Dairy of Winifred Frances Wynne for 1916." Manuscripts and Archives Research Library, Trinity College Dublin. https://www.tcd.ie/library/1916/the-diary-of-winifred-frances-wynne-for-1916/.
Gleeson, C. 2015. "Horses and Greyhounds Allocated € 74m in Budget 2016." *Irish Times,* October 13. https://www.irishtimes.com/news/politics/horses-and-greyhounds-allocated-74m-in-budget-2016-1.2390818.
Gmelch, S. 1975. *Tinkers and Travellers.* Montreal: McGill-Queen's University Press.
Goffman, E. 1961. *Asylums.* New York: Anchor.
Golden Eagle Trust. n.d. "Reintroduction of Wildlife." http://goldeneagle.ie/index.php?option=com_k2&view=item&layout=item&id=660&Itemid=195.
Gourley, B. 1995. "Vegetarian Society of Ulster." *EVU News,* 3–4. https://ivu.org/news/evu/news95/ulster.html.
Gove, M. 2017. "Environment Secretary Confirms Sentience of Animals Will Continue to Be Recognised and Protections Strengthened When We Leave the EU." Gov.uk, November 23. https://www.gov.uk/government/news/environment-secretary-confirms-sentience-of-animals-will-continue-to-be-recognised-and-protections-strengthened-when-we-leave-the-eu.
Green, M. 1992. *Animals in Celtic Life and Myth.* London: Routledge.
Greenpeace. 2019. *Feeding the Problem.* Brussels: Greenpeace European Unit. https://storage.googleapis.com/planet4-eu-unit-stateless/2019/02/83254ee1-190212-feeding-the-problem-dangerous-intensification-of-animal-farming-in-europe.pdf.
Gregory, J. 2007. *Of Victorians and Vegetarians.* New York: Tauris.
Griffin, B. 1994. "'Mad Dogs and Irishmen': Dogs and Rabies in the Eighteenth and Nineteenth Centuries." *Ulster Folklife* 40:1–15.
Griffin, D. 2017. "Gull Control Approved in Dublin despite No Evidence of Threat.'" *Irish Times,* July 17. https://www.irishtimes.com/news/environment/gull-control-bird-swooped-and-took-chip-from-baby-s-mouth-1.3159958.
Griffith, G. 2002. *Socialism and Superior Brains: The Political Thought of George Bernard Shaw.* New York: Routledge.
Grogan, E., G. Eogan, J. Rees, V. Butler, and J. Henderson. 1987. "Lough Gur Excavations by Seán P. Ó Ríordáin: Further Neolithic and Beaker Habitations on Knockadoon." *Proceedings of the Royal Irish Academy: Archaeology, Celtic Studies, History, Linguistics, Literature* 87:299–506.
Guenther, L. 2012. "Beyond Dehumanization: A Post-humanist Critique of Intensive Confinement." *Journal of Critical Animal Studies* 10 (2): 46–68.
Gunn-King, B. 1996. "Jack McClelland." *Vegan,* Spring, 7.
Hackett, P. 2017. "Who Protects Ireland's Animals?" Paper presented at the Irish Philosophical Society's Annual Conference, Dublin, November 4.

Hall, L. 2010. *On Their Own Terms: Bringing Animal-Rights Philosophy Down to Earth*. Darien, CT: Nectar Bat.
Halley, J. O'M. 2012. *The Parallel Lives of Women and Cows*. London: Palgrave Macmillan.
Hamilton, C. L. 2019. *Veganism, Sex and Politics*. Bristol: HammerOn.
Hamilton, L. 1994. *Report of the Tribunal of Inquiry into the Beef Processing Industry*. Dublin: Government of Ireland.
Harbison, P. 1976. *The Archaeology of Ireland*. New York: Scribner's.
Harper, A. B. 2010. "Race as a 'Feeble Matter' in Veganism: Interrogating Whiteness, Geopolitical Privilege, and Consumption Philosophy of 'Cruelty-Free' Products." *Journal for Critical Animal Studies* 8 (3): 5–27.
Harris, M. 1989. *Cows, Pigs, Wars, and Witches*. New York: Vintage.
Harte, L. 1997. "Creeping Privatization of Irish Co-operatives: A Transaction Cost Explanation. In *Strategies and Structures in the Agro-food Industries*, edited by J. Nilsson and G. van Dijk, 32–54. Assen, Neth.: Van Gorcum.
Harvey, S. 2000. "Celtic Creatures: A Bestiary of Ancient Ireland." *The World and I* 15 (6): 210–21.
Harvey, W. 1866. "Cattle Plague, and Smallpox amongst Sheep." *Dietetic Reformer and Vegetarian Messenger*, no. 18, 16–19.
Hatton, H. E. 1993. *The Largest Amount of Good: Quaker Relief in Ireland, 1654–1921*. Montreal: McGill-Queen's University Press.
Haughton, J. 1849. "Letter from James Haughton." *Liberator* 19 (41): 162.
———. 1861. "Dietetic Reform.—Personal Experience." *Dietetic Reformer and Vegetarian Messenger*, no. 1, 21–23.
———. 1863. "Diseased Cattle." *Dietetic Reformer and Vegetarian Messenger*, no. 10, 53–54.
———. 1864. "A Word for Vegetarians and Their Supporters. To the Editor of the *Irish Times*." *Dietetic Reformer and Vegetarian Messenger*, no. 16, 124–25.
———. 1865. "Non-stimulating Treatment of Disease." *Dietetic Reformer and Vegetarian Messenger*, no. 28, 38–44.
Haughton, S. 1877. *Memoir of James Haughton*. Dublin, IE: E. Ponsonby.
Hayes, B. C., and I. McAllister. 2007. "Public Support for Political Violence and Paramilitarism in Northern Ireland and the Republic of Ireland." *Terrorism and Political Violence* 17 (4): 599–617.
Helleiner, J. 2000. *Irish Travellers: Racism and the Politics of Culture*. Buffalo, NY: University of Toronto Press.
Henchion, M., and B. McIntyre. 2000. "Regional Imagery and Quality Products: The Irish Experience." *British Food Journal* 102 (8): 630–44.
Henderson, G. 1948. "Actotem: A Summary of Recent Events." *Vegan* 4 (1): 2.
Hickey, Kate. 2019. "The Fascinating 8,000-year History of Irish Cuisine." *Irish Central*, June 28. https://www.irishcentral.com/culture/food-drink/history-of-irish-cuisine.

Hickey, Kieran. 2013. *Wolves in Ireland: A Natural and Cultural History*. Dublin: Four Courts.
Higgins, S. 2017. "Ciara Kelly Declares Violence Acceptable." Go Vegan World. https://goveganworld.com/ciara-kelly-declares-violence-acceptable-newstalk-debate-sandra-higgins/.
———. 2020. "Irish Farmers' Association Attempts to Malign Animal Sanctuary as It Cannot Deny the Truth of Vegan Campaign." Go Vegan World, January 9. https://goveganworld.com/irish-farmers-association-attempts-to-malign-animal-sanctuary-as-it-cannot-deny-the-truth-of-vegan-campaign.
Higginbotham, P. 2008. *The Workhouse Cookbook*. Stroud: History.
Hill, E. C. 1978. *George Bernard Shaw*. Boston: Twayne.
Hilliard, M. 2020. "Up to 600 Meat-Plant Workers Have COVID-19." *Irish Times*, May 15. https://www.irishtimes.com/news/health/up-to-600-meat-plant-workers-have-covid-19-1.4253819.
Hillis, G. 2012/2013. "A Trip Down Memory Lane." *Irish Vegetarian*, no. 137, 6.
Hinnant, C. J. 1987. *Purity and Defilement in "Gulliver's Travels."* New York: Palgrave Macmillan.
Historyo, R. n.d. "Ron Historyo Presents the Belfast Bulldog." Wrestling Heritage. http://www.wrestlingheritage.co.uk/belfastbulldog.htm.
Hobson-West, P. 2007. "Beasts and Boundaries: An Introduction to Animals in Sociology, Science, and Society." *Qualitative Sociology Review* 3 (1): 23–41.
Hodson, G., K. Dhont, and M. Earle. 2020. "Devaluing Animals, 'Animalistic' Humans, and People Who Protect Animals." In *Why We Love and Exploit Animals*, edited by K. Dhont and G. Hodson, 267–86. Abingdon, UK: Routledge.
Hoff, J., and M. Yeates. 2000. *The Cooper's Wife Is Missing: The Trials of Bridget Cleary*. New York: Basic Books.
Holroyd, M. 1997. *Bernard Shaw: The One-Volume Definitive Edition*. London: Chatto and Windus.
Hoogvelt, A. 2001. *Globalization and the Postcolonial World*. Baltimore: Johns Hopkins University Press.
Hogan, T. 2012. "Native Animals 'At Risk of Extinction' as Pollution and Overfishing Take Toll." *New Irish News*, June 26. http://www.independent.ie/irish-news/native-animals-at-risk-of-extinction-as-pollution-and-overfishing-take-toll-26868955.html.
hooks, b. 1982. *Ain't I a Woman: Black Women and Feminism*. London: Pluto.
———. 1992. *Black Looks*. Boston: South End Press.
Hooton, E. A., and C. W. Dupertuis. 1955. *The Physical Anthropology of Ireland*. Cambridge, MA: Museum [Peabody Museum of Archaeology and Ethnology].
Horses and Ponies Protection Society. 1963. "The Irish Traffic." *Vegan*, Autumn.
Ignatiev, N. 2009. *How the Irish Became White*. New York: Routledge.
Ingpen, R., and W. Peck. 1965. *The Complete Works of Shelley*. New York: Gordian.
Irish Independent. 2013. "Good News for Local Suppliers and Farmers as Aldi Continues to Grow." March 3. http://www.independent.ie/regionals/goreyguardian/news/

good-news-for-local-suppliers-and-farmers-as-aldi-continues-to-grow-29124164.html.

Irish Nutrition and Dietetic Institute. 2004. *A Guide to Vegetarian Eating.* https://www.indi.ie/healthy-eating,-healthy-weight-and-dieting/506-eating-well-on-a-vegetarian-diet.html.

Irish Press. 1949. "Day to Day." February 26, 6.

Irish Prisoners. 1916a. "Letter from Irish Prisoners, Frongoch to William O'Brien, Esq., MP, 11 October 1916." *Letters 1916–1923.* http://letters1916.maynoothuniversity.ie/item/358.

Irish Prisoners. 1916b. "Letter from Irish Prisoners, Frongoch to William O'Brien, Esq., MP, 14 October 1916." *Letters 1916–1923.* http://letters1916.maynoothuniversity.ie/item/361.

Irish Society for the Prevention of Cruelty to Animals. n.d. "Who We Are." https://www.ispca.ie/who_we_are.

Irish Times. 1998. "Grants Awarded to Animal Groups." December 23. http://www.irishtimes.com/news/grants-awarded-to-animal-groups-1.228295.

———. 2001. "Animal Rights Activist Dies after Hunger Strike." November 5. https://www.irishtimes.com/news/animal-rights-activist-dies-after-hunger-strike-1.402644.

———. 2017a. "Record Number of Irish Horses Flown from Shannon to China." January 8. https://www.irishtimes.com/business/agribusiness-and-food/record-number-of-irish-horses-flown-from-shannon-to-china-1.2929342.

———. 2017b. "Europol Arrests 66 People in Horsemeat Investigation." July 16. https://www.irishtimes.com/news/crime-and-law/europol-arrests-66-people-in-horsemeat-investigation-1.3156669.

Irish Wildlife Trust. n.d. "IWT Policies and Submissions." https://iwt.ie/what-we-do/campaigns/policy/.

Jannaway, K. 1975. "Vegetarian Centre in Northern Ireland." *Vegan* 22 (2): 19.

Johnston, H. 1994. "New Social Movements and Old Regional Nationalisms." In *New Social Movements: From Ideology to Identity*, edited by E. Larana, H. Johnston, and J. R. Gusfield, 267–86. Philadelphia: Temple University Press.

Joyce, J. 1922. *Ulysses.* Mineola, NY: Dover.

Joyce, P. W. 1906. *A Smaller Social History of Ancient Ireland.* New York: Longmans, Green.

Kasperbauer, T. J. 2018. *Subhuman: The Moral Psychology of Human Attitudes to Animals.* Oxford: Oxford University Press.

Kaufman, M., and H. J. Kaufman. 1972. "Henry Bergh, Kit Burns, and the Sportsmen of New York." *New York Folklore Quarterly* 28 (1): 15–29.

Kean, H. 1995. "The 'Smooth Cool Men of Science': The Feminist and Socialist Response to Vivisection." *History Workshop Journal* 40 (1): 16–38.

Keenan, M. 2012. "It's a Tough Business Running Dublin Zoo." *Independent*, September 27. http://www.independent.ie/business/irish/its-a-tough-business-running-dublin-zoo-28814581.html.

Keenan-Thomson, T. 2010. *Irish Women and Street Politics, 1956–1973*. Dublin: Irish Academic Press.

Keery, A. 2014. "Becoming Vegetarian is Increasingly Popular." *Irish Catholic*, July 17.

Keet-Black, J. 2013. *Gypsies of Britain*. Oxford: Shire.

Kelleher, L. 2017. "7,618 Horses Killed for Meat in Ireland." *Irish Examiner*, March 28. http://www.irishexaminer.com/ireland/7618-horses-killed-for-meat-in-ireland-446276.html.

———. 2019. "Almost 30,000 Male Calves Slaughtered at 10 Days Old Last Year." *Irish Examiner*, December 5. https://www.irishexaminer.com/breakingnews/ireland/almost-30000-male-calves-slaughtered-at-10-days-old-last-year-968607.html.

Kellogg, J. H. 1923. *The Natural Diet of Man*. Battle Creek, MI: Modern Medical.

Kelly, A. C. 2007. "Gulliver as Pet and Pet Keeper: Talking Animals in Book 4." *ELH* 74 (2): 323–49.

Kelly, F. 1997. *Early Irish Farming*. Dublin, IE: Dublin Institute for Advanced Studies.

Kelly, J. 1992. "Scarcity and Poor Relief in Eighteenth-Century Ireland." *Irish Historical Studies* 28 (109): 38–69.

———. 2014. *Sport in Ireland, 1600–1840*. Dublin: Four Courts.

———. 2017. *Food Rioting in Ireland in the Eighteenth and Nineteenth Centuries*. Dublin: Four Courts.

Kennedy, R. 1972. "The Social Status of the Sexes and Their Relative Mortality in Ireland." In *Readings in Population*, edited by W. Peterson, 121–36. New York: Macmillan.

Keralis, S. C. 2012. "Feeling Animal: Pet-Making and Mastery in the Slave's Friend." *American Periodicals* 22 (2): 121–38.

Kettrick, T. 1913–21. "Statement by Witness Document No. W.S. 872." *Bureau of Military History, 1913–21*. https://www.militaryarchives.ie/collections/online-collections/bureau-of-military-history-1913-1921/reels/bmh/BMH.WS0872.pdf.

Kevany, S., and M. Busby. 2020. "'It Would Be Kinder to Shoot Them': Ireland's Calves Set for Live Export." *Guardian*, January 20. https://www.theguardian.com/environment/2020/jan/20/it-would-be-kinder-to-shoot-them-irelands-calves-set-for-live-export.

Kheel, M. 1995. "License to Kill: An Ecofeminist Critique of Hunters' Discourse." In *Animals and Women*, edited by C. J. Adams and J. Donovan, 126–48. Durham, NC: Duke University Press.

Kiely, M. 2001. "Summary Report." *North/South Ireland Food Consumption Survey*. Dublin: Food Safety Promotion Board.

Kiernan, P. 1999. "ISPCA Branch May Face Dis-affiliation over Blood Sports Stance." *Animal Watch* 11 (Spring/Summer).

Kijewska, A., and A. Bluszcz. 2016. "Analysis of Greenhouse Gas Emissions in the European Union Member States with the Use of an Agglomeration Algorithm." *Journal of Sustainable Mining* 15 (4): 133–42.

Kilkenny People. 2016. "Sulky Racing Now Banned as New Bylaws Come into Force." January 20. http://www.kilkennypeople.ie/news/home/201408/Sulky-racing-now-banned-as-new.html.

King, A. 2013. "Inside the Mouse House: Animal Testing in Irish Labs." *Irish Times*, October 17. https://www.irishtimes.com/news/science/inside-the-mouse-house-animal-testing-in-irish-labs-1.1562866.

King, C., and L. Kennedy. 1994. "Irish Co-operatives: From Creameries at the Crossroads to Multinationals." *History Ireland* 4 (2): 36–41.

Kinmonth, C. 2006. *Irish Rural Interiors in Art*. New Haven, CT: Yale University Press.

Kirkpatrick, K. 2015. "Quick Red Foxes: Irish Women Write the Hunt." In *Animals in Irish Literature and Culture*, edited by K. Kirkpatrick and B. Faragó, 26–41. London: Palgrave Macmillan.

Kneafsey, M. 1998. "Tourism and Place Identity: A Case-Study in Rural Ireland." *Irish Geography* 31 (2): 111–23.

Kneafsey, M., and R. Cox. 2002. "Food, Gender and Irishness: How Irish Women in Coventry Make Home." *Irish Geography* 35 (1): 6–15.

Knox, D. B. 2017. *The Curious History of Irish Dogs*. Dublin: New Island.

Ko, A. 2019. *Racism as Zoological Witchcraft*. New York: Lantern.

Ko, A., and S. Ko. 2017. *Aphro-ism: Essays on Pop Culture, Feminism, and Black Veganism from Two Sisters*. New York: Lantern.

Kramer, W. 2010. *Filid, Fairies and Faith: The Effects of Gaelic Culture, Religious Conflict and the Dynamics of Dual Confessionalisation on the Suppression of Witchcraft Accusations and Witch-Hunts in Early Modern Ireland, 1533–1670*. MA thesis, California Polytechnic State University, San Luis Obispo, CA.

Kraut, A. M. 1994. *Silent Travelers: Germs, Genes, and the 'Immigrant Menace.'* Baltimore: Johns Hopkins University Press.

Langan-Egan, M. 1999. *Galway Women in the Nineteenth Century*. Dublin: Open Air.

Larsen, E. 2003. "Cú Chulainn: God, Man, or Animal?" *Proceedings of the Harvard Celtic Colloquium* 23:172–83.

Laurence, A. 1988. "The Cradle to the Grave: English Observation of Irish Social Customs in the Seventeenth Century." *Seventeenth Century* 3 (1): 63–84.

Layte, R., and D. Landy. 2018. "The Fighting Irish? Explaining the Temporal Pattern of Social Protest during Ireland's Fiscal Crisis." *Sociology* 52 (6): 1270–89.

Leahy, E., S. Lyons, and R. Tol. 2010. "National Determinants of Vegetarianism." Working paper, Economic and Social Research Institute, Dublin.

LeDuff, C. 2000. "At a Slaughterhouse, Some Things Never Die." *New York Times*, June 16.

Leneman, L. 1997. "The Awakened Instinct: Vegetarianism and the Women's Suffrage Movement in Britain." *Women's History Review* 6 (2): 271–87.

Lentin, A. 2006. "Anti-racism in Ireland." In *Social Movements and Ireland*, edited by L. Connolly and N. Hourigan, 190–209. New York: Manchester University Press.

Li, P. 2017. "The 'Dog Meat' Trade in China's Urban-Based Development." In *Animal Oppression and Capitalism*, edited by D. Nibert, 1:118–39. Santa Barbara, CA: Praeger.
Lillington, K. 2016. "Sad Realities of Our Domestic Puppy-Farming Industry." *Irish Times*, August 5. https://www.irishtimes.com/news/crime-and-law/sad-realities-of-our-domestic-puppy-farming-industry-1.2745436.
Linden, J. 2016. "Irish Gain a Taste for Poultry Meat." *WATTAgNet.com*, January 11. http://www.wattagnet.com/articles/25516-irish-gain-a-taste-for-poultry-meat.
Lindsey, P. A., G. Chapron, L. S. Petracca, D. Brunham, M. W. Hayward, P. Henschel, A. E. Hinks, S. T. Garnett, D. W. Macdonald, E. A. Macdonald, W. J. Ripple, K. Zander, and A. Dickman. 2017. "Relative Efforts of Countries to Conserve World's Megafauna." *Global Ecology and Conservation* 10:243–52.
Linklater, A. 1980. *An Unhusbanded Life: Charlotte Despard*. London: Hutchinson.
Lloyd, D. 2003. "After History: Historicism and Irish Postcolonial Studies." In *Ireland and Postcolonial Theory*, edited by C. Carroll and P. King, 46–62. Cork: Cork University Press.
Lobell, J. A., and S. S. Patel. 2010. "Clonycavan and Old Croghan Men." *Archaeology* 63, no. 3. http://archive.archaeology.org/1005/bogbodies/clonycavan_croghan.html.
Locke, T. 2017. *Tales of the Irish Hedgerows*. Dublin: History Press Ireland.
Lonergan, A. 2018. "No Proof? How the Infamous 'No Irish, No Blacks, No Dogs' Signs May Never Have Existed." *Irish Post*, January 26. https://www.irishpost.com/life-style/infamous-no-irish-no-blacks-no-dogs-signs-may-never-have-existed-148416.
Love Irish Food. 2014. About Us. http://www.loveirishfood.ie/about-us/.
Lucas, A. T. 1960. "Irish Food before the Potato." *Folk Life* 3 (2): 8–43.
Luddy, M. 1997. "'Abandoned Women and Bad Characters': Prostitution in Nineteenth-Century Ireland." *Women's History Review* 6 (4): 485–503.
———. 2007. *Prostitution and Irish Society, 1800–1940*. Cambridge: Cambridge University Press.
Lundblad, M. 2013. *The Birth of a Jungle: Animality in Progressive-Era U.S. Literature and Culture*. New York: Oxford University Press.
Lux Research. 2015. "Alternative Proteins to Claim a Third of the Market by 2054." Press release, February 24. https://www.luxresearchinc.com/press-releases/alternative-proteins-to-claim-a-third-of-the-market-by-2054.
Lynch, M. 1913–921. "Statement by Witness Document No. W.S. 511." *Bureau of Military History, 1913–21*. https://www.militaryarchives.ie/collections/online-collections/bureau-of-military-history-1913-1921/reels/bmh/BMH.WS0511.pdf.
Lyons, S. 2015. "Food Plants, Fruits and Foreign Foodstuffs: The Archaeological Evidence from Urban Medieval Ireland." In *Food and Drink in Ireland*, edited by E. FitzPatrick and J. Kelly, 111–16. Dublin: Royal Irish Academy.

Mac Coitir, N. 2006. *Irish Wild Plants: Myths, Legends and Folklore*. Cork: Collins Press.
———. 2010. *Ireland's Animals: Myths, Legends and Folklore*. Cork: Collins Press.
Mac Con Iomaire, M. 2003. "The Pig in Irish Cuisine Past and Present." In *The Fat of the Land: Proceedings of the Oxford Symposium on Food and Cookery, 2002*, edited by H. Walker, 207–15. Bristol: Footwork.
———. 2008. "Searching for Chefs, Waiters and Restaurateurs in Edwardian Dublin." *Petits Propos Culinaires* 86: 92–126.
MacConnell, C. 2016. "Everything You Know about the St. Patrick's Day Shamrock Is a Lie." *Irish Central*, March 10. http://www.irishcentral.com/opinion/others/truths-about-the-shamrock-for-st-patricks-day-everything-you-think-you-know-about-the-symbol-of-irishness-is-a-lie-198438781-238173881.html.
MacInnis, C. C., and G. Hodson. 2017. "It Ain't Easy Eating Greens: Evidence of Bias toward Vegetarians and Vegans from Both Source and Target." *Group Processes and Intergroup Relations* 20 (6): 721–44.
MacLysaght, E. 1979. *Irish Life in the Seventeenth Century*. Dublin: Irish Academic Press.
Mahon, D., and C. Cowan. 2004. "Irish Consumers' Perception of Food Safety Risk in Minced Beef." *British Food Journal* 106 (4): 301–12.
Main, L. 2003. "Tribute to the Late Kathleen Jannaway." *Vegan*, Summer, 8–9.
Malamud, R. 2017. "The Problem with Zoos." In *The Oxford Handbook of Animal Studies*, edited by L. Kalof, 397–410. New York: Oxford University Press.
Mallory, J. P. 2016. *In Search of the Irish Dreamtime: Archaeology and Early Irish Literature*. London: Thames and Hudson.
María, G. A., B. Mazas, F. J. Zarza, and G. C. Miranda de la Lama. 2017. "Animal Welfare, National Identity and Social Change." *Journal of Agricultural and Environmental Ethics* 30 (6): 809–26.
Marine Institute. 2009. *Atlas of the Commercial Fisheries around Ireland*. Galway: Marine Institute.
Marlow, J. 1973. *Captain Boycott and the Irish*. New York: Saturday Review Press.
Marx, K. (1844) 2000. "Economic and Philosophical Manuscripts." In *Karl Marx: Selected Writings*, edited by D. McLellan, 83–121. Oxford: Oxford University Press.
———. (1846) 2000. "The German Ideology." In *Karl Marx: Selected Writings*, edited by D. McLellan, 175–208. Oxford: Oxford University Press.
———. (1848) 2000. "Speech on Free Trade." In *Karl Marx: Selected Writings*, edited by D. McLellan, 295–96. Oxford: Oxford University Press.
———. (1867) 2000. "On Ireland." In *Karl Marx: Selected Writings*, edited by D. McLellan, 638–40. Oxford: Oxford University Press.
Marx, K., and F. Engels. (1848) 1962. "Manifesto of the Communist Party." In *Marx/Engels Selected Works*, 98–137. Moscow: Foreign Languages Publishing House.
Mason, J. 1993. *An Unnatural Order: Uncovering the Roots of Our Domination of Nature and Each Other*. London: Simon and Schuster.
Mason, P. 1997. *The Brown Dog Affair*. London: Two Stevens.

Martin, M. 1916. "Letter from Marie Martin to Mary Martin, 17 September 1916." *Letters 1916-1923*. http://letters1916.maynoothuniversity.ie/item/116.

Mauger, A. 2017. *The Cost of Insanity in Nineteenth-Century Ireland*. London: Palgrave Macmillan.

Mauss, M. 2004. *The Gift: The Form and Reason for Exchange in Archaic Societies*. New York: Routledge.

Mayall, D. 2009. *Gypsy-Travellers in Nineteenth-Century Society*. Cambridge: Cambridge University Press.

Mayorga-Gallo, S. 2018. "Whose Best Friend? Dogs and Racial Boundary Maintenance in a Multiracial Neighborhood." *Sociological Forum* 33 (2): 505–28.

McCall, B. 2015. "Strong Growth Continues for Mushroom Industry." *Irish Times*, February 2. http://www.irishtimes.com/sponsored/strong-growth-continues-for-mushroom-industry-1.2085451.

McCarthy, Á. 2004. "Hearts, Bodies and Minds: Gender Ideology and Women's Committal to Enniscorthy Lunatic Asylum, 1916–25." In *Irish Women's History*, edited by A. Hayes and D. Urquhart, 115–25. Portland, OR: Irish Academic Press.

McCarthy, N. 2019. "The Most Vegan-Friendly Cities Worldwide." *Forbes*, October 10. https://www.forbes.com/sites/niallmccarthy/2019/10/10/the-most-vegan-friendly-cities-worldwide-infographic/.

McComb, A. M. G., and D. Simpson. 1999. "The Wild Bunch: Exploitation of the Hazel in Prehistoric Ireland." *Ulster Journal of Archeology* 58: 1–16.

McCormick, F. 1983. "Dairying and Beef Production in Early Christian Ireland: The Faunal Evidence." In *Landscape Archaeology in Ireland*, edited by T. Reeves-Smyth and F. Hamond, 253–68. Oxford: British Academy.

———. 1991. "The Dog in Prehistoric and Early Christian Ireland." *Archaeology Ireland* 5 (4): 7–9.

McCulloch, S. P., and M. J. Reiss. 2017. "Bovine Tuberculosis and Badger Culling in England: A Utilitarian Analysis of Policy Options." *Journal of Agricultural and Environmental Ethics* 30 (4): 511–33.

McDonagh, D. 2017. "Tayto Park Argues Release of Animal Death Data Would Damage Business." *Irish Times*, December 21. https://www.irishtimes.com/news/ireland/irish-news/tayto-park-argues-release-of-animal-death-data-would-damage-business-1.3335013.

McDonagh, P., and P. Commins. 1999. "Food Chains, Small-scale Food Enterprises and Rural Development: Illustrations from Ireland." *International Planning Studies* 4 (3): 349–71.

McDonald, T., and D. Vandersommers, eds. 2019. *Zoo Studies*. Montreal: McGill-Queen's University Press.

McGrath, S. 2013. "Some Notes on the History of Vegetarianism in Dublin, Pt. I (1866–1922)." *Come Here to Me! Dublin Life and Culture* (blog), May 21. https://comeheretome.com/2013/05/21/some-notes-on-history-of-vegetarianism-in-dublin-pt-i-1866-1922/.

McKeown, M. 2019. "Global Data on Key Innovation Trends in Dairy: Part 1—Plant-based Dairy." *Food Alerts*, October 4. https://www.bordbia.ie/industry/news/food-alerts/globaldata-on-key-innovation-trends-in-dairy-part-1--plant-based-dairy/.

McLaren, D. 2003. "Environmental Space, Equity and the Ecological Debt." In *Just Sustainabilities*, edited by J. Agyeman, R. D. Bullard, and B. Evans, 19–37. New York: Earthscan.

McMahon, Á. 2017. "More than 1,500 Dogs 'Destroyed' in Irish Dog Pounds Last Year." *Irish Times*, July 20. https://www.irishtimes.com/news/social-affairs/more-than-1-500-dogs-destroyed-in-irish-dog-pounds-last-year-1.3161790.

McNally, F. 2019. "From a Vegetarian Restaurant in Dublin to the Presidency of India." *Irish Times*, April 19. https://www.irishtimes.com/opinion/from-a-vegetarian-restaurant-in-dublin-to-the-presidency-of-india-1.3865990.

McNeur, C. 2011. "The 'Swinish Multitude': Controversies over Hogs in Antebellum New York City." *Journal of Urban History* 37 (5): 639–60.

———. 2014. *Taming Manhattan*. Cambridge, MA: Harvard University Press.

McNulty, F. 2015. "Should Horse Sulky Racing Be Banned?" *RTÉ News*, July 23. https://www.rte.ie/news/primetime/2015/0723/716729-prime-time-sulky-racing/.

Meagher, A. 2013a. "Social Horse Projects: 'I Couldn't Live Anywhere without a Horse.'" *Changing Ireland*, no. 43 (Autumn): 8.

———. 2013b. "Experience Points to Embracing Our Urban Cowboys: Reframing Sulky Riding in a Positive Context." *Changing Ireland*, no. 43 (Autumn): 4.

Meens, R. 2002. "Eating Animals in the Early Middle Ages: Classifying the Animal World and Building Group Identities." In *The Animal-Human Boundary*, edited by A. N. H. Creager and W. C. Jordan, 3–28. New York: University of Rochester Press.

Merrill, W. M., ed. 1979. *The Letters of William Lloyd Garrison*. Vol. 4. Cambridge, MA: Belknap Press of Harvard University Press.

Miele, M., and J. Lever. 2013. "Civilizing the Market for Welfare Friendly Products in Europe?" *Geoforum* 48: 63–72.

Miller, I. 2015. "Nutritional Decline in Post-Famine Ireland, c. 1851–1922." In *Food and Drink in Ireland*, edited by E. FitzPatrick and J. Kelly, 307–23. Dublin: Royal Irish Academy.

———. 2016. "Why H-Block Hunger Strikers Were Not Force-Fed." *Irish Times*, July 5. https://www.irishtimes.com/culture/books/why-h-block-hunger-strikers-were-not-force-fed-1.2706786.

Mintz, S. W. 1996. *Tasting Food, Tasting Freedom*. Boston: Beacon Press.

Moane, G. 2011. *Gender and Colonialism*. Rev. pbk. ed. London: Palgrave Macmillan.

Mooney, J. 2010. "Representations of the Irish in American Vaudeville and Early Film." *Networking Knowledge* 3 (2): 1–21.

Moore, F., and A. Dixon. 1921. *Call for New Members to Join the Royal Zoological Society of Ireland*. Manuscripts and Archives Research Library, Trinity College Dublin. IE TD MS 10608/24/1.

Monk, M. 2013. "The First Farmers." In *Secrets of the Irish Landscape*, edited by M. Jebb and C. Crowley, 103–11. Cork: Atrium.
Montgomery, W. I., M. G. Lundy, and N. Reid. 2012. "'Invasional Meltdown': Evidence for Unexpected Consequences and Cumulative Impacts of Multi-species Invasions." *Biological Invasions* 14 (6): 1111–25.
Moran, C. 2017. "'British-Only Beef' Campaign Sparks Export Fears for Farmers." *Independent*, May 4. http://www.independent.ie/business/farming/beef/britishonly-beef-campaign-sparks-export-fears-for-farmers-35678998.html.
Morgan, K., and Cole, M. 2011. "The Discursive Representation of Nonhuman Animals in a Culture of Denial." In *Humans and Other Animals: Critical Perspectives*, edited by B. Carter and N. Charles, 112–32. London: Palgrave.
Morin, K. M. 2018. *Carceral Space, Prisoners and Animals*. New York: Routledge.
Morris, H. 1939. "St. Martin's Eve." *Folklore of Ireland Society* 9 (2): 230–35.
Morton, T. 2006. "Joseph Ritson, Percy Shelley and the Making of Romantic Vegetarianism." *Romanticism* 12 (1): 52–61.
Mulhall, E. 2016. "'Shot like a Dog': The Murder of Francis Sheehy Skeffington and the Search for Truth." *Century Ireland*, September. http://www.rte.ie/century ireland/images/uploads/further-reading/Ed84-Mulhall-Skeffington-Full.pdf.
Mullen, P. 1913–21. "Statement by Witness Document No. W.S. 621." *Bureau of Military History, 1913–21*. https://www.militaryarchives.ie/collections/online-collections/bureau-of-military-history-1913-1921/reels/bmh/BMH.WS0621.pdf.
Murphy, D. 2015. "The Vegans Are Coming." *Dublin Inquirer*, June 2. http://dublininquirer.com/2015/06/02/the-vegans-are-coming/.
Murphy, M. O'R. 2015. *Compassionate Stranger: Asenath Nicholson and the Great Irish Famine*. Syracuse, NY: Syracuse University Press.
Murphy, M., and M. Stout. 2015. *Agriculture and Settlement in Ireland*. Dublin: Four Courts.
Murrin, J. M. 2002. "'Things Fearful to Name': Bestiality in Early America." In *The Animal-Human Boundary*, edited by A. N. H. Creager and W. C. Jordan, 115–56. Rochester, NY: University of Rochester Press.
Mushroom Bureau. n.d. *Healthy Eating with Mushrooms*. https://www.justadd mushrooms.com/.
Mussetter, S. 1977. "An Animal Miniature on the Monogram Page of *The Book of Kells*." *Mediaevalia* 3:119–30.
Nance, S. 2015. *The Historical Animal*. Syracuse, NY: Syracuse University Press.
Nationalist. 2013. "Ban Sulky Racing before Someone Is Killed Warning." October 23. http://www.nationalist.ie/news/local-news/156376/Ban-sulky-racing-before-someone-is.html.
Newman, R. C. 2011. *Brian Boru*. Cork: Mercier.
Nibert, D. 2002. *Animal Rights/Human Rights: Entanglements of Oppression and Liberation*. New York: Rowman and Littlefield.
———. 2003. "Humans and Other Animals: Sociology's Moral and Intellectual Challenge." *International Journal of Sociology and Social Policy* 23 (3): 5–25.

———. 2013. *Animal Oppression and Human Violence: Domesecration, Capitalism, and Global Conflict*. New York: Columbia University Press.

Nicholson, A. 1835. *Nature's Own Book*. 2nd ed. New York: Wilbur and Whipple.

Ní Chonchuir, S. 2015. "Pros and Cons of a Vegan Diet." *Irish Examiner*, August 8. http://www.irishexaminer.com/lifestyle/foodanddrink/features/pros-and-cons-of-a-vegan-diet-346767.html.

Ní Chríodáin, L. 2018. "A History of Irish Lunacy." *Irish Times*, December 7. https://www.irishtimes.com/life-and-style/health-family/a-history-of-irish-lunacy-intermarriage-tea-drinking-and-eating-potatoes-1.3708092.

Noonan, K. M. 1998. "'The Cruel Pressure of an Enraged, Barbarous People': Irish and English Identity in Seventeenth-Century Policy and Propaganda." *Historical Journal* 41 (1): 151–77.

Norris, M. 2017. "Tatters, Bloom's Cat, and Other Animals in *Ulysses*." *Humanities* 6 (3): 1–9.

Ó Briain, M. 1991. "The Horse-Eared Kings of Irish Tradition and S. Brigit." In *Crossed Paths: Methodological Approaches to the Celtic Aspect of the European Middle Ages*, edited by B. Hudson and V. Ziegler, 83–113. New York: University Press of America.

O'Brien, T. 2017a. "Seaweed Shown to Reduce 99% Methane from Cattle." *Irish Times*, July 16. https://www.irishtimes.com/news/ireland/irish-news/seaweed-shown-to-reduce-99-methane-from-cattle-1.3156975?.

———. 2017b. "Brexit Biggest Threat to Food Industry 'Since Economic War.'" *Irish Times*, February 28. https://www.irishtimes.com/news/politics/brexit-biggest-threat-to-food-industry-since-economic-war-1.2992437.

———T. 2017c. "Irish Cattle Slaughtered in Conditions 'Breaching EU Law.'" *Irish Times*, April 2. https://www.irishtimes.com/news/ireland/irish-news/irish-cattle-slaughtered-in-conditions-breaching-eu-law-1.3033583?mode=amp.

O'Callaghan, S. 2000. *To Hell or Barbados*. Dublin: Brandon.

O'Connor, M. 2010. *The Female and the Species: The Animal in Irish Women's Writing*. Bern: Peter Lang.

———. 2013. "Vegetable Love: The Syncretic Nation in the Writings of Margaret Cousins and Eva Gore-Booth." *Journal of Irish Studies* 28:18–33.

O'Donoghue, M. 1913–921. "Statement by Witness Document No. W.S. 1741." *Bureau of Military History, 1913–21*. https://www.militaryarchives.ie/collections/online-collections/bureau-of-military-history-1913-1921/reels/bmh/BMH.WS1741%20PART%201.pdf.

O'Donovan, J. 2014. "Climate Change and Agriculture." *Irish Vegetarian*, no. 143, 22.

———. n.d. "101 Million Animals Are Killed in Ireland Every Year." *Vegan Sustainability Magazine*. http://vegansustainability.com/101-million-animals-are-killed-in-ireland-every-year/.

O'Donovan, P., and M. McCarthy. 2002. "Irish Consumer Preference for Organic Meat." *British Food Journal* 104 (3/4/5): 353–70.

O'Halloran, M. 2017. "Ireland Is 'Puppy Farm Capital' of Europe." *Irish Times*, May 26. https://www.irishtimes.com/news/politics/oireachtas/ireland-is-puppy-farm-capital-of-europe-1.3097931.

———. 2019. "Rural TDs Criticise Varadkar for Comments on Eating Meat." *Irish Times*, January 15. https://www.irishtimes.com/news/politics/rural-tds-criticise-varadkar-for-comments-on-eating-meat-1.3758647.

Ó hAodha, M. 2011. *"Insubordinate Irish": Travellers in the Text*. New York: Manchester University Press.

O'Kelly, M. J. 2001. *Early Ireland*. Cambridge: Cambridge University Press.

Okey, T. (1930) 1990. "Holidays: I." In *Shaw*, edtied by A. Gibbs, 211–13. Iowa City: University of Iowa Press.

O'Mahony, J. 2009. "Ireland's EU Referendum Experience." *Irish Political Studies* 24 (4): 429–46.

O'Malley, P. 1990. *Biting at the Grave: The Irish Hunger Strikes and the Politics of Despair*. Boston: Beacon.

O'Mara, F. 2008. *Country Pasture/Forage Resource Profiles*. http://www.fao.org/agriculture/crops/news-events-bulletins/detail/en/item/121919/icode/.

O'Reilly, M. 2013. "ARAN Live Exports Rally." *Irish Vegetarian*, no. 139, 16.

O'Reilly, S. 2015. "World Vegan Month in Full Swing." *College Tribune*, November 30. http://collegetribune.ie/world-vegan-month-in-full-swing/.

Ó Ríordáin, S. P., and M. MacDermott. 1949. "Lough Gur Excavations." *Journal of the Royal Society of Antiquaries of Ireland* 79 (1/2): 126–45.

O'Sullivan, K. 2017. "Serious Rise in Irish Greenhouse Gas Emissions, Figures Show." *Irish Times*, November 27. https://www.irishtimes.com/news/environment/serious-rise-in-irish-greenhouse-gas-emissions-figures-show-1.3306961.

O'Sullivan, M. 2013. "Press Release from the Vegetarian Society of Ireland: Growth in Vegetarianism in Ireland after Horse Meat Scandal." *Irish Vegetarian*, no. 139, 19.

———. 2014. "World Vegetarian Day 2014: Some Legal Matters for Vegetarians and Vegans to Consider." *Irish Vegetarian*, no. 143, 13–14.

O'Toole, F. 2017. "We Are Still Living within a Mindset Forged by the Church." *Irish Times*, March 14.

Owen, J. 2014. "Did St. Patrick Really Drive Snakes Out of Ireland?" *National Geographic*, March 15. http://news.nationalgeographic.com/news/2014/03/140315-saint-patricks-day-2014-snakes-ireland-nation/.

Owens, D. 2008. *'Courageous Negro Servitors' and Laboring Irish Bodies: An Examination of Antebellum Era Modern American Gynecology*. PhD diss., University of California, Los Angeles.

Parker, L. 2019. "Who Let the Dogs In? Antiblackness, Social Exclusion, and the Question of Who Is Human." *Journal of Black Studies* 50 (4): 367–87.

Pavee Point Traveller and Roma Centre. 2014. *Submission on the Control of Horses Act 1996*. http://www.paveepoint.ie/wp-content/uploads/2013/11/Submission-on-the-Control-of-Horses-Act-1996.pdf.

Pearson, G. 1983. *Hooligan: A History of Respectable Fears*. London: Macmillan.
Peggs, K. 2012. *Animals and Sociology*. New York: Palgrave Macmillan.
Pemberton, N., and M. Worboys. 2007. *Mad Dogs and Englishmen: Rabies in Britain, 1830–2000*. London: Palgrave Macmillan.
Peters, C. N. 2015. "'He Is Not Entitled to Butter': The Diet of Peasants and Commoners in Early Medieval Ireland." In *Food and Drink in Ireland*, edited by E. FitzPatrick and J. Kelly, 79–109. Dublin: Royal Irish Academy.
Phelps, N. 2007. *The Longest Struggle: Animal Advocacy from Pythagoras to PETA*. New York: Lantern.
Philadelphia Inquirer. 1916. "Mrs. C. E. White, Humanitarian, Dies." September 8, 5.
Pichler, R., and G. Blackwell. 2007. "How Many Veggies . . . ?" *European Vegetarian Union*.
Plock, V. M. 2007. "Modernism's Feast on Science: Nutrition and Diet in Joyce's *Ulysses*." *Literature and History* 16 (2): 30–42.
Pollak, S. 2017. "Irish Greyhounds Face Brutal Treatment Abroad, Group Says." *Irish Times*, July 18. https://www.irishtimes.com/news/social-affairs/irish-greyhounds-face-brutal-treatment-abroad-group-says-1.3159448.
Pollard, J. 2015. "A Community of Beings: Animal and People in the Neolithic of Southern Britain." In *Animals in the Neolithic of Britain and Europe*, D. Serjeantson and D. Field, 135–48. Oxford: Oxbow.
Poole, K. 2013. "Horses for Courses? Religious Change and Dietary Shifts in Anglo-Saxon England." *Oxford Journal of Archaeology* 32 (3): 319–333.
Pope, C. 2016. "Graveyard Shift: A Day with the Dead of Glasnevin Cemetery." *The Irish Times*, March 26. Retrieved from: https://www.irishtimes.com/life-and-style/graveyard-shift-a-day-with-the-dead-of-glasnevin-cemetery-1.2585917
Potts, D. 2015. "'Room for Creatures': Francis Harvey's Bestiary." In *Animals in Irish Literature and Culture*, edited by K. Kirkpatrick and B. Faragó, 165–81. London: Palgrave Macmillan.
Power, J., and V. Clarke. 2019. "Brexit €100m Beef Fund for Farmers Announced." *Irish Times*, July 29. https://www.irishtimes.com/news/politics/brexit-100m-beef-fund-for-farmers-announced-1.3970515.
Pramaggiore, M. 2015. "The Celtic Tiger's Equine Imaginary." In *Animals in Irish Literature and Culture*, edited by K. Kirkpatrick and B. Faragó, 214–30. London: Palgrave Macmillan.
Prior, P. M. 2003. "Dangerous Lunacy: The Misuse of Mental Health Law in Nineteenth-Century Ireland." *Journal of Forensic Psychiatry and Psychology* 14 (3): 525–41.
Prowse, K. 2004. "Mushrooms." *Vegan*, Winter, 14–15.
Prunty, J. 1998. *Dublin Slums, 1800–1925*. Dublin: Irish Academic Press.
Public Record Office of Northern Ireland. n.d. *The Great Irish Famine*. Education Leaflet 3. Belfast: Public Record Office of Northern Ireland.
Purdon, H. S. 1896. "The Thyroid Treatment of Psoriasis." *Dublin Journal of Medical Science* 102: 379–84.

Read, D. H. M. 1916. "Some Characteristics of Irish Folklore." *Folklore* 27 (3): 250–78.
Regan, M. M. 2009. "'Weggebobbles and Fruit': Bloom's Vegetarian Impulses." *Texas Studies in Literature and Language* 51 (4): 463–75.
Reinhard, J. R., and V. E. Hull. 1936. "Bran and Sceolang." *Speculum* 11 (1): 42–58.
Retail News. 2011. "EUROSPAR: The Super Easy Supermarket." July/August, 38–39.
Reynolds, J. D. 1988. "Crayfish Extinctions and Crayfish Plague in Central Ireland." *Biological Conservation* 45 (4): 279–85.
Rhatigan, P. 2009. *Irish Seaweed Kitchen*. Rotterdam: Booklink.
Rice, C. A., and J. F. Benson. 2005. "Hungering for Revenge: The Irish Famine, the Troubles and Shame-Rage Cycles, and Their Role in Group Therapy in Northern Ireland." *Group Analysis* 38 (2): 219–35.
Ritvo, H. 1989. *The Animal Estate*. Cambridge, MA: Harvard University Press.
Rolleston, T. 1890. Introduction to *An Address to the Irish People*, by Percy Bysshe Shelley, 11–24. Edited by T. Wise. London: Reeves and Turner.
Ross, E. B. 1987. "An Overview of Trends in Dietary Variation from Hunter-Gatherer to Modern Capitalist Societies." In *Food and Evolution*, edited by M. Harris and E. B. Ross, 7–56. Philadelphia: Temple University Press.
Royal Zoological Society of Ireland. 1929. Address to the Zoological Society of London from the president of the Royal Zoological Society of Ireland, April 29, 1929. Item no. IE TCD MS 10608/24/1 in the Archives of the Zoological Society of Ireland, Manuscripts and Archives Research Library of Trinity College Dublin. Digital no. MS10608-24-1_46.
Russell, G. W. 1916. *The National Being: Some Thoughts on an Irish Polity*. New York: Macmillan.
———. (1913) 1978. "Food Values." In *Selections from the Contributions to "The Irish Homestead,"* edited by H. Summerfield, 374–77. Gerrards Cross, UK: Smythe.
Ryan, L. 2004. "The Press, Police and Prosecution: Perspectives on Infanticide in the 1920s." In *Irish Women's History*, edited by A. Hayes and D. Urquhart, 137–51. Portland, OR: Irish Academic Press.
Ryan, P. 2004. "The Coming-Out of the Gay Movement in Ireland 1970–80." In *Social Movements and Ireland*, edited by L. Connolly and N. Hourigan, 86–105. London: Manchester University Press.
Ryder, R. D. 1989. *Animal Revolution*. Oxford: Blackwell.
Sage, C. 2003. "Social Embeddedness and Relations of Regard: Alternative 'Good Food' Networks in South-West Ireland." *Journal of Rural Studies* 19 (1): 47–60.
Saha, J. 2017. "Colonizing Elephants: Animal Agency, Undead Capital and Imperial Science in British Burma." *British Journal for the History of Science* 2: 169–89.
Salaman, R. N. 1985. *The History and Social Influence of the Potato*. Cambridge: Cambridge University Press.
Salt, H. (n.d.) 1990. "'A Tall, Thin Young Man'." In *Shaw*, edited by A. Gibbs, 259–62. Iowa City: University of Iowa Press.
Sanderson, J. 1963. Editorial. *Vegan*, Autumn, 1.

———. 1965. "Survival Test—Then Nuts and Salad for Jack." *Vegan*, Winter, 6.
———. 1970. Editorial. *Vegan* 17 (4): 105–6.
Sands, B. 1981. *The Writings of Bobby Sands*. Belfast: Sinn Fein Prisoner of War Department.
Sappol, M. 2002. *A Traffic of Dead Bodies: Anatomy and Embodied Social Identity in Nineteenth Century America*. Princeton, NJ: Princeton University Press.
Sartin, J. S. 2004. "J. Marion Sims, the Father of Gynecology: Hero or Villain?" *Southern Medical Journal* 97 (5): 500–505.
Saunderson, G. W. 1961. "Butterwitches and Cow Doctors." *Ulster Folklife* 7: 72–73.
Semple, R. 1897. "Annual Report 1897: Ireland." *Vegetarian Federal Union 1889–1911*. https://ivu.org/history/vfu/1897-report-ireland.html.
Sexton, R. 1995. "'I'd Ate It Like Chocolate!': The Disappearing Offal Food Traditions of Cork City." In *Disappearing Foods: Studies in Foods and Dishes at Risk: Proceedings of the Oxford Symposium on Food and Cookery, 1994*, edited by H. Walker, 172–88. Devon, UK: Prospect Books.
———. 2002. "Food and Drink at Irish Weddings and Wakes. In *Food and the Rites of Passage: Leeds Symposium on Food History*, edited by L. Mason, 115–42. Devon, UK: Prospect.
———. 2013. "Plant Foods in Ireland before AD 1500." In *Secrets of the Irish Landscape*, edited by M. Jebb and C. Crowley, 155–63. Cork: Atrium.
———. 2015. "Food and Culinary Cultures in Pre-famine Ireland." In *Food and Drink in Ireland*, edited by E. FitzPatrick and J. Kelly, 257–306. Dublin: Royal Irish Academy.
Sharkey, O. 1987. *Old Days Old Ways: An Illustrated Folk History of Ireland*. Syracuse, NY: Syracuse University Press.
Shaw, G. B. (1896) 1990. "An Exam Paper." In *Shaw*, edited by A. Gibbs, 22–29. Iowa City: University of Iowa Press.
———. (1898) 1990. "Vegetarianism." In *Shaw*, edited by A. Gibbs, 401–3. Iowa City: University of Iowa Press.
Sheen, M. 2006. *Harvesting Justice: Mushroom Workers Call for Change*. Dublin: Migrant Rights Centre Ireland.
Sheridan, R. B. 1994. *Sugar and Slavery*. Kingston, JM: Canoe.
Shprintzen, A. D. 2013. *The Vegetarian Crusade*. Chapel Hill: University of North Carolina Press.
Siggins, L. 2017a. "Minister Welcomes 8% Rise in Value of Whitefish Quotas for Irish Fleet." *Irish Times*, December 13. https://www.irishtimes.com/news/ireland/irish-news/minister-welcomes-8-rise-in-value-of-whitefish-quotas-for-irish-fleet-1.3325763.
———. 2017b. "What's Happening with Our Seaweed and Why Should We Care?" *Irish Times*, July 28. https://www.irishtimes.com/life-and-style/people/what-s-happening-with-our-seaweed-and-why-should-we-care-1.3160359.
Simms, K. 1986. "Nomadry in Medieval Ireland: The Origins of the Creaght or Caoraighacht." *Peritia* 5: 379–91.

Simoons, F. J. 1994. *Eat Not This Flesh: Food Avoidances from Prehistory to the Present*. Madison: University of Wisconsin Press.
Sjoestedt, M.-L. 2000. *Celtic Gods and Heroes*. Mineola, NY: Dover.
Skonieczny, A. 2010. "Interrupting Inevitability: Globalization and Resistance." *Alternatives* 35 (1): 1–28.
Slater, B. 2011. "New Local Meetup Group: The Cork Vegans." *Irish Vegetarian*, no. 133, 20.
Smith, G. 1880. *Gipsy Life*. London: Haughton.
Smith, J. 2004. "Transnational Processes and Movements." In *The Blackwell Companion to Social Movements*, edited by D. A. Snow, S. A. Soule, and H. Kriesi, 311–36. Oxford: Blackwell.
Smithers, R. 2020. "Shiitake Happens: Vegans Fuel Boom in Exotic Mushrooms." *Guardian*, January 25. https://www.theguardian.com/lifeandstyle/2020/jan/25/vegan-veganism-exotic-mushrooms-shiitake-meat-substitute.
Smyth, J., and R. P. Evershed. 2015. "The Molecules of Meals: New Insight into Neolithic Foodways." In *Food and Drink in Ireland*, edited by E. FitzPatrick and J. Kelly, 27–46. Dublin: Royal Irish Academy.
Sneddon, A. 2012. "Witchcraft Belief and Trials in Early Modern Ireland." *Irish Economic and Social History* 39 (1): 1–25.
Socha, K. 2014. *Animal Liberation and Atheism*. Minneapolis: Free Thought.
Socha, K., and L. Mitchell. 2014. "Critical Animal Studies as an Interdisciplinary Field." In *Defining Critical Animal Studies*, edited by A. Nocella, J. Sorenson, K. Socha, and A. Matsuoka, 110–34. New York: Peter Lang.
Speedy, A. W. 2003. "Global Production and Consumption of Animal Source Foods." *Journal of Nutrition* 133 (11): 4048S–53S.
Spence, L. 1999. *The Magic Arts in Celtic Britain*. Mineola, NY: Dover.
Spillane, M., and M. O'Sullivane. 1913–21. "Statement by Witness. Document No. W.S. 862." *Bureau of Military History, 1913–21*. https://www.militaryarchives.ie/collections/online-collections/bureau-of-military-history-1913-1921/reels/bmh/BMH.WS0862.pdf.
Stack, L. 2015. "Guinness Is Going Vegan." *New York Times*, November 4. http://www.nytimes.com/2015/11/05/business/guinness-is-going-vegan.html.
Stănescu, V. 2010. "'Green' Eggs and Ham? The Myth of Sustainable Meat and the Danger of the Local." *Journal for Critical Animal Studies* 8 (1/2): 8–32.
Steinfeld, H., P. Gerber, T. Wassenaar, V. Castel, M. Rosales, and C. de Haan. 2006. *Livestock's Long Shadow*. Rome: Food and Agriculture Organization of the United Nations.
Stewart, F. 2014. "The Outcasts: Punk in Northern Ireland during the Troubles." In *Tales from the Punkside*, edited by G. Bull and M. Dines, 33–44. London: Itchy Monkey.
Stogre, M. 1992. *That the World May Believe: The Development of Papal Social Thought on Aboriginal Rights*. Sherbrooke, QC: Éditions Paulines.

Stopper, A. 2006. *Monday at Gaj's: The Story of the Irish Women's Liberation Movement*. Dublin: Liffey Press.
Stout, M. 2015. "The Early Medieval Farm." In *Agriculture and Settlement in Ireland*, edited by M. Murphy and M. Stout, 14–27. Dublin: Four Courts.
Suzuki, Y. 2017. *The Nature of Whiteness: Race, Animals, and Nation in Zimbabwe*. Seattle: University of Washington Press.
Swanson, M. 2014. "How 'Humane' Labels Harm Chickens." In *Confronting Animal Exploitation*, edited by K. Socha and S. Blum, 204–22. Jefferson, NC: McFarland.
Swift, J. 1729. *A Modest Proposal for Preventing the Children of Poor People in Ireland from Being a Burden to Their Parents or Country, and for Making Them Beneficial to the Public*. Dublin: S. Harding.
———. (1726) 1900. *Gulliver's Travels into Several Remote Nations of the World*. New York: D. C. Heath.
Taylor, N., and Z. Sutton. 2018. "For an Emancipatory Animal Sociology." *Journal of Sociology* 54 (4): 467–87.
Taylor, S. 2017. *Beasts of Burden: Animal and Disability Liberation*. New York: New Press.
Teagasc Mushroom Stakeholder Consultative Group. 2013. *Mushroom Sector Development Plan to 2020*. Carlow, IE: Agriculture and Food Development Authority.
TeBrake, J. K. 1992. "Irish Peasant Women in Revolt: The Land League Years." *Irish Historical Studies* 28 (109): 63–80.
Thejournal.ie. 2019a. "Water Quality in Almost Half of Ireland's Lakes and Rivers Deemed Unsatisfactory." December 10. https://www.thejournal.ie/water-in-irish-lakes-and-rivers-deteriorating-4923996-Dec2019/.
———. 2019b. "'Where's the Beef Ya Vegan?' Taoiseach Met with Protests from Farmers in Cork City." May 1. https://www.thejournal.ie/taoiseach-farmer-protest-cork-4614331-May2019/.
———. 2019c. "Almost 6,000 Greyhounds Killed in Ireland Every Year, New RTÉ Documentary Reveals." June 26. https://www.thejournal.ie/rte-investigates-greyhounds-being-killed-4697196-Jun2019/.
Thomas, K. 1991. *Man and the Natural World*. New York: Penguin.
Tipp FM. 2017. "Tipp Travellers Hit Back at Sulky Criticism." News, February 2. http://tippfm.com/news/tipp_travellers_hit_back_at_sulky_criticism/.
Tipperary Star. 2014. "New Era for Traveller Horse Owners in Tipp." *Tipperary Star*, March 21. http://www.tipperarystar.ie/news/local-news/166194/New-era-for-Traveller-horse-owners.html.
Torres, B. 2007. *Making a Killing: The Political Economy of Animal Rights*. Oakland, CA: AK Press.
Tovey, H. 1991. "'Of Cabbages and Kings': Restructuring in the Irish Food Industry." *Economic and Social Review* 22 (4): 333–50.

———. 1993. "Environmentalism in Ireland: Two Versions of Development and Modernity." *International Sociology* 8 (4): 413–30.

———. 1997. "Food, Environmentalism and Rural Sociology: On the Organic Farming Movement in Ireland." *Sociologia Ruralis* 37 (1): 21–37.

———. 2000. "Milk and Modernity: Dairying in Contemporary Ireland." *Research in Rural Sociology and Development* 8: 47–73.

———. 2002. "Risk, Morality and the Sociology of Animals: Reflections on the Foot and Mouth Outbreak in Ireland." *Irish Journal of Sociology* 11 (1): 23–42.

———. 2003. "Theorising Nature and Society in Sociology: The Invisibility of Animals." *Sociologia Ruralis* 43 (3): 196–215.

———. 2006. "New Movements in Old Places? The Alternative Food Movement in Rural Ireland." In *Social Movements and Ireland*, edited by L. Connolly and N. Hourigan, 168–89. New York: Manchester University Press.

———. 2007. *Environmentalism in Ireland: Movement and Activists*. Dublin: Institute of Public Administration.

Tovey, H., and P. Share. 2000. *A Sociology of Ireland*. Dublin: Gill and Macmillan.

Townsend, S. L. 2015. "Porcine Pasts and Bourgeois Pigs: Consumption and the Irish Counterculture." In *Animals in Irish Literature and Culture*, edited by K. Kirkpatrick and B. Faragó, 55–72. London: Palgrave Macmillan.

Tuan, Y. 2009. *Dominance and Affection: The Making of Pets*. New Haven, CT: Yale University Press.

Turner, M. 1996. *After the Famine: Irish Agriculture, 1850–1914*. New York: Cambridge University Press.

Unti, B. 2002. *The Quality of Mercy: Organized Animal Protection in the United States, 1866–1930*. PhD diss., American University, Washington, DC.

———. 2008. "The Foremother to American Animal Advocacy: Caroline Earle White." *AV Magazine*, Spring, 6–9.

Urfer, S. R., C. Gaillard, and A. Steiger. 2011. "Lifespan and Disease Predispositions in the Irish Wolfhound: A Review." *Veterinary Quarterly* 29 (3): 102–11.

van Dooren, T. 2011. "Invasive Species in Penguin Worlds: An Ethical Taxonomy of Killing for Conservation." *Conservation and Society* 9 (4): 286–98.

van Wijngaarden-Bakker, L. H. 1974. "The Animal Remains from the Beaker Settlement at Newgrange, Co. Meath: First Report." *Proceedings of the Royal Irish Academy: Archaeology, Celtic Studies, History, Linguistics, Literature* 74:313–83.

Vegan. 1963. "Jack McClelland's Great Swim." *Vegan*, Autumn, 9–11.

———. 1968. "Vegan Sportsmen." *Vegan*, Autumn, 73–75.

———. 1969. "Sportsmen." *Vegan* 16 (3): 12.

———. 1974. "News of Members." *Vegan* 21 (1): 14.

Vegan Society. 1971. "Minutes of the 27th Annual Meeting of the Vegan Society." *Vegan* 18 (9): 1–10.

———. 1973. "News of Members." *Vegan* 20 (1): 3.

———. 1996. "BSE—Set to Run. . . ." *Vegan*, Summer, 4–5.
Vegetarian. 1890. "The Federal Union." September 20.
Vegetarian Magazine. 1893. "Vegetarian Congress, Chicago, June 1893." https://ivu. org/congress/1893/report3.html.
———. 1908. "Progress of the Movement." Vol. 11 (9): 24.
———. 1909. "Vegetarian Industries." Vol. 13 (3): 31.
Villanueva, G. 2018. *A Transnational History of the Australian Animal Movement, 1970–2015*. London: Palgrave.
Viney, M. 2015. "Another Life: Lynx on the Loose? That'll Add a Frisson to a Forest Ramble." *Irish Times*, May 9. https://www.irishtimes.com/news/environment/another-life-lynx-on-the-loose-that-ll-add-a-frisson-to-a-forest-ramble-1.2205411.
Wahidin, A. 2016. *Ex-combatants, Gender and Peace in Northern Ireland*. London: Palgrave Macmillan.
Walker, M. R. 2008. *Suicide among the Irish Traveller Community, 2000–2006*. Wicklow County Council.
Walsh, O. 2004. "Gender and Insanity in Nineteenth-Century Ireland." *Clio Medica* 73: 69–93.
Ward, B. 2017. *Imagining Alternative Irelands in 2012*. Dublin: Four Courts.
Weaver, H. 2013. "'Becoming in Kind': Race, Class, Gender, and Nation in Cultures of Dog Rescue and Dogfighting." *American Quarterly* 65 (3): 689–709.
Webb, J. J. 1913. *Industrial Dublin since 1698, and The Silk Industry in Dublin: Two Essays*. Dublin: Maunsel.
Wedderburn, P. 2016. "Ireland's Problem with Overpopulation of Dogs." *Gorey Guardian*, June 11. https://www.independent.ie/regionals/goreyguardian/lifestyle/irelands-problem-with-overpopulation-of-dogs-34776850.html.
Wells, R. 1994. Review of *The Largest Amount of Good: Quaker Relief in Ireland, 1654–1921*, by H. E. Hatton. *Canadian Journal of History* 29 (1): 208–11.
Went, A. E. J. 1971. "The Dublin Zoo." *Dublin Historical Record* 24 (4): 101–11.
White, C. 1913. "An Item of Past History." *Journal of Zoöphily* 22: 35–36.
Wilde, O. (1882) 2000. "To Charles Godfrey Leland." In *The Complete Letters of Oscar Wilde*, M. Holland and R. Hart-Davis, 170. New York: Holt.
———. (1887) 2000. "To Violent Fane." In *The Complete Letters of Oscar Wilde*, edited by M. Holland and R. Hart-Davis, 334. New York: Holt.
Wiley, A. S. 2011. *Re-imagining Milk*. New York: Routledge.
———. 2017. "Growing a Nation: Milk Consumption in India since the Raj." In *Making Milk*, edited by M. Cohen and Y. Otomo, 41–60. New York: Bloomsbury Academic.
Wilmer, L. A. 1859. *Our Press Gang: A Complete Exposition of the Corruptions and Crimes of the American Newspapers*. Philadelphia: J. T. Lloyd.
Woodworth, P. 2016a. "Are We Culling Badgers Needlessly?" *Irish Times*, October 15. https://www.irishtimes.com/news/environment/are-we-culling-badgers-needlessly-1.2825443.

———. 2016b. "Golden Eagles and Ireland's Uplands Crisis." *Irish Times*, January 9. https://www.irishtimes.com/news/environment/golden-eagles-and-ireland-s-uplands-crisis-1.2489767.

Wrenn, C. L. 2013. "Nonhuman Animal Rights, Alternative Food Systems, and the Non-profit Industrial Complex." *Phaenex* 8 (2): 209–42.

———. 2016. *A Rational Approach to Animal Rights*. London: Palgrave.

———. 2017. "Toward a Vegan Feminist Theory of the State." In *Animal Oppression and Capitalism*, edited by D. Nibert, 2:201–30. Santa Barbara, CA: Praeger.

———. 2019. *Piecemeal Protest: Animal Rights in the Age of Nonprofits*. Ann Arbor: University of Michigan Press.

Wright, L. 2015. *The Vegan Studies Project*. Athens, GA: University of Georgia Press.

———. 2021. *Routledge Handbook of Vegan Studies*. New York: Routledge.

Yalden, D. 1999. *The History of British Mammals*. London: Academic Press.

Yates, R. 2011. "Criminalizing Protests about Animal Abuse: Recent Irish Experience in Global Context." *Crime, Law and Social Change* 55:469–82.

———. 2015. "Tim Barford's VegFestUK Helping to Bring the Vegan Animal Rights Grassroots Together and to the Fore." *On Human Relations with Other Sentient Beings* (blog), November 11. http://onhumanrelationswithothersentientbeings.weebly.com/the-blog/tim-barfords-vegfestuk-helping-to-bring-the-vegan-animal-rights-grassroots-together-and-to-the-fore.

York, R., and P. Mancus. 2013. "The Invisible Animal: Anthrozoology and Macro-sociology." *Sociological Theory* 31 (1): 75–91.

Zoophilist and Animals' Defender. 1904. "Notes and Notices." Vol. 24 (8): 150.

———. 1905a. "Obituary: Mr. Richard P. White." Vol. 25 (2): 36.

———. 1905b. "Ireland: List of Registered Places." Vol. 25 (2): 35.

Index

Adams, Carol, 11, 13, 184
Africa, 8, 47, 49–50, 68, 70, 78, 95, 122–23
Alliance for Animal Rights, 133, 197
American Humane Association, 100
anarchism, 116
animal advocacy, 64, 69, 80–86, 88–89, 92–93, 98, 100, 102, 105–108, 109–10, 113, 115, 116–23, 130, 134–37, 139, 157, 181–82, 190, 201–204, 205, 207
animals and society, 2, 8, 181–82
animalization, 14, 39, 46, 49–50, 52, 54, 58–64, 74–76, 77–78, 81, 82, 95, 100, 103, 104, 107, 121–29, 182, 184, 186–87, 199, 202
Animal Liberation Front, 134–36
animal rights, 7, 80–81, 83–85, 88, 116, 134–35, 166, 181, 190, 200, 203–204, 207
see also Animal advocacy
Animal Rights Action Network, 116, 136, 200
animism, 20–23, 40, 42–43, 181–82
anthroparchy, 7, 10–11, 13, 19, 21, 25, 27, 36–37, 39, 41–42, 43, 56, 59, 66, 75, 76, 167, 195
see also anthropocentrism
anthropocentrism, 7, 17, 21, 23, 34, 43, 56, 70, 130, 181–82
Anti-vivisection League, 98

Asia, 151, 174–75, 194, 197, 200
see also China and India
Australia, 62, 122–23, 186, 202

badgers, 160, 195–96
bears, 24, 69, 85, 102, 160
beasts, 5, 22, 36, 60–62, 68, 74, 100
bees *see* insects
Belfast, 91–92, 112–14, 116, 126, 169–70
Bergh, Henry, 99–102
Besant, Annie, 6, 98–99, 106
birds, 23, 24, 25, 30, 32, 34–35, 37, 38, 40, 53, 56, 69, 72, 75, 76, 82–83, 86, 88, 94, 115, 125–27, 160–61, 195, 205
see also chickens
Book of Kells, 34
Bourdieu, Pierre, 14, 21, 28
Britain, 1, 4–6, 11, 12, 14, 16, 19, 25, 29, 34, 43–44, 45–47, 50–54, 59–62, 64, 66–68, 70–78, 80–82, 83, 86, 92, 94, 96–99, 106–107, 109–10, 111, 112–13, 115, 120–21, 124, 127–28, 134–37, 139, 141, 144–46, 148–49, 152–53, 157, 162–63, 169–70, 174–75, 177, 181, 182–84, 185–86, 188–89, 190, 196, 200, 201, 202, 206, 207

239

British Union for the Abolition of
   Vivisection, 94
Burns, Kit, 100–102, 182
butter, *see* dairy
"Buy Irish," 144–45, 154–56, 162,
   165

cannibalism, 22, 54
capitalism, 10, 14, 65, 72, 77,
   106–107, 137, 144, 153, 161,
   163, 167, 169, 174, 176, 187,
   188, 193, 195, 197–98, 200–201,
   202–203
Caribbean, 47–50, 61, 78, 186
cats, 22, 24, 27, 34, 37, 42, 100, 132,
   146, 162, 191
cattle-raiding, 19, 21, 24, 26, 27–28,
   31
Celts, 21, 23, 24, 28–29, 34, 37, 42,
   50, 67, 73, 74, 124, 146, 160,
   182
chickens, 36, 38, 56, 58, 64, 72, 76,
   82, 83, 88, 142, 143, 148, 150,
   156, 159, 162, 173, 182, 205,
   206
   see also eggs
children, 40, 41, 42, 76, 77, 82, 94,
   104, 115, 119, 130, 159, 165,
   167, 186, 190, 194, 205
China, 142, 194, 197
Christianity
   see religion; Church and monasteries
Church and monasteries, 8, 29, 32,
   33–34, 38–39, 45, 64–65, 184,
   186, 205
circus, 191
civilizing process, 6, 14, 20, 26, 39,
   64, 69–70, 81–82, 86–87, 90,
   121, 129, 146
civil rights, 107–108, 109–10, 114,
   125, 139, 185, 189, 203
   see also social justice

class, 14, 19, 20, 25, 29–31, 32,
   37–39, 43–44, 46, 48–60, 62–64,
   66–67, 68–69, 72–73, 79–80,
   82, 83–84, 87, 88, 91, 95,
   97–98, 100, 103–105, 106–107,
   120, 122–25, 145–46, 149–50,
   152–54, 157, 160, 175, 178, 184,
   186, 188, 190, 193, 200, 202,
   205
Cobbe, Frances 94
colonialism, 5, 6–7, 8–9, 10, 12,
   13–14, 20–21, 43–44, 46–80,
   81–82, 84, 87, 90–91, 94, 98–99,
   105–107, 109, 114–17, 120–21,
   124, 126, 131–32, 134, 137, 139,
   140, 144, 149, 152–53, 159, 161,
   163, 165, 169, 172, 177–78,
   182–86, 200, 202–203
Connolly, James 144
consumption, 7, 10, 29–33, 38–39,
   44, 46–48, 50–57, 61, 79–80,
   85, 88–89, 91, 98, 114–17, 138,
   141–44, 146, 148, 149, 153–54,
   165, 167, 169, 172, 177–78, 186,
   189, 194, 197–98, 202
   see also food
cooking, 24–26, 29–30, 32, 37, 51,
   55, 86, 91, 92, 99, 111, 145,
   154, 169, 175, 177
Cork, 4, 47, 120, 134, 169
Cousins, Margaret, 98–99
cows and bulls, 4, 19, 26, 27, 28, 29,
   30–31, 34, 35–36, 41, 47–48, 51,
   53, 56, 58, 61, 62, 65, 72, 73,
   82, 83–84, 85, 88, 94, 103–105,
   113, 122–23, 130–31, 142–45,
   147, 148–49, 151–52, 153–54,
   157–59, 162, 166–67, 173, 175,
   182, 188–89, 192, 194, 195, 196,
   198
crime and incarceration, 46, 70, 74,
   107, 125–30, 132, 149, 205, 207

Index | 241

critical animal studies, 4, 12–25, 18, 20–31, 69, 114–15, 164, 181
Cú Chulainn, 22, 23, 31
Cumann na mBan, 148, 172

dairy, 30–31, 32, 40–41, 47, 52, 53, 57, 61, 62, 78, 82, 87, 102–104, 110, 130, 132, 142–46, 149–51, 158, 160, 163, 165, 173, 174, 176–77, 188–89, 191–92, 193, 194
butter 28, 30, 34, 40–41, 47–48, 51, 57, 88, 145, 147
milk 19, 28, 30–31, 32, 36–37, 40–41, 51, 58, 91, 104–105, 130–31, 142, 144, 146–47
deers, 22, 25, 38, 64, 68, 72–73, 133, 148–49, 162, 198, 205, 206
denial, 185
Despard, Charlotte 6, 96, 98
disability, 36–37, 39, 42, 58–60, 67, 70, 90, 106, 156, 185, 186, 202
disease, 37, 41, 51, 56, 60, 62, 64, 67, 69, 71, 75, 86–87, 90, 102–104, 121, 124, 134, 143, 145, 147, 153, 156–57, 162, 170, 175, 178–79, 187–88, 194, 195–96, 205, 207
dogs, 22, 24, 27, 38, 56, 64, 65–67, 72–73, 83–84, 93, 94, 95, 98, 100–102, 103, 121, 123, 125, 132, 149, 187, 191, 197–98
domestication, 3, 26–33, 39, 67, 70, 121, 168
donkeys, 81, 133, 146, 206
Drummond, William, 83–86, 106, 206
Dublin, 30, 32, 34, 68–72, 75, 79–80, 83, 85, 92, 99, 110, 111, 133–34, 169, 171–73, 188–89, 200, 206

economy, 2, 12, 15, 18, 20, 27, 42, 43–44, 45, 54, 56–57, 62, 69, 78, 100, 117, 130, 136, 138, 141, 143, 147, 149–55, 158–59, 161, 163–65, 173, 175–78, 183, 184, 186, 187, 189, 190, 192, 194, 203–204
eggs, 51, 146
elephants, 70–71
Elias, Norbert, 6, 70
environment, 15, 109, 111, 113, 114, 139–40, 151–53, 158–59, 161, 165, 169, 176, 178–79, 187, 189, 190, 191–94, 194, 195, 200, 203, 207
eugenics, 46, 67–68, 147, 159, 167–68, 194
Europe, 29, 39–40, 42, 45, 66, 109, 174–75, 191, 192, 196, 197, 205
European Union, 136, 137, 139–40, 143, 150–56, 158, 160, 168, 188, 191–93, 194, 196, 199–200
euthanasia, 119, 197

farming, 15, 31, 36, 40–42, 43–44, 45, 51–55, 57, 59, 62, 65, 66, 73–74, 79, 81–82, 88, 91, 130–32, 139–40, 141–44, 146, 150–54, 156–57, 159–65, 167, 173, 176–78, 182–83, 186, 187, 188–89, 190, 191–94, 195–96, 197, 202–203, 205
Farplace Animal Rescue, 170
feminism, 6, 8–9, 18, 41, 76, 88, 90, 98–99, 109, 115, 145, 149, 170–71, 201
  see also vegan feminism
Fettes, Christopher, 112, 138
fishes and fishing, 30, 32, 53, 55, 56, 72, 142, 147, 149, 151, 158–61, 170, 175, 187–88, 195, 205

folklore, 5, 21, 26, 31, 33–35, 39–42, 43, 160
food, 5–6, 11, 19, 24–25, 26, 27–33, 37–39, 41, 44, 45, 46–48, 50–58, 61, 68, 79, 85–86, 88–89, 91, 103–105, 106, 110, 114–16, 125, 129–30, 133, 139, 141–42, 143–44, 146–52, 154–56, 158–59, 160, 163–65, 167, 173, 176–79, 182–83, 188, 191–93, 194, 196, 197–98, 199, 202, 205
see also cooking; cows; consumption; dairy; deers; domestication; farming; fishes and fishing; goats; grains; Great Famine; horses; hunger strikes; hunting; meat; mushrooms; nutrition; nuts; oceans; pigs; rabbits; seaweed; sheeps; veganism; vegetables; vegetarianism
foxes, 64, 72–73, 123, 134, 195, 198
fur, 24, 47, 90
fruit, 32, 111, 142, 170, 178

Galway, 113, 134, 169
gender, 20, 24, 27, 40–42, 43, 57, 58–60, 62, 69, 73–74, 75, 76, 85, 92–93, 95, 104–105, 117, 119–20, 148–49, 167, 177, 184, 186, 189, 206
Giddens, Anthony, 183
Goffman, Erving, 59, 69–70
globalization, 45, 138, 139–40, 142–43, 145, 149–50, 152–53, 165, 178–79, 187–88, 189, 194, 197–200, 202–203
goats, 29, 68, 94
Gore-Booth, Eva, 6, 98–99
Go Vegan World, 130, 132, 133, 136, 188–89, 190, 201, 207
Gunn-King, Brian and Margaret, 111–13

grains, 32, 37, 51–53, 55–56, 58, 111, 142, 144–45, 146, 148, 158–59, 176, 178
Gramsci, Antonio, 3, 65, 109, 140, 141, 177
Great Famine, 6, 51–57, 59, 61, 68, 85, 88, 114, 134, 143–44, 158, 185
Green Party, 138, 161, 192

Haughton, James and Samuel, 86–88, 106
hegemony, 3, 140, 141, 163, 177, 179, 202
horses, 14, 22–23, 26, 36–37, 38–39, 41, 42, 72–73, 75, 82, 85, 100, 116–21, 134, 146, 153–54, 157, 187, 197–99
hunger strikes, 6, 128, 135
hunting, 12, 24–25, 28, 30, 32, 38, 40–41, 64, 65, 66, 72–73, 81, 82–83, 94, 124, 133, 134, 147, 148–49, 160–61, 183, 195–96, 197, 198–99, 206

immigration, 47–48, 53, 61, 64, 67, 74–75, 77, 100, 102–107, 124–25, 141, 174, 182, 186, 202
independence, 57, 60–61, 66, 68, 73–78, 85, 92, 98, 106, 130, 137, 139, 144, 146–47, 152–53, 162, 172–73, 177–78, 183, 196
India, 8, 52, 70, 98, 106, 114, 142, 171–73
insects, 34, 37–38, 40, 126, 187
institutions, 48, 51, 58–60, 76, 78, 157, 168–69, 182, 184, 186, 200–201, 205, 207
intersectionality, 6, 8–11, 12, 15, 18, 20, 24, 28, 39, 40–41, 43, 46, 48, 50, 57, 58, 60–62, 64–68,

70, 76, 79, 88, 89, 94–95,
  98–99, 103, 105, 109, 114–18,
  120, 124, 125–27, 129, 134,
  139, 149, 167, 170–71, 174–75,
  182–85, 187–88, 193, 199, 202
invasive species, 159, 161, 187–88
Irish Anti-Vivisection Society, 138
Irish Council against Blood Sports,
  134, 207
Irish Horse Welfare Trust, 116
Irish Farmer's Association, 196
Irish Union against Vivisection, 110
Irish Vegan Festival, 170
Irish Wildlife Trust, 133, 136–37,
  206
Irish Whale and Dolphin Group, 206

Jannaway, Kathleen, 112
Joyce, James, 146, 149, 170

Kilkenny, 119, 134
Ko, Aph, 10, 13, 54, 182, 184, 203

Late, Late Show, 130
land reform, 6, 45, 47, 55, 56, 72,
  78, 82, 91, 121–22, 144, 150,
  176, 184
language, 4, 17, 28, 76
laws, 38–39, 53, 56, 59, 80–82, 94,
  98, 103, 106–107, 120–21, 128,
  153, 156–57, 160–61, 169, 175,
  177, 196, 197–98, 200
leather, 24, 29, 34, 35, 51, 73, 78
Lee, Ronnie, 135
Limerick, 169
live export, 99, 116, 122–23, 194

mac Cumhaill, Fionn, 22, 25
Martin, Richard, 80, 106
Marx, Karl and Marxism, 2–3, 11,
  12, 14, 20, 26, 27, 43, 48, 49,

77–78, 106–107, 116–17, 153,
  163, 165, 178, 184–85, 203–204
McCaughey, Leonard, 170, 172–73
McClelland, Jack, 112–14, 116, 139
meat, 29–30, 33, 37, 44, 47–48,
  52–54, 55, 58, 61, 62–63, 73,
  78, 79, 85–87, 90, 91, 94, 99,
  115, 130, 132, 142–51, 154,
  157–58, 160, 163, 165, 167,
  173–77, 184, 188–89, 191–94,
  196, 197, 199, 205, 207
  see also chickens; cows; deers; food;
  horses; hunting; fishes and fishing;
  pigs; rabbits
mice, 37, 94, 124, 162
  see also pests
milk, *see* dairy
modernization, 58, 141–42, 146, 154,
  183–84, 187, 193
monsters, *see* beasts
moral panics, 118–19
Morrígan, 23, 31
mushrooms, 32, 173–75, 190, 193

National Anti-vivisection Society, 94,
  206
nationalism, 8, 11, 66, 85, 115–16,
  122–25, 130, 132, 134, 142–48,
  155, 163, 166, 169–71, 176–78,
  183, 184, 188–89, 196, 203, 206
Nibert, David, 3, 11, 20, 27, 52, 141,
  162, 164, 169, 178, 184, 189
Normans, 5, 24–25, 45, 64–65, 66,
  74
nutrition, 32, 38, 51, 54–60, 61, 67,
  85, 112–14, 140, 141, 145, 147,
  163, 168–69, 194
nuts, 32, 110–11, 142, 163, 174, 178,
  189

oceans, *see* water

otters, 22, 160
oxen, 94

pacifism, 149
patriarchy, *see* gender; feminism; vegan feminism
pests, 37, 75, 77, 102, 124, 148, 160–61, 187, 195
pets, 67, 100, 132, 157, 191, 197, 199
   see also cats; dogs
pigs, 4, 22, 24, 25, 26, 27, 28–29, 30, 37, 38, 48, 51, 56, 62–64, 76, 86, 104, 127, 142, 153–54, 157, 159, 162, 182, 187, 199
Power, Jenny Wyse, 172
protest, 6, 49–50, 51, 57, 59–61, 64, 74, 78, 96–98, 106–108, 122–23, 127–28, 134–35, 137–39, 141, 144–47, 153, 176, 196, 200, 203–204
prison, *see* crime and incarceration

rabbits, 25, 40–41, 47, 53, 72, 103, 134, 162, 198
race, 8, 9, 47–50, 54, 64, 66, 67–69, 70, 74, 77, 95, 100, 102–104, 105, 118, 122, 124, 141–42, 147, 164, 182, 183, 184, 186–87, 188, 193, 197, 206
racing, 65, 72, 73, 117–20, 134, 139, 174, 183, 191, 197–99
rats, 94, 101–102, 124, 162, 182
   see also mice; pests
Regan, Tom, 130
Republicanism, 6, 76–77, 79–80, 96, 98, 115, 125–27, 134, 139, 146–47, 171
   see also independence; protest; Troubles
religion, 21, 27, 29, 33–39, 41, 42, 43, 55, 76, 80, 83, 86, 88, 90, 103, 114, 116, 124, 128, 146, 170, 177, 205
restaurants, 88, 90, 116, 169–73, 177, 178–79
rivers, *see* water
Russell, AE, 145–46, 149

Salt, Henry, 88–90, 147
Sands, Bobby, 125–29
science, 12–13, 18, 60, 67–70, 83, 88–89, 90, 93–95, 99, 103, 113, 125, 136, 140, 145, 183, 194–95, 206
Scotland, 110–11, 132
seals, 30, 151, 161
seaweed, 55, 113, 148, 175–76, 190
Shaw, George, 88–92, 96, 98, 146–47
Sheehy-Skeffington, Francis, 149
sheeps, 26, 27, 29, 30, 37, 51, 53, 57, 62, 81–82, 90, 122–23, 143, 148–49, 151, 152, 159, 162, 189
Shelley, Percy, 79–80, 206
silk and silkworms, 30, 47
simianism, 62–63, 74–75, 104, 131, 187
   see also animalization
Sinn Féin, 126, 171
   see also Republicanism; Sands; Troubles
slavery, 9, 28, 46, 47–50, 122, 206
snakes, 37, 199
social justice, 7–10, 84, 88, 96, 106, 109, 114–17, 128, 130, 164–65, 170–71, 184–85, 190, 193, 201–203
social movements, *see* protest
sociology, 2, 13, 15, 16–17
SPCA, 80–81, 83, 92–93, 99–100, 102, 117, 119, 133, 157, 197
speciesism, 2, 12, 65, 75, 78, 80, 99–100, 109, 130, 132, 134, 139–40, 150, 156–57, 159–61,

164–65, 168, 177–78, 183–84, 185, 187–88, 189, 193, 197–98, 202, 207
see also anthroparchy; anthropocentrism
sports, 4, 64, 65, 66, 69, 72–74, 82, 83–84, 85, 89, 100–102, 112–13, 121, 139, 182–83, 191, 206
see also hunting; Irish Council against Blood Sports
squirrels, 24, 47, 115, 161, 205
Stănescu, Vasile, 167–68, 194
state, 3, 11, 136–38, 143–44, 146, 152, 157–58, 164–65, 168–69, 173, 177–79, 185, 188, 189, 190, 191–94, 198, 201, 202–203
sustainability, 7, 11, 27, 111, 140, 151–54, 156–60, 163, 167–69, 175, 177–78, 187, 191–94, 195, 203, 207
see also environment
Swift, Jonathan, 13–14, 62, 146, 203

Tipperary Traveller Horse Owners Association, 118–19
tourism, 4, 8, 152, 173, 195, 198
Travellers, 116–25, 182, 184
Troubles, 6, 74–76, 114, 116, 125–30, 134–35, 207
Turkey, 194

United Kingdom, *see* Britain
United States of America, 47, 55, 62–64, 67, 68, 74–75, 77, 92, 95, 98, 99, 99–107, 110–11, 112, 114, 115, 134–35, 137, 138, 169, 181, 186, 190, 202, 207

veganism, 7, 8, 18, 33, 38–39, 59, 88, 107, 110–13, 116, 130–32, 133–34, 143, 168–70, 173–74, 176–79, 188–90, 191–93, 201–202, 203–204

vegan feminism, 9–11, 12, 18, 20, 25, 27, 28, 30, 42, 57, 77, 79, 90, 98, 106, 115–16, 174, 177, 181, 184
Vegan Information Project, 134, 200, 207
vegan societies, 110–13, 133, 135–36, 139, 157, 173, 201, 206, 207
vegetables, 32, 51–53, 55–56, 59, 88, 91, 111, 115, 142, 146–48, 163, 170–72, 174, 178
see also seaweed
vegetarianism, 33, 38–39, 51–52, 54–55, 78–80, 85–91, 94, 98–99, 106, 113–15, 130, 145–47, 148, 149, 168–70, 177, 185–86, 192, 205
see also veganism
vegetarian societies, 91–92, 110–14, 133, 135–36, 138, 139, 157, 170, 190
vermin, *see* pests
Vikings, 30, 45
vivisection, 83, 85, 88–89, 93–95, 98, 99, 106, 136, 145, 182–83, 186, 206

war, 23, 24, 26, 27–28, 61, 68, 76, 92, 109–10, 115, 142, 143–44, 146–49, 172, 177, 207
Warzone, 116
water, 27, 30, 33, 36, 56, 104, 113, 133, 135, 137–38, 148, 151, 158–61, 175–76, 187, 194, 201
see also fishes and fishing; wildlife
Waterford, 29
welfare, 34, 64–65, 69, 76, 79–81, 85–86, 89, 92–94, 99–102, 106–107, 110, 115–22, 132–33, 137–38, 140, 156–57, 159, 163, 165–66, 169, 178, 189, 190, 192, 193, 194, 196, 197–98, 203
see also animal advocacy

White, Caroline Earle and Richard, 92–93
Wilde, Oscar, 115, 146
wildlife, 4, 8, 21, 23–25, 28–29, 34, 69–73, 133, 151–52, 158–61, 187, 195, 201, 205
  see also wolves; bears; beasts; birds; deers; environment; fishes and fishing; hunting; water
witchcraft, 40–42
wolves, 24, 62, 160

wool, 29, 57, 165
  see also sheeps
women, 6, 9–10, 12, 20, 28, 40–43, 52, 57–59, 62, 68, 75, 76, 94, 128, 145, 148, 174, 183, 184, 185, 186, 193, 201, 202
  see also gender; feminism; vegan feminism

Yates, Roger, 170

zoos, 65, 68–72, 74, 78, 88, 183

www.ingramcontent.com/pod-product-compliance
Ingram Content Group UK Ltd.
Pitfield, Milton Keynes, MK11 3LW, UK
UKHW041933140426
5217IPUK00014B/451